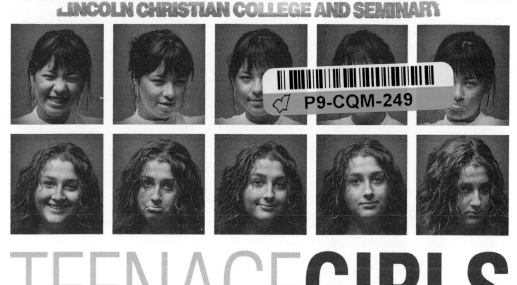

TEENAGE GIRLS

Exploring Issues Adolescent Girls Face and Strategies to Help Them

Ginny Olson

ZONDERVAN™

GRAND RAPIDS, MICHIGAN 49530 USA

ZONDERVAN.COM/
AUTHORTRACKER

Youth Specialties

www.youthspecialties.com

Youth Specialties

Teenage Girls: Exploring Issues Adolescent Girls Face and Strategies to Help Them
Copyright © 2006 by Ginny Olson

Youth Specialties products, 300 South Pierce Street, El Cajon, CA 92020 are published by
Zondervan, 5300 Patterson Avenue Southeast, Grand Rapids, MI 49530.

Library of Congress Cataloging-in-Publication Data

Olson, Ginny.
  Teenage girls : exploring the issues that adolescent girls face and the strategies to help them /
by Ginny Olson.
     p. cm.
  Includes bibliographical references.
  ISBN-10: 0-310-26632-7 (pbk.)
  ISBN-13: 978-0-310-26632-7 (pbk.)
  1. Church work with teenagers. 2. Teenage girls–Religious life. I. Title.
  BV4447.O485 2006
  259'.23–dc22

                                                                        2006003986

Web site addresses listed in this book were current at the time of publication. Please contact
Youth Specialties via e-mail (YS@YouthSpecialties.com) to report URLs that are no longer
operational and replacement URLs if available.

*Creative Team: Dave Urbanski, Laura Gross, Heather Haggerty, Janie Wilkerson, and Mark
Novelli*
Cover design by Burnkit
Printed in the United States

06 07 08 09 10 • 10 9 8 7 6 5 4 3 2 1

ACKNOWLEDGMENTS

I've worked with, ministered to, and studied adolescent girls since I was an adolescent myself, so having the chance to write this book is a dream come true. And as is the case with most dreams realized, there are many people who've helped bring it into being, and I am deeply indebted to them. A huge round of thanks belongs to the team at Youth Specialties: Jay Howver, for the opportunity to take on this challenge and having the confidence in me that I could do it; Roni Meek, who graciously kept me moving forward and gave her excellent guidance to the process; Dave Urbanski, who with his amazing talent always makes me sound better than I deserve; Laura Gross, who meticulously combed through the details to make sure the manuscript was accurate (any errors are mine, not hers); and of course the rest of the YS team who give so much of their lives to figuring out how to best support those in the youth ministry trenches.

I am also grateful for my colleagues at the Center for Youth Ministry Studies at North Park University. Jim Dekker and Alison Burkhardt selflessly stepped in to carry the lion's share of the load at school to allow me time to research and write. They have been amazing encouragers along this journey. And I am so appreciative for the rest of the Dekker clan who supported me along the way with encouragement, insights, and unbelievable home-cooked meals.

This process would have been much more difficult if it weren't for a small group of friends who committed to pray for me and constantly communicated their support as I was in my "writing cave": Alise Barrymore (and the Emmaus Community), Debbie Blue, Justine Conley, Janice Knight, Andrea Sanderson, Terryl Scarbrough, and Gerald and Cynthia Stewart (and the Faith Community of St. Sabina). I am thankful for their friendship in ways they will never know. And of course, I owe a large debt of thanks to the numerous youth workers and adolescent girls who willingly and graciously shared their stories with me over the months and years. Their insights proved to be invaluable.

And finally, this book is dedicated to my mother, who patiently loved and prayed two daughters through the journey of adolescence. Through her life, she showed us what it meant to be a woman of God and to dream big dreams. And for that I am extremely grateful.

—Ginny Olson

CONTENTS

Contents

INTRODUCTION
NO TOURISTS NEED APPLY

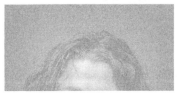

Anthony, the youth pastor, stood chatting with a couple of middle school students after church when Kayla slipped by on the other side of the hall. Anthony stopped in mid-sentence and called out, "Hey Kayla, when's your next game?"

The tall, lithe seventh-grader looked at him in surprise. She almost never came to youth group except when she was dragged by her parents. She didn't even know the youth pastor knew her name, much less that she played basketball.

"Wednesday," she stammered. "Three thirty. It's a home game." Anthony nodded and went back to the conversation with the rest of the students. Kayla walked away puzzled and skeptical. No one ever came to the games except a sprinkling of parents and teachers.

But Wednesday afternoon arrived, and Anthony and a female small group leader were planted on the hardwood bleachers, cheering Kayla on. At the beginning of the game, Kayla glanced back from the bench and shyly smiled at the new visitors. Gradually, her mild bewilderment at their presence gave way to a confident grin of appreciation.

That game was a turning point for Kayla. After that she never missed a youth group gathering. Not only was she a committed regular, she brought her friends, too. One night there were about 90 students at youth group, and Anthony was trying to divide them into three teams for a game. He then realized that more than a third of the students were Kayla's friends. He ended up having to beg a few to go to the other teams.

What seemed to be a simple, solitary act—cheering on a student at a game—was in reality a very powerful example of the ministry of presence. What Kayla needed was someone to show up for her, to take an interest in entering her world. Anthony was willing to take up the challenge, and Kayla responded.

Our adolescent girls aren't looking for tourists—adults who are only interested in seeing the beautiful spots, taking a few quick pictures, and then leaving after a week to go back to their comfortable lives at home. Rather, these girls are looking for pilgrims like Anthony who will wade into the muddy, adventurous mess of a journey of adolescence with them. Pilgrims who aren't looking for the comfortable, easy path but are willing to take the hard road of understanding the issues that adolescent girls face, issues that are unprecedented in their magnitude.

Adolescent girls are longing for mentors who will try to comprehend the impact of wildly fluctuating hormones, rapidly changing bodies, morphing identities, and a culture that pushes them toward early sexualization. They want those who will grasp that these girls, or at least their friends, are likely encountering eating disorders, self-injury, fracturing families, a shifting spirituality, and a proclivity toward depression. Whether or not these girls will admit it, they are famished for someone to show up for them.

This book is intended to assist those who are interested in showing up in adolescent girls' lives. Those who are willing to walk with girls as they deal with pressures they feel, the stress they shoulder, the changes they encounter.

This book is designed to help those who consider themselves pilgrims to come along for the journey and help girls not just survive adolescence—but thrive in it.

A LITTLE HISTORY

What is adolescence? It comes from the Latin verb *adolescere*, which means "growing up." Even though the term *teenager* is a relatively recent creation (it was coined by advertisers on Madison Avenue in the 1940s to describe a new consumer group), the word *adolescent* has been around for a long time. The word first showed up in English literature around

1440, about 90 years before the term *adult* was seen.[1] Well before that, philosophers and educators such as Aristotle, Plato, and Rousseau discussed the idea of adolescence. They and many others have spent time musing and speculating over this season of human development. As Aristotle said during the fourth century BC:

> The young are in character prone to desire and ready to carry any desire they may have formed into action. Of bodily desires it is the sexual to which they are most disposed to give way, and in regard to sexual desire they exercise no self-restraint... They are passionate, irascible, and apt to be carried away by their impulses...Their lives are lived principally in hope. They have high aspirations; for they have never yet been humiliated by the experience of life, but are unacquainted with the limiting force of circumstances. Youth is the age of when people are most devoted to their friends, as they are then extremely fond of social intercourse. If the young commit a fault, it is always on the side of excess and exaggeration, for they carry everything too far, whether it be their love or hatred or anything else.[2]

In the realm of research and psychology, however, adolescence is a relatively new phenomenon. It wasn't until the early 1900s that a season of adolescence was first researched in depth. In 1904 G. Stanley Hall produced a two-volume book that's now considered foundational for the field of adolescent research.[3] He looked at everything known about adolescents at that time, including how they were portrayed in literature and history. In doing so, Hall established himself as the first person to scientifically research adolescents. His categorization of adolescence as being a time of "storm and stress"[4] (or *Sturm und Drang* in German) is descriptive to say the least. Adolescence is a time of conflict with authority figures, of trying on new identities and discarding old ones, of mood swings, and of exploring new territory.

While research of adolescence is relatively new, the research of *female* adolescence is brand new. For example, as recently as 1980 the *Handbook on Adolescent Psychology* didn't contain even one chapter devoted to girls.[5] In fact, researchers who predominantly studied males—and Caucasian males at that— developed most of what's known in adolescent theory.

Dr. Carol Gilligan, a psychologist and feminist ethicist (who has taught at Harvard, New York University, and the University of Cambridge), has added much to the field of knowledge about adolescent females in her books, especially *In a Different Voice: Psychological Theory and Women's Development* (1982). As both a researcher and a theorist, she has helped others in her field to rethink the gender bias in developmental theory.

Another key voice in the study of adolescent girls is Dr. Mary Pipher, a clinical psychologist. She brought the discussion of the current state of adolescent girls into the forefront with her insightful and groundbreaking book, *Reviving Ophelia* (1995). More and more research on adolescent girls is being done, and more is needed if we are to understand this population.

> "Psychology has a long history of ignoring girls this age. Until recently adolescent girls haven't been studied by academics, and they have long baffled therapists. Because they are secretive with adults and full of contradictions, they are difficult to study. So much is happening internally that's not communicated on the surface."[7]
> —Dr. Mary Pipher, *Reviving Ophelia*

"There is increasing awareness and increasing evidence that most major developmental theories, written as they are from the male perspective, may reflect a gender bias. The reasons are numerous; partly because the creators of these theories have been predominantly male; partly because the theoretical models have been based on research data collected from males; partly because female data have not easily fit into the established male model...and partly because cultural prejudice and stereotypes may have influenced psychological and developmental thinking in the past."[6] —Rolf E. Muss, *Theories of Adolescence*

"Girls are the world's most squandered gift. They are precious human beings with enormous potential, but across the world, they are generally the last to have their basic needs met and the first to have their basic rights denied."[11] —World Vision's *Girl Child Report*, 2001

A FEW NUMBERS

According to the 2000 census, there are approximately 20 million girls living in the United States between the ages of 10 and 19.[8] The majority are White (almost 14 million); approximately three million are Black; and another three million are Latina. Close to 700,000 are Asian; 130,000 are Native American, Eskimo, or Aleut; and 35,000 are Native Hawaiian or other Pacific Islander. Worldwide, there are more than 578 million girls between the ages of 10 and 19.[9] Looking ahead, the U.S. Census Bureau projects that by the year 2015, there will be almost 30 million girls between the ages of five and 17.[10]

Internationally, the state of girls is not a pretty one, especially if they live in developing countries. World Vision's *Girl Child Report* discusses how girls are "the least likely to be treated with justice."[12] They are subject to early matrimony, which often means early pregnancy and increases health risks, such as hemorrhaging, toxemia, anemia, and infection.[13] Girls also suffer from genital mutilation. The World Vision report cites that "between 85 and 114 million women worldwide are victims of female genital mutilation. Each day, another 6,000 girls are 'circumcised'—two million per year."[14]

The preference for boys over girls, often resulting in female infanticide, is another discouraging fact internationally. Girls are expected to perform household labor, and this prevents them from receiving an education. Many girls are subject to sexual exploitation, being sold—sometimes by their own families—for the sake of money. According to Anita Botti, somewhere between 700,000 to one million women and children are sold internationally into some type of slavery or bondage with about 50,000 of them being brought to the United States for sweatshops, as well as sexual and domestic purposes.[15] In Africa teenage girls care for entire families due to the HIV/AIDS pandemic that killed the adults in their families. Some are forced to engage in risky sexual behavior just to survive.[16]

A FEW BASIC QUESTIONS

In light of girls struggling with life-or-death matters such as AIDS, sex trafficking, and genital mutilation, issues such as body image and self-esteem seem relatively minor. But to an adolescent girl, they are cause for concern in her world. She has entered a season of her life where change is constant—this can be thrilling and terrifying all at the same time. Think of riding a giant roller coaster. At first you're laboring up a track and can't see over the top. You wonder if this ride will be worth the time you spent waiting in line. Suddenly, within the very next second, you're free-falling and shrieking with joy and with terror. That's an adolescent girl's life.

For the next few years, her focus will primarily encompass three areas:

1. Identity: Who is she?

2. Significance: Does she matter?

3. Purpose: Why is she here and where is she going?

These three questions are woven throughout her adolescence as she tries to figure out what her body is doing, how she relates to her friends and family, how she's connected to God and the church, and what she thinks and feels about the past, the present, and her future.

As she journeys through adolescence, she wants to know that her physical development is normal and that she's safe from abuse. She wants to have relationships where there's trust and love, both with friends and with her family. She wants female—and male—role models who will guide and help her figure out how to live life. She wants to relate to adults who will respect her and help her become a competent adult herself. She wants to be emotionally well and to have a healthy perspective on her sexuality. She wants to know that she's loved, she belongs, she's competent, and she's worth something.

A COUPLE OF CAVEATS

This book is intended to act as an early warning system. It's not designed as a tool for diagnosis, but rather one that gives an overarching look into the lives of adolescent girls today. I'm not a licensed therapist, but I have ministered to and with adolescent girls for many years, and I've spent quite a bit of time researching them.

Because I'm a female writing about females, I've made sure to include some male voices in the book. Sprinkled throughout are quotes and insights from male youth workers—both rookies and veterans. There are also insights from adolescent girls, some statistics and hard research, and personal anecdotes. The result is an eclectic web of biology, sociology, theology, psychology—and a bunch more "-ologies"—that will give youth workers a better sense of what adolescent girls struggle with and what they celebrate.

CHAPTER ONE
IDENTITY MATTERS

Elise watched Karla drift into the youth room with a swarm of boys surrounding her, basking in her glow. With a flip of her dark brown hair, she'd smile at the ones who made her laugh—and they were all trying. Her short denim skirt was slung low around her hips, her long legs seemed to stretch into oblivion, and one strap of her black knit tank top was resting provocatively off one shoulder. Even the guy leaders turned their heads when she walked in. Elise just shook her head. Karla was only 15, but she'd already mastered the art of flirting.

They were starting small groups that night, and Elise was dismayed to learn that Karla was in her group. If Elise were honest, she'd admit that Karla intimidated her. She had never really talked to Karla, as the girl only attended youth group in spurts. Plus, Elise had never felt comfortable around "girly girls." She was an athlete who'd broken a few school records when she was in college. How on earth was she going to connect with someone like Karla? Elise had vague misgivings that this group was going to focus more on makeovers and boy-toys than on anything substantial.

Later that evening, as they sat in tiny orange plastic chairs around the linoleum table in the second grade Sunday school room, the girls in Elise's group were sharing their stories. Elise had to hide her surprise as Karla talked about how much time basketball required, and how it was taking her away from church and her studies. She was hoping to win a much-needed scholarship for college, but she was debating whether or not it was worth the cost. When Karla asked the group to pray for her, Elise thought, "They need to be praying for *me*."

Even though she believed she was seeing the whole picture, Elise had seen only one of Karla's personas. An adolescent girl is multifaceted, and which facet she chooses to show all depends on her mood. She's wavering in a world where some days she wishes she could still play with her dolls, yet she recognizes that her body is now able to bear children. She's in a constant state of flux, wondering who she is right now, and who she'll be tomorrow. Some days she'll feel as though she's 21. Other days, she's 10 again. It's a season of setting aside her childhood props and grieving that loss, while at the same time eagerly rejoicing as she becomes an adult. This isn't a one-day decision; it's a process that takes place over her adolescent years, as she constantly tries on new personalities and casts off others.

During this phase of her life, change is the only constant; every relationship is shifting, and every belief is questioned. What she once knew was solid ground now feels as though an earthquake hit it. She's not quite sure where to find the stability of her childhood, or if she even wants to. In the midst of this chaos, she's screaming the question of adolescence: "Who am I?" Tied to that question is a whole series of other questions: Who is she in relation to her friends? To her family? To her community? She's seeking to find *her* identity.

BACKGROUND

Erik Erikson is the name most frequently associated with the topic of identity development in adolescents. Erikson, a researcher in the area of human development, divided the human life span into phases, and a key issue marks each phase. According to Erikson, the adolescent phase of life deals with the issue of "identity versus identity confusion."[1] In other words, during her adolescent years it's healthy for a teenage girl to try to figure out who she is and how she fits into her surrounding context. The unhealthy alternative (or "identity confusion") occurs when a girl reaches the end of adolescence (around her early 20s), and she hasn't made a commitment to any identity.

Identity formation is why it's normal for a girl to walk into youth group one month dressed in black Goth attire (and an attitude to match), while next

-Dancers?

month she's wearing polo shirts and Shetland sweaters. She's researching different personas to see what she likes and what others respond to affirmatively (in her judgment). Ideally, according to Erikson's theory, by the time she's reached young adulthood, she'll have made choices and commitments about her beliefs, her values, and her goals in life. All of these help form an identity that's acceptable to her, as well as to her larger community.

However, if at age 22 she's still walking into church wearing a punk outfit one Sunday and hip-hop the next, those are indicators that she's not moving in a healthy direction. Those kinds of drastic, external persona changes are a sign that she's floundering internally and having a difficult time committing to an identity. She's probably still waffling about what she believes, what she really values, and what she wants to do with her life. She's emerging from adolescence without a committed answer in any of these areas.

This uncertainty about who she is as she heads into young adulthood results in what Erikson would call "identity confusion." Erikson doesn't claim that adolescence is the only time people deal with their identities; discerning one's identity is a lifelong process. However, adolescence is when the questions about identity are at the forefront of life and most critical to a person's future development.

Some theorists and researchers have challenged Erikson's theories, saying his research is biased toward males. They propose that adolescent girls place a higher value on intimacy and forming an identity *in relationship with others* than adolescent boys do, and that a girl will forgo pursuing goals and opportunities if it requires sacrificing a relationship. But gender influences on identity development seem to be dissipating.[2]

"We are…most aware of our identity when we are just about to gain it and when we (with that startle which motion pictures call a 'double take') are somewhat surprised to make its acquaintance; or, again, when we are just about to enter a crisis and feel the encroachment of identity confusion."[3] —Erik Erikson, *Identity and the Life Cycle*

INFLUENCES ON IDENTITY DEVELOPMENT

In the past, a girl developed her sense of self among those she knew: family (including her extended family), friends, and people in her community. She took part in traditions, such as rites of passage, where she learned about her culture and received input from the elders in the community so she would understand that she was part of a legacy of a long line of strong women. She would receive religious guidance—not just from her pastor, but also from others in her community. She would receive role training from her mother, grandmother, aunts, older sisters, and other women in the community. All this was done with only minimal input from the outside world.

Then came the advent of television, videos, print media geared toward adolescent girls, cell phones, and especially influential—the Internet. An adolescent girl is now influenced by a multitude of sources, and they're not just from her community but, quite literally, from around the world. And these sources are sending her a variety of messages, many of which are contradictory:

- "Love your body the way it is…but make sure you're tall and thin."

- "Don't let your sexuality be the only thing that defines you…but be sexy and attractive to guys."

- "Be happy with your natural beauty…but we'll define 'beauty' by the models in the magazines."

- "Don't get an STD…but if you're normal, you're sexually active."

- "Be confident and outspoken…but not too aggressive or abrasive, or people will call you a 'bitch.'"

- "Embrace your ethnicity…but we'll still hold up a white European ideal."

Our girls struggle to discern which voices to give credence to, as all of these opinions are being screamed at them. No wonder so many girls enter young adulthood confused about who they are.

THE CONTEXTS OF IDENTITY DEVELOPMENT

As an adolescent girl forms her sense of self, it's important to understand that she sees herself not just as one consistent person traveling through the different settings of her life; rather, she has multiple selves that occur in a variety of contexts. She's subconsciously asking identity-searching questions:

- "Who am I as a daughter? As a stepdaughter? As a sister?"

- "Who am I as a friend? As a girlfriend?"

- "Who am I at school in the classroom? In the lunchroom? On the sports field? In the choir room?"

- "Who am I when I'm at church?"

- "Who am I as a second-generation Korean American (or as a Latina, Native American, Black, or White) girl?"

- "Who am I when I'm by myself?"

These are just a few of the contexts that influence the identity of an adolescent girl. They, and several others, are explored in greater depth throughout the rest of the book.

The Context of Family

A girl's family context is the most influential on her identity development. It's here that she wrestles with a dilemma—the desire to please her parents and earn their approval, as well as the desire to be independent and no longer be seen as "our darling baby girl." At the same time her parents are grappling with how to help her develop into an independent adult yet

protect her from the real and perceived dangers of
adolescence.

It's easy to see that conflict is bound to happen in
this pushing-away/pulling-closer context. Parents set
rules and boundaries for the safety and well-being of
their daughter, and she naturally pushes against those
rules and boundaries. Remember, she's developing
her capability to think abstractly, and one way she's
exercising that competence is to question the rules,
as well as the motivation and logic behind them.
Sometimes parents feel as though they're living with
a lawyer. Every decision they make seems up for debate. However, her social skills usually haven't yet
developed enough for her to ask these questions in
a gracious manner that might elicit a more positive
response from her parents.

In other words, the discussion usually sounds
something like this, "We want you home by midnight."

(Defiantly) "Why? None of my friends have to be
in that early."

(A more authoritarian parental tone) "We're not
your friends' parents, we're yours."

(Louder, more disgusted tone) "You still treat me
like a child!" And from there the discussion declines
rapidly, ending with the slamming of a door.

The parents are dumbfounded; they believe
they've made a reasonable demand in order to keep
their child safe. However, their daughter sees her
curfew as her parents' lack of trust in her emerging
adult judgment. A conflict of opinions, a conflict of
power, a conflict of perceived identities: Is she still a
child or is she an emerging adult?

This dialogue exemplifies the internal trial-and-
error she's working through. She's trying on an older
identity—the ability to go out with friends and self-
determine when it's okay to come home—and testing

Mothers and fathers play key roles in the identity development of their daughters. Their impact on an adolescent girl's life is explored further in chapter 9 on family matters.

that identity with her parents. She's also questioning the voice of authority that, previously, she had always assumed was correct. Again, because of her increasing abstract-thinking skills, she's able to look at several sides of an issue and is weighing which one she wants to accept, even if that means disagreeing with her family.

For example, she may have been committed to the same political party as her parents. But now she's reading more newspapers, listening to political debates, exploring issues such as justice and fairness, and she decides she'll back a different political point of view. This can create family conflict if her parents regard her choice as an act of disloyalty. Healthy parents are able to accept this kind of change as their daughter's assertion of her own thoughts and opinions—just another step she's taking toward her identity development. She's now deciding what she believes—not just because someone told her to, but because she explored the options and came to her own conclusions. Hopefully, her parents will see her decision-making process as an identity skill that will serve her well in the future.

The Context of Church

Karen and Jackie were sitting in the back pew passing notes to each other. Cynthia was sitting next to them, text-messaging Chris who was sitting with his grandmother on the other side of the church. If you asked any of them what they got out of the Sunday service, they wouldn't have been able to tell you. But whether or not they were aware of it, they were being formed by their church that day—and every Sunday before that. They were learning their roles as Christians in that community. For as long as they've been going to church, they've been learning whether or not it's okay for them to have a leadership role. They've been absorbing whether women can have a voice or if they must stay silent. They've been picking up that it's okay for women to be up front if they're singing a solo but not if they're preaching, or that it's okay for a woman to work in the nursery but not to chair the board. Or perhaps they've learned that women are called and gifted to play any role in the church.

They've also been learning if it's okay to ask questions and to wrestle with doubt by watching how the rest of the congregation handles it when someone doesn't accept what's being taught from the pulpit. They're learning if it's better to give grace or to sit in judgment by watching how the church deals with the college girl who came home pregnant. They're noticing that they only worship with people who look like them and that church visitors who don't look like them don't stay.

In this culture of church, adolescent girls are having their faith formed from an early age. It's not just the teaching and preaching that gives them input, but it's also the conversations at the church potluck and observing how people talk about each other. This community is a tangible representation of who God is and what their relationship with God should be like. It's here that girls learn how to rejoice, how to grieve, how to forgive, how to pray, and how to lament. The voice of the church carries a heavy influence in the life of an adolescent girl.

The Context of Culture, Ethnicity, and Race

"But I don't see you as Black," exclaimed Katie. "I look at you and see my friend Charise."

"Please!" Charise retorted. "If you don't see my skin color then you don't see me." Katie had a hurt and bewildered look on her face. Charise took a deep breath and continued, "Katie, my color is part of who I am. Yes, I am female. I am a Christian. I am a straight-A student. And I am your friend. I am ALL of those things. But I am also Black. When you say you don't see me as Black, you deny my story, my history."

It's said that girls often define themselves according to their relationships with others. Usually they take that to mean relationships with peers. But it's also in relationship with their culture and history. They haven't come to this place in the timeline of the world without ancestors.

Some girls in minority cultures grow up strongly identifying with their ethnic groups while others find themselves just awakening to it during adolescence. Jean Phinney has done quite a bit of work in the area of identity formation in adolescents. She's found that they have four basic ways of responding to their ethnicity:

1. *Assimilation.* This is when someone chooses to ignore her ethnic background and blends into the population that surrounds her. "I don't like the label 'Korean American.' I just consider myself American."

2. *Marginality.* This occurs when someone neither accepts her own culture nor feels accepted by the majority culture. She doesn't feel at home when she's with her family, and she feels as though she stands out when she's with her majority culture friends.

3. *Separation.* When someone rejects the majority culture altogether and chooses only to associate with people of her own culture. This is often seen in older immigrants who live in the same area, speak the same language, go to the same church and shop at the same grocery stores that carry items from their culture. It is also seen in adolescents who refuse to interact with people from a different culture.

4. *Biculturalism.* A girl who is bicultural is at home both in the majority culture and in her culture of origin. She sees strengths in both cultures and can easily move back and forth and feel as though she's staying true to herself.[4]

Because adolescence is a time of self-reflection, for the first time girls who are members of minority cultures may find themselves getting in touch with the injustices their relatives were exposed to over the centuries. Thus, they may be angry or depressed. As youth workers, we can design experiences where they can develop plans of action to help them deal with current injustices and help them research their pasts, as well as celebrate them. Girls need to understand what they've gained by being part of an ethnic group: What are they proud of? What do they appreciate or enjoy about their ethnicities or cultures? What roles have they been told they need to take on because of their cultural backgrounds (for example, caregiver of the little ones or the elderly, advocate of causes, girlfriend, daughter, wife)? Which roles do they *want* to take on, and which *don't* they?

We also need to develop a diverse curriculum that integrates various ethnicities. Check to see how many video clips show only majority culture students. Are illustrations only of one ethnicity? Are there role models and examples of leadership from only one ethnicity? We can create environments where girls from the majority culture get in touch with the issues facing girls of color and learn to embrace their own ethnic identity, as well as their friends'.

The Context of Peers

Peers are sometimes the loudest voice of influence during adolescence. They're often the audience that an adolescent girl plays to, adapting her identity based on the feedback she receives. Positive relationships with her peers prove to her that she has the social skills to make commitments to other people and she's capable of intimacy and forming lasting friendships. They can give her a sense of confidence and increase her level of self-esteem. Good peer relationships also help her develop a sense of understanding and empathy toward others. Healthy friendships teach her how to share herself and how to support

"Studies of the major [television] networks have shown that the majority of positive character traits are modeled by Caucasian [characters], while negative traits are usually modeled by African American [characters] or other minorities."[5] —*This Is My Reality: The Price of Sex*

others. These relationships can be a source of knowledge as they teach her about the world and about perspectives other than those of her family.

Peer relationships can also damage her identity through betrayal, hurt, aggression, or snubbing. Not having or keeping friends during adolescence can result in an adult who's more likely to be unemployed or who suffers from poor mental health.[6]

Robert Weiss talks about two different forms of loneliness: social loneliness and emotional loneliness.[7] *Social loneliness* deals more with feeling as though one lacks "enough" friends. This can be addressed, say, if a girl gets involved in a ministry or in a small group and develops more relationships where she feels connected. On the other hand, *emotional loneliness* isn't determined by the quantity of relationships, but by the quality. Girls feel lonely if the relationships they have aren't sufficiently deep or if their preferred level of sharing just isn't happening.

Friends can often act as a support during identity development. They can encourage a girl's values, relationships, and dreams. In analyzing the data from the National Study of Youth and Religion, Christian Smith found that, "Teenagers' friendships seem related to their religious lives in important, if not always unexpected ways…the more religiously serious and involved a teenager is, unsurprisingly, the more their good friends seem to be. Moreover, parents of less religious U.S. teenagers are more likely to say that their teenagers' friends are a negative influence on them, while parents of religiously devoted teenagers think their teenagers' friends are a positive influence."[8] Youth ministries can often play a role in connecting girls with these positive peer relationships.

SELF-ESTEEM

All of these contexts have spoken into a girl's life and helped her form her identity, her image of herself. Self-esteem is how *she* views herself. What does she think of her identity? Is she proud of who she is? Embarrassed? Does she wish she were something more or something less? Who does she hope she will eventually be and who does she dread becoming?

Sometimes, when a girl is dissatisfied with her identity or has low self-esteem, she'll seek to hide her true self behind a mask of a false self. She may wear the mask of "perfection," striving to perform at unrealistic levels in all that she does: the essay must be flawless, the speech must get an A, the competition must be won, or the room must be spotless. Anything less than perfect means she's to blame. She forgets that *no one* is perfect, and that God loves her for who she is, not for what she does.

A girl might put on the mask of "the good girl." This is similar to the mask of perfection, except "perfection" focuses on tasks while this mask focuses on relationships. She must always win the approval of others—especially those in authority—even if it means losing her own self-approval. She avoids conflict, even to the point of denying her beliefs because it may cause a rift in the relationship. She goes the extra mile because that's what a "good Christian girl" does. She operates without concern for her own emotional, spiritual, or physical well-being. The worst thing someone can say to someone wearing this mask is, "I'm so disappointed in you." Those words can devastate her. For her, Romans 3:23 is a daily reality. Everyone may have sinned and fallen short of the glory of God, but her sin is worse. That's why she must work so hard for approval. She wonders if she'll ever get the approval and affirmation she needs. She doesn't understand that God's grace and love are free for the asking.

STRATEGIES FOR DEVELOPING GIRLS WITH STRONG IDENTITIES

- Help girls become media savvy so they can discern the media's messages about how they should look and behave. Help them understand their focus on the external versus the internal person.

- Assist girls in developing their personal competence. Help them succeed by giving them responsibilities in a variety of areas. Help them learn about natural consequences by not bailing them out when they don't succeed. Afterward, talk through what happened so the "failure" becomes a learning experience. Understand that adolescents like the challenge of high goals. Too often we expect too little from them. They will meet our expectations, whether high or low.

- Develop accountability structures with older female mentors in which girls can begin to see progress in their lives.

CONTINUED >

She may wear the mask of "strong girl" when she wants to communicate that she's tough and confident. When she wears this mask, her feelings of inadequacy and insecurity are hidden. She doesn't cry, doesn't feel lonely, doesn't need anyone else's help. She's FINE. When a girl wears this mask, she becomes Leah—covering up her pain over not being chosen and needing to be loved. But she forgets that Hannah sobbed her heart out over not having a child; that Esther was terrified at having to take a stand; that Ruth must have felt horribly lonely after leaving the place where she grew up; and that the woman who was bleeding for so many years felt such desperation that she would reach out and touch God in public, just for the chance to be healed.

These and other masks can hide an adolescent girl's true self. The difference between wearing these masks and trying on identities, covered earlier in the chapter, is that wearing a mask is all about gaining other people's approval for our identities rather than our own approval. When a teenage girl is trying on a mask, she's seeing if someone else likes her better with it on, and she'll hide her true self behind it. But when she's trying on an identity, she's testing to see if she likes who she is: Is this a part of her persona that she hasn't realized yet? Does this feel authentic to her or not? This isn't an easy process, and there can be pain and confusion as she wrestles with who she is and who she's becoming. It's difficult for her to realize that her identity is constantly forming. It's not to be "achieved"; it's a *process*.

THE YOUTH WORKER'S ROLE

As youth workers, it's crucial that we surround girls with positive messages about who they are and who they can become. They sometimes need us to dream with them about what God envisions for their lives. I was having coffee with Tessa one day, and we were talking about her life. Tessa had a rough time growing up. Many of the contexts mentioned earlier in this chapter were negative ones for her. Her father abandoned her, teachers overlooked her, and the local church was absent in her family's life.

I'd known Tessa for quite a while. She's a remarkable young woman. Even with all the negative forces she'd dealt with growing up, she survived. She's amazingly gifted and could choose a number of paths in life; we talked about those. What if she became a lawyer and advocated for abandoned children? What if she became a doctor and worked with the disenfranchised? What if she became a pastor and reached out to girls like her? Any of those were viable options for her.

As we were leaving the diner at the end of our conversation, she stopped me. "Can we do this again sometime? I've never had anyone dream with me before." We need to dream with our girls, helping them envision identities that are grounded in Scripture and developed in God's love.

CONTINUED >

- Teach the girls how different cultures define identity and self-esteem.

- Create environments where girls can begin to comprehend how unique and how normal they are.

- Have girls write down their dreams and then develop plans for how to achieve them.

- Laugh! Laughter is great for boosting self-confidence.

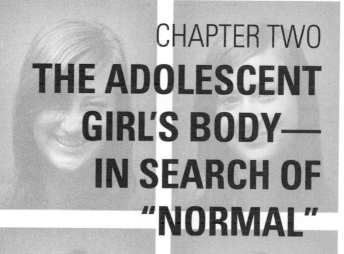

CHAPTER TWO
THE ADOLESCENT GIRL'S BODY—
IN SEARCH OF
"NORMAL"

"Where have the little girls gone?" the summer staff person asked me in disbelief.

It was "transition" day at our church camp, and we were saying good-bye to our sixth-grade girls and welcoming our seventh- and eighth-grade girls. The camp is located on a rugged site in the north woods of Michigan's Upper Peninsula. In other words, we had no electricity and no running water, just outhouses and bucket showers with water that was fire-heated each morning.

It was a perfect place for middle school girls to escape the pressures of their normal worlds. Because of our remote setting, there was no way the bus drivers could drive the girls directly into the camp. Instead they would park about a mile down the river on the opposite bank, and the camp staff would ferry the girls across by boat—the incoming girls on one trip, and the departing girls on the return trip. There was a constant flow of activity as we hugged the younger girls who were leaving, and then cheered and welcomed the older girls arriving on the return trip. It was an afternoon filled with celebration and emotion.

It was also an afternoon spent observing the dramatic changes that happen to girls during early adolescence. We sent home young girls with stuffed animals and sleeping bags covered with cartoon characters tucked under their arms, some wearing the same outfit they'd worn all week. And we welcomed young women who arrived bearing massive amounts of luggage—even make-up kits—and wearing bikini tops and low-slung shorts designed to show off their new curves. They were a marked contrast to the girls who had just left. Where we hugged departing little girls with boyish figures, messy hair, and craft projects firmly grasped in hand, we greeted young women who were noticeably taller and curvier, and who visibly struggled between exhibiting a cool detachment and a girlish giddiness upon being back at camp.

It was at this point that the staff person, upon experiencing this transition for the first time, looked around at the new arrivals and asked his question—a question packed with more layers of insight than he probably intended.

Indeed, he posed the question that delineates adolescence, "Where have the little girls gone?"

HER BODY IS CHANGING

One of the most easily identifiable indicators that a girl is hitting adolescence is the change in her body. Prior to that, she looks pretty similar to little boys her age, except for her clothes and hairstyle. As my high school biology teacher used to quip, "The only difference at this point is indoor and outdoor plumbing." However, once puberty begins, the transformation is drastic. Externally, her body starts changing months, if not years, before menarche (the onset of her first period). But internally, the changes begin even earlier.

Sometime between the ages of seven and 11, a girl's hormones start telling the rest of her body that it's time to move toward adulthood. The hypothalamus (a gland about the size of a grape) in the front part of her brain grows active and sets in motion some of her other glands, such as the pituitary gland (about the size of a pea) located below her hypothalamus and her ovaries, otherwise known as *gonads* or *sex glands* (these appear as testes in boys). Now her body begins producing female sex hormones, such as estrogen and progesterone. And it's these hormones that start her body on the track to puberty.

Going Up…

Starting about two years before menarche, a girl's body will hit a growth spurt that rivals the time when she was a baby. This growth surge usually occurs when she's around 10 to 12 years of age, but it can happen anytime between eight to 14 years of age.

FEMALE SEX HORMONES

- The term *estrogens* means "to produce mad desire or frenzied passion."

- Estrogens are a group of sex hormones produced by the ovaries. They're strategic to a girl's development of secondary sex characteristics, such as breast and pubic hair growth. They also heighten her sense of smell, which is most sensitive halfway between her periods.

- Also produced by the ovaries, progesterone is a key hormone when it comes to a girl's period. It determines the length of her cycle and prepares her uterus for pregnancy.

YOUTH WORKER TIP

Because of the size advantage that most middle school girls have over the boys, plus the physical awkwardness of early adolescents in general, never pit them against each other in games where winning requires physical prowess. Rather, even out the playing field by changing the rules of the game. For example, play softball with a canoe paddle and a big rubber ball or have the runners run the bases backwards. Play volleyball with a big sheet hung over the net so the teams can't see their opponents and have no idea where the ball is coming from. By taking standard games and tweaking the rules, the students are free to focus on the fun rather than on how they're doing when compared with the rest of the group.

During childhood, boys are slightly taller than girls. However, in early adolescence, girls grow faster than boys, until the girls reach about age 13 or 14. That's when the boys' growth spurt kicks in. The boys eventually catch up and pass the girls at around age 14 or 15, but until that point it can make for some interesting middle school pictures as many of the girls tower almost a full head over the boys.

A girl's height significantly increases anywhere from a year to six months before she starts her period. At her peak, she will grow about three and one-half inches in a year. This can be a real drain on the family budget when it comes to shopping for clothes and shoes. After that surge, her growth will slow down quite a bit. By the time she's done growing at around age 16 or 17, she'll have added almost 10 inches of height since adolescence began.

Sometimes a girl may be terrified that she'll grow too tall, especially if she matures early. She may hunch her shoulders and wear baggy clothes in order to hide her body, particularly if she's significantly taller or more noticeably developed than her female peers. The reality is, however, that a girl who matures early is more likely to be shorter in the long run than one who matures later. This is due to the fact that her sex hormones will signal her pituitary gland to reduce the production of growth hormones. Once a girl finishes her major growth spurt, she'll probably only grow another inch or so. If she's concerned about her height, a visit with a physician may reassure her. The doctor can usually offer a close estimate of her final height.

This physical transformation impacts different parts of her body at different times. Her hands, head, and feet are the first to grow, followed by her arms and legs. The long, leggy look typically seen among middle school girls is due to the fact that their legs are growing much faster than their torsos. All of this seemingly random growth can create a sense of awkwardness. Girls often trip over their own feet as they're walking down the hall and will bump into desks and lockers.

I saw this exemplified during a visit to a local junior high school. I was visiting with a seventh-grade girl I knew from church, and she had a cast on her wrist. When I asked her what happened, she sheepishly admitted that she was running through a doorway, accidentally banged her arm into the doorjamb, and broke a bone. She laughed and shrugged her shoulders as if to say, "Things like this happen when you're a junior high girl." This clumsiness is understandable when you consider the fact that young teenage girls are growing so quickly. It takes a while to learn how to coordinate all those extra inches of flesh and bone.

Not only is an adolescent girl growing taller, but her face is also starting to change, especially her jaw line. She's shifting away from the round, babyish look of a little girl and developing the sharper and more distinct facial features of a young woman. Her face takes on clearer definition as her mouth widens, her lips fill out, and her nose loses its childlike look.

After all of this, the last area to be impacted by her growth spurt is the trunk of her body. Her torso finally lengthens and her shoulders broaden, although not as much as a boy's. She no longer resembles a little girl but is finally taking on the look of a young woman.

Beneath the Surface

During this time of growth, a girl is also putting on a layer of fat right below the skin. This, along with the widening of her hips and the filling out of her thighs, gives her a woman's body shape. The impact of this can be difficult if she's part of a community (ethnic or socioeconomic) that prefers a more straight-line figure to a curvy one. (We'll discuss this further in chapter 3.)

DID YOU KNOW...?

If a girl gets blemishes before she hits puberty, then she's more likely to have serious skin problems than a girl who doesn't see blemishes until mid-adolescence.[1]

Besides her growing body, an adolescent girl's skin is also changing. Skin-care product manufacturers are well aware of this fact and thus have turned it into a huge niche market. When a girl turns 11 or 12, her skin becomes noticeably oilier because her hormones are telling her skin and scalp to produce more oil. This can result in blemishes and greasy hair. Most people will experience acne at some point in their adolescence (85 percent, according to the National Institute of Arthritis and Musculoskeletal and Skin Diseases.[2]) Most cases are mild and can be treated with over-the-counter medications and treatments. (Note: Your assurance that the "mountain" of a pimple on her forehead is noticeable only to her is minimally helpful to a young adolescent and usually will be met with a look of disdain.) However, sometimes the blemishes are severe enough to require medical treatment.

Because teenagers are so focused on outward appearance, it's important that a girl suffering with severe acne sees a doctor for treatment. If she doesn't, she can withdraw from friends and social situations, and she may eventually become clinically depressed. Besides an increase in oil production, an adolescent girl's sweat glands also start producing a fatty substance with a distinct aroma. In other words, she develops body odor—a scent you'll instantly recognize if you've ever walked into a room full of seventh-grade girls the morning after a sleepover, or if you've ever been a cabin counselor at camp. If a girl doesn't have a parent or older sister to help her establish some hygiene routines, she may be oblivious to her own odor and unaware that she needs to take showers more frequently and use deodorant. Sometimes a kind *female* youth worker needs to step in and help her out, especially if the girl is being teased.

HER SECONDARY SEX CHARACTERISTICS

As a girl's body changes, her secondary sex characteristics are much more visible than her primary sex charactcristics, which we'll discuss in the next section. Although secondary sex characteristics are not critical for reproduction, they do play a crucial role. These secondary traits are what visibly differentiate the female from the male bodies. These are also the features that adolescents use to measure themselves against their peers to see if they're "normal." While girls' bodies are changing rapidly, they're obsessed with finding out what's average and discovering if they fit into those parameters. In gym class they'll covertly glance around and wonder if their breasts are too small or too big or the right shape. They try to discern if they're wearing the right kind of bra. They question if they have too much or too little pubic hair. They struggle with when they should start shaving their legs, or how to deal with the fact that they come from a culture in which women don't shave, or with mothers who adamantly insist they're still too young to shave. Although it may not relieve the stress entirely, it can be comforting for a girl to realize it's normal for girls to develop their secondary sexual features in different ways and at different times.

One of the first secondary sexual characteristics to appear is pubic hair. Pubic hair can begin growing anywhere from age eight to age 14, but on average it usually shows up, albeit sparsely, when a girl is around 12. As a girl grows older, her pubic hair becomes dark, curly, and coarser. Eventually, it fills into the shape of a triangle around her pubic area and inner thighs. About two years after hair begins to grow in the pubic region, underarm hair appears. A girl can be anywhere from 10 to 16 years old when this starts.

Shortly after the arrival of pubic hair (although sometimes before), a girl's breasts begin developing, usually around nine or 10 years of age. They show up as small bumps known as "breast buds." It's not abnormal to have only one appear first, although it can be frightening for a young adolescent. For example, one young girl was afraid she had a cancerous

DID YOU KNOW…?

"The word *puberty* is derived from the Latin word *pubescere* which means 'to grow hairy.'"[3]

breast tumor because of this phenomenon. A trip to her (very sensitive) doctor reassured her that this was normal for a girl her age. For some girls, it might take a while until their breasts balance out, usually a year or so after their first period. However, some never do; so her doctor may suggest cosmetic surgery after her breasts have stopped developing.

HER PRIMARY SEX CHARACTERISTICS

Although the development of secondary sex characteristics is very noticeable, they don't significantly impact a female's ability to reproduce. However, the primary sex characteristics, which are much less obvious, are critical to her ability to procreate some day. Puberty brings about the development of a girl's primary sex characteristics, meaning it entails the development of the internal sex organs: vagina, uterus, ovaries, and fallopian tubes. Her external sex organs are known collectively as the "vulva." Some parts of the vulva include the labia majora (larger, outer lips), labia minora (smaller, inner lips), and the clitoris.

Ovulation

Included in the development of her sex organs is a girl's ability to develop eggs. A female infant is born with about 400,000 undeveloped eggs inside her ovaries. By the time she hits puberty that number has decreased to about 160,000. When she has her period, she develops one mature egg every menstrual cycle. This means she releases anywhere from 400 to 500 mature eggs throughout her reproductive lifetime. The exception is during the first year or so of a girl's menstrual cycle, when ovulation is erratic and sometimes nonexistent. During this time she may not start ovulating regularly, possibly not until the third or fourth year of her period. This information can lead some girls to believe they can't get pregnant when they're first starting to menstruate. It's important to emphasize that because of the inconsistent nature of her fertility, it may indeed be possible for her to become pregnant. And besides pregnancy, she also needs to be concerned about sexually transmitted diseases (STDs).

Menstruation—Her Period

The onset of menstruation, or menarche, is a significant sign of passage for adolescent girls. A girl is balancing on the precipice between childhood and adulthood. Whereas up until now the changes in her body have been fairly gradual, getting her period is a sudden and unmistakable sign that her body is transitioning from that of a girl's to that of a woman's. The reality is that, whether or not she's ready emotionally, her body is now able to conceive and bear children. There's excitement and anticipation as she prepares to enter this chapter, but also a certain degree of anxiety. Her body is indicating to her that she's moving toward womanhood, but part of her may desire to remain cocooned in her childhood world.

At the beginning of the twentieth century, a girl living in a Western nation used to begin menstruation at around age 15, if not later. However, since about 1970, the average age for a girl's first period is between 12 and 13 years of age, although it can occur anywhere from nine to 18 years of age. Besides better nutrition and health care, there are several other factors that influence when a girl gets her period. For example, if she's carrying extra body fat, then she might begin earlier than other girls. If she's an active athlete, then the onset of her period might be delayed. Or if a girl is African American, chances are she'll probably reach menarche anywhere from several months to a year before a Caucasian girl of the same age.

Getting a first period is greeted sometimes with anticipation, other times with indifference, and occasionally even with fear. Many girls see it as the entry into the grown-up world and breathe a sigh of relief that they finally get to catch up with their friends. So much of adolescence is checking around to make

FAMILY INFLUENCE ON MENARCHE

- The more active a father is in his daughter's life, and with the family as a whole, the later the onset of menarche.

- Girls from divorced families start their periods earlier than girls from intact families.[7]

dances

"Each time I have a period...I have the feeling that in spite all of the pain, unpleasantness, and nastiness, I have a sweet secret and that is why, although it is nothing but a nuisance to me in a way, I always long for the time that I shall feel that secret within me again."[8] —Anne Frank, *The Diary of a Young Girl*

HOW DO YOU PREPARE THE GIRLS IN YOUR MINISTRY FOR THEIR PERIODS?

We talk to the girls in our ministries about sex and dating and careers and quiet times—everything but getting your period. That topic we leave up to the families and to the school systems to explain. Sometimes that's adequate, but what if it's not?

Here are some ideas for how to talk to girls about getting their periods:

- Prepare her for what happens physiologically (e.g., the big picture of what's happening to her body, what actually happens when a girl starts her period, how it feels, and so on). Reassure her that this is a normal process that a healthy body goes through.

- Create an emotionally supportive environment. Author Anita Diamant, in her book *The Red Tent*, writes about the significance of women in ancient times gathering when they were menstruating. They would dwell together

CONTINUED >

sure one is progressing "normally" (as defined by her peer group) and getting her period is one of the most, if not *the* most, momentous markers that she is truly growing up. If a girl is one of the last in her peer group to get her period, she can feel frustrated and embarrassed. In fact, research has found that after a girl gets her period, her social standing with her peers increases, as does her sense of self-esteem.[9]

While some girls might celebrate getting their period, other girls have an opposite reaction. They dread it or even fear it because they don't like what's happening to their body (cramps, moodiness, weight gain, strange sensations of wearing a pad or a tampon). They hide in shame and hope no one notices that suddenly they have to carry a purse and run to the bathroom during class. They hate that now they have to plot their cycles and figure out whether or not they'll wear their new white jeans to the party.

If a girl hasn't had someone explain what's happening to her physiologically, it can be a time of terrifying confusion and embarrassment. This is especially true if she develops earlier than her friends and doesn't have any peer support. In some families a girl's first period is a hushed and awkward event, a secret only between mother and daughter, if that. Women have told horror stories of having no information about menstruation and upon getting their first period fearing they had cancer or were internally wounded and hemorrhaging to death. Others talk about how they felt as though their childhood had ceased and the future of being a woman was a necessary burden rather than a joy.

Since menarche is the most obvious and clearly defined of the changes that occur as a girl enters puberty (one day she doesn't have it, the next she does), many cultures acknowledge menarche with honor and celebration. For example, among certain people groups in Africa and South America, at the onset of a girl's period, she's removed from her parents' home and placed in the company of the elders in order to prepare her for her future. The belief is that it's important to separate her from her family so she can learn about the identity and responsibilities that her community requires of her as a woman. In this time of seclusion, she's taught the traditions and values of the community and spends time absorbing the wisdom of the older women. Toward the end of this initiation rite there is a celebration with friends and extended family to mark her passage into womanhood and readiness to take on her new responsibilities in society. She enters back into her society no longer a girl but as a woman.[10]

Although a much smaller unit than a tribe or clan, Western families also understand the importance of this event in a girl's life. They're creating new rites to help mark the experience in their daughters' lives. *The Cosby Show* was one of the first on television to openly talk about menarche in a celebratory fashion. In the episode where Rudy gets her first period, Mrs. Huxtable explains the family tradition of "Women's Day." When each of the girls got her first period, the mother and daughter would celebrate by doing whatever the daughter wanted to do. It also provided a chance for the daughter to ask questions and to bond with her mom.

Some families celebrate by having "period parties." For example, Maya is a high school girl who lives with her dad most of the time. She related the experience of getting her first period while staying at his place, "When I got my period, my dad was like, 'Should I go out and buy you some tampons?' Then he baked me a cake and told me that I was now a woman." She laughed softly as she added, "It was so cute, but he just didn't get it."

Whether or not Maya could appreciate it at this point in her life, her father was awkwardly and graciously attempting to commemorate her menarche as an empowering occasion. Perhaps he realized that adolescent girls receive very few positive messages about their bodies these days and wanted to counter-

CONTINUED >

in the red tent when they got their periods— perhaps for religious reasons, but most importantly for emotional and relational support. One ministry in the Pacific Northwest holds a retreat to empower girls. One of the things they talk about during the weekend is viewing your period as an empowering event, rather than one of shame and embarrassment.

- Give her helpful tips for managing her period (for example, always be prepared by carrying a tampon and a pad, even before you get your first period). Being prepared can help lessen her anxiety. Talk practically about hygiene issues.

DID YOU KNOW...?

In the 1940s Walt Disney produced a cartoon called, "The Story of Menstruation." Rather than serving popcorn, they served chocolate bars. (Okay, that last part isn't true, but it should be!)

"I noticed this girl kept going to the bathroom all the time and that our toilet paper was running out. It took me awhile to realize that she was having her first period and didn't bring anything with her," observed a middle school camp counselor.

It seems that on any kind of retreat, camp, or trip you take with your students, there will always be a girl who gets her period but isn't prepared for it. Packing a large box of pads and tampons with the rest of the supplies will save you a midnight trek to the local store. Make sure the female counselors know where this box is stored so they can access the supply, if necessary.

"Just listen! Don't try to fix it. Generally it's bad to 'leap before you listen.' On these days, listen for a *long* time. Gift her with your listening composure. Your composure gives her the context to vent the tensions of her very real world of emotions." —PMS advice from a youth worker who's also a husband and the father of two teenage girls.

act the negative messages. By celebrating her menarche, he was taking part in an ancient tradition of marking this rite of passage for his daughter.

PMS

Anyone who's worked with adolescent girls is familiar with PMS (premenstrual syndrome). It occurs the week before a girl's period and can cause cramps, bloating, tender breasts, weight gain, backaches, fatigue, and skin breakouts. Some girls get slightly depressed, moody, and prickly right before it comes. Others crave chocolate. For some girls, PMS is severe enough to warrant a visit to the doctor and possible medication. Other girls experience no symptoms at all. The key is to be patient during this time and not to discount what a girl is feeling. As one high school senior said, when asked what advice she'd give to youth workers, "Be patient with us, especially when we're PMSing and our moods are all over the place."

EARLY MATURATION

Take a look at a group of eighth-grade girls and you can quickly see the differences—one looks as though she's still a tomboy—skinny, all arms and legs, not a curve on her. The girl next to her could pass for a high school junior. I saw this clearly one afternoon when I was back at my old junior high school. I was there in the role of "youth pastor," seeking to connect with the students from our ministry. As I stood in the cafeteria chatting with one of my former math teachers, a young woman walked by and we exchanged greetings. She was an eighth-grader who had visited our ministry a few times. Tall, blonde, and beautiful, she had a number of small junior high boys bobbing in her wake like puppies begging for attention. She sat down at a long Formica table with a cluster of her friends who were more typical-looking eighth-grade girls. My former math teacher shook his head and remarked, "You know her? She's only 14, but she looks like she's about 22. She's in for a heap of trouble." And he was right. Soon after that encounter, we discovered she was dating a much older high school boy and making dangerous decisions. The last I heard of her story was that she eventually dropped out of high school and was traveling around the United States as a rock band groupie.

Unfortunately, girls who develop much earlier than their peers usually end up with a poor self-image compared to those girls who develop later. (This is the opposite of what happens to boys.[11]) Early maturing girls are more likely to have a negative view of their bodies and to suffer from an eating disorder or substance use. And, they're more likely to have conflict both at school and at home.

There are many possible explanations for these negative outcomes of early maturation. One is that even though a girl may physically look like a woman, emotionally and mentally she's still a young girl. The tendency is for adults and older peers to treat her based on how old she looks, rather than how old she actually is. She's unsure of how to handle this attention; and because her decision-making skills are still underdeveloped, she ends up making poor choices that place her at risk, or she modifies her behavior in order to meet their expectations and obtain their attention and favor.

A second possible explanation is that the earlier she matures, the more likely she is to get attention from boys, older boys in particular. Yet because of her young age, she isn't prepared to deal with that attention—emotionally or socially. In addition, these girls are sometimes rejected by their peers. So while it seems as though an early maturing girl might be more confident, the opposite is actually true. She will tend to be more submissive and unsure of her identity. Consequently, she may seek friendships with the older crowd that seemingly accepts her, while at the same time introduces her to a variety of behaviors and situations where she doesn't have the maturity to discern what may cause her harm.

And finally, a third possibility is that girls who mature early also tend to be heavier and shorter. This is antithetical to the media's ideal of tall and willowy, and it might also explain why early maturing girls are more prone to eating disorders. They're seeking to fit the norm of what society says is acceptable. However, it's important to note that this third reason might be limited to Caucasian girls. Research has found that Latinas and African American girls aren't as negatively impacted by early maturation as Caucasian girls are.[12] Perhaps it's because their cultures don't buy into the thin ideal to the same degree that a Caucasian girl's culture does. (We'll discuss more about eating disorders later on in the book.)

It's important for youth workers to realize that even though a girl may look older and even hang around with older students, there are parts of her that are still very young and have yet to develop (for instance, her decision-making and discernment abilities). An early-maturing girl needs special attention because of the potential concerns she faces that could place her at risk. It would be wise to pair her with a female volunteer or a woman in the church who understands the difficulties inherent in maturing early. This mentor could help a young girl navigate these difficult waters until her peers catch up with her. It's encouraging to note that the effects of early maturing tend to dissipate by the time a girl is in late adolescence.

LATE MATURATION

There were shrieks of laughter in the locker room as the seventh-grade girls got ready for gym class. "Ohmigosh Kara! You're still wearing an undershirt! When are you ever going to get a bra?" Kara knew the teasing from her close friends was good-natured and she laughed along, but her bright red face revealed how the words had hit a little too close to home. Most late-maturing girls get impatient with their bodies. They want to "grow up" faster, to reach the marks of puberty along with their peers, rather than always being the last one to arrive. They will try everything from chest exercises to "special lotions" and "guaranteed vitamins" to try to encourage breast development. Others may resort to stuffing tissue or padding into their bras. And still others buy into the urban legends that hold no promise of reality to a late developer, as they try to urge their periods along by running or eating lots of beets.

The good news is that in the long run, girls who develop later tend to be much more satisfied with their looks than their peers who develop early. They don't have as many of the issues to contend with as early maturing girls do, except for the teasing and embarrassment of being behind in achieving the "norm" of their peer group. By the time they hit late adolescence, they're usually much taller and leaner than their peers and have a much better body image.

STRATEGIES FOR YOUTH WORKERS

When it comes to dealing with adolescent girls and their bodies, a youth worker is venturing into a field full of potential land mines. When do you talk to a girl about how she looks? When do you stay silent? When do you intervene and offer help or suggestions? When do you confer with her parents?

When it comes to girls' physiology, part of our role as youth workers is helping girls understand that they're *in process*. Several years ago (before WWJD), there was a small, round, white pin that was popular among Christians. Unassuming blue block letters spelled out, "PBPGINFWMY," and it stood for, "Please be patient. God is not finished with me yet." This is the promise that adolescent girls need to hear again and again. They need to be assured and reassured that God isn't finished with them yet. Their

ADVICE FOR LATE-MATURING GIRLS

Have them talk to their mothers about when and what they experienced during puberty. Girls who feel as though they're developing slowly may be reassured to know that they'll usually follow their mother's timeline.

A MALE YOUTH WORKER'S PERSPECTIVE...

Q: "What do you wish you'd known about teenage girls before you started in ministry?"

A: "I wish I had known (for both guys and girls) about the tremendous physiological changes occurring in teenagers. But with girls, for me it was like dealing with someone from another planet. I'd say it's important to pay attention to the fact that what's developing on the inside is so much more delicate and crucial than what we see on the outside (*and I thought the outside was the biggest issue*)."

- "'Beauty magazines only make you feel ugly.' You will never fully understand the truth of this phrase."

- "Sixth-grade girls are some of the coolest people on the earth and you will never ever understand them."

CONTINUED >

bodies won't always be so awkward and their faces won't always be in a perpetual state of breaking out. But they *are* beautifully designed by the One who created the world.

There can be a lot of anxiety surrounding the development of girls' bodies, especially during early adolescence and particularly if they don't know what to expect. Some girls are excited by the changes and can't wait to show off their curves. They relish the fact that their new figures draw the guys' attention. On the other hand, some girls are unnerved and embarrassed by the transformation of their bodies. Terrified and mystified by the changes, they aren't quite sure how to handle them. Plus, it doesn't help that some adolescent boys are great at singling out those girls who vary from the norm, especially during middle school. Their favorite pastime of snapping a girl's bra can make walking down the hallway extremely traumatic. They'll tease girls who develop early *and* girls who develop late (as will other girls). Girls who become the target of teasing may react by wearing baggy sweatshirts and loose fitting jeans in an attempt to disappear inside their clothes.

THE YOUTH WORKER'S ROLE

It's critical that in our youth ministries we have a zero-tolerance policy when it comes to any kind of teasing, including any that might come from our leadership team—*especially* them! Our ministries need to be safe and affirming places where it's made clear that people are accepted as they are. One joking comment about a girl's appearance by a youth worker can negate months of teaching about being made in the image of God.

One way that youth workers can help assuage anxiety that adolescent girls have about bodily changes is to prepare younger students for what's ahead. Talk to them about the physical changes that are taking place. Teach them what's normal and in what circumstances they might need to seek a doctor. Let the girls know it's not unusual to spend hours in front of the bathroom mirror examining their bodies and wondering if they've inherited their father's nose or their mother's hips, if that gap in between their front teeth is endearing or ugly, or if their pores are too big and their ear lobes are too small.

It doesn't matter how many times you tell them they're beautiful—to them perception is reality. So if they perceive themselves as being ugly, that's the reality they live in. An adolescent girl needs constant reassurance that God doesn't make mistakes and creates each person with a sense of beauty and uniqueness. If she hears this enough, it will hopefully penetrate the massive number of negative messages she receives—both from herself and from those around her.

As youth workers, it's important to be aware that in addition to being hypercritical of their own bodies, adolescent girls also are hypercritical of those around them. In the same way they hold themselves to an unattainable standard, they also hold others to that same standard—including youth workers—and they don't always know how to filter their judgmental statements. For example, a couple of junior high small group leaders were talking with their students after youth group when one of the girls put her face just inches from her leader's face. The group got quiet as the girl suddenly blurted out, "Did you know you have a mustache?" The leaders rolled their eyes at each other in embarrassed good humor. They knew that comments like that are just part of the price you pay when you work with adolescent girls. Not only do they view their bodies under a microscope, but yours as well.

In our youth ministries, it's important to teach students what it means to have a healthy body and a healthy body image. Discuss with the girls about how God views their changing bodies. Be careful about complimenting a girl on her body—in fact, don't do

CONTINUED >

- "Compliment female students often. Make your compliments about their character and intentions. When you're older, it will be more appropriate for you to comment on their beauty. You'll know you are older because the kids in your group will tell you how old you are."

it. Instead, learn to compliment her on her character. And if you compliment one girl, make sure to affirm all the rest within hearing range. Otherwise they'll wonder what's wrong with them. Educate girls to know what's normal and what isn't. Engage parents in the dialogue. Ask how you can assist them as their daughters are in constant physical flux. Perhaps some of the parents who have older children in their late teens and 20s can mentor some of the parents who are experiencing these changes for the first time. Be aware that single fathers may especially need help when it comes to understanding and dealing with the physical development of their daughters.

And above all, seek to love these girls the way God loves them. With their pimples and greasy hair and body odor, can you see them through the eyes of God? Can you hold the hope for them that God is not finished with them and they are indeed beautiful, even when they can't see it for themselves? Can you help them focus on their character development as much as they focus on their physical development? Esther was known for her beauty, but it was her character and courage that were crucial in the end. If she had solely focused on her external appearance, God would not have been able to use her the way he did. As it says in 1 Samuel 16:7 (*The Message*), "God judges persons differently than humans do. Men and women look at the face; God looks into the heart."

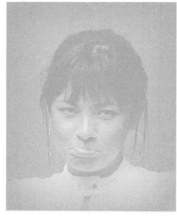

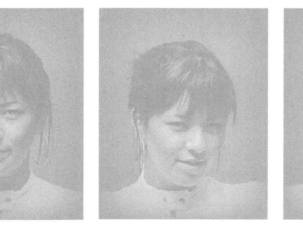

CHAPTER THREE

THE ADOLESCENT GIRL'S BODY— BODY ISSUES

"Thinness is a visual code that speaks to young women about the power of being aloof rather than desirous, cool rather than hot, blasé rather than passionate, and self-contained rather than needy."[1] —Susan Bordo, *Unbearable Weight: Feminism, Western Culture, and the Body*

Jamie was sitting with her girls around the dining table at the church retreat. When Asha got up to get another helping of mashed potatoes, Jamie heard two of the other girls whispering, "No wonder she's such a fat cow!"

"I know! Doesn't she know how she looks in those jeans?"

The crass comments took Jamie by surprise. She hadn't heard her girls slam each other in such a derogatory fashion before. Besides that, their comments puzzled Jamie. In her estimation, Asha was a normal high school girl, just a little curvier than some of the other girls who had stick-thin, almost boyish figures.

Her radar up, Jamie began to notice what the rest of the girls were eating. Even though the girls had been climbing on the ropes course all afternoon, they had vastly different portions on their plates. Emily had much smaller portions than the rest. She passed up the homemade bread and the mashed potatoes. She subtly counted the peas on her plate and cut her meatloaf into tiny portions—pushing some to the side. Up until now, Jamie had figured that perhaps she wasn't feeling well or maybe she was homesick. She'd also never really thought about Clarissa's trips to the bathroom right after every meal—she just assumed the girl had an overactive bladder. Of course it irritated her that Jenny knew the calorie count and fat percentage of every food item and would announce it to the rest of the table whenever possible, but Jamie had chalked it up to being a high school girl who was concerned about her figure. Jamie was beginning to realize that her previous assumptions might be off.

What Jamie was picking up on is what every youth worker who works with adolescent females needs to be aware of: body image issues—how girls see their own bodies and those around them. Although it would seem that Western culture is becoming more diverse, unfortunately this is rarely reflected in adolescent culture (using the term *culture* in the broadest sense). Rather than becoming more accepting of diverse body types and broadening the description of beauty, it seems as if adolescent culture is narrowing its definitions and becoming more stringent in delineating what is and isn't socially acceptable when it comes to body type. Jamie and other youth workers like her have to be aware that female body images have narrowed regarding "acceptability."

BODY IMAGE

Anyone who works with adolescent girls knows that one of the biggest sources of angst for them is the way their bodies look, or rather the way they *perceive* their bodies look. As we learned previously, it's a normal part of physical development for a girl to begin to put on a layer of fat. Her stomach becomes more rounded as she heads into puberty and this may cause her to worry that she's heading for obesity. It's a sign that she's developing *normally*. As she continues to mature, the tummy fat shifts to her hips and breasts, giving her the curves of a woman. However, not all girls understand or appreciate that part of having a growing body means there will be some weight gain. A report by the National Center on Addiction and Substance Abuse (CASA) revealed that while only 15 percent of girls and boys under the age of 18 are overweight, 62.3 percent of teenage girls said they're trying to lose weight (while only 28.8 percent of boys are doing the same).[2]

However, even if a girl knows in her head that the weight gain is a normal sign of development, the media, her friends and sometimes even her family, may not support this progression toward "normal." In grade school, most girls are confident about their bodies. They're comfortable with how they're built and they don't spend a lot of time thinking or caring about whether or not their bodies match others' or what the media says is the model. (The exception to this is if they portray an extreme— taller, shorter,

CONSIDER YOUR MINISTRY

Step back and look at the girls in your group. By what criteria are they judged by their peers? By their parents? By their youth leaders? How is "pretty" defined in your community? How about "unattractive"? What messages is the youth ministry sending them? Must they reach a certain standard of attractiveness if they're to be in up-front leadership positions? Do the prettier girls get more privileges? More attention? How will you strategize so all girls are affirmed? How will you communicate in a way that helps adolescent girls understand that God delves beneath the skin and cares about their hearts?

MEDIA DECODING

Ask the girls in your small group or ministry to record their observations as they watch television.

- If a girl is smart, how is she depicted? Is she accepted in that culture or seen as a misfit?

- If a girl is overweight, how is she depicted? Is she accepted in that culture or seen as a misfit?

- What activities are girls portrayed as participating in?

- How often are girls shown playing sports?

- How often do girls have a serious conversation that doesn't involve boys, shopping, or body image?

- What is the ideal body image portrayed for girls? Is there a difference between ethnicities?

larger, smaller—when compared with their peers.) They play freely and easily shrug off any thought about what others think, especially boys.

However, there is evidence that this carefree attitude might be changing, and that the increased pressure on appearance is invading even the younger girls' worlds. In the same CASA study mentioned earlier, researchers found that 40 percent of girls in first through fifth grades reported that they were trying to lose weight.[3] Girls as young as age seven have been identified with eating disorders. The pressure to be thin is slowly creeping into the younger ranks. One girl who's now a high school senior spoke about going over to a friend's house when she was nine. Her friend pointed out the treadmill and announced, "We're going to work out." When she questioned her friend as to why (it didn't really fit into her idea of a fun afternoon), her friend replied, "Because we have to be thin."

Whatever the emphasis is on body image among younger girls, it increases dramatically when she reaches early adolescence. Any confidence she might have had as a young girl fades away, and she becomes extremely self-conscious about her body. As David Elkind notes in *All Grown Up and No Place to Go* (1997), adolescents believe they're on center stage and everyone is watching them, even if the reality is that no one is. They're playing to an imaginary audience that feels very real to them. In an adolescent girl's mind, this audience is judging her to see if she fits the socially acceptable body type for her peer group. Girls are highly attuned to relationships; if they don't feel as though they're matching up to peer, family, or even cultural expectations, then some girls will take drastic measures to begin to change the shape of their body through cosmetic surgery, over-exercising, or even an eating disorder.

Media Impact

Not only are girls very attuned to what their peers think, but they are also well aware of what the media says is acceptable and what isn't. In the words of Margaret Mead, "Today our children are not brought up by parents, they are brought up by the mass media."[4] For example, in a study of 548 middle school and high school girls, 59 percent reported that they were displeased with their bodies. And even though only 29 percent of the girls in the study were overweight, 66 percent said they wanted to lose weight. When the researchers investigated the impact of women's fashion magazines on the girls, they found that 69 percent of the girls said that the way the models looked in the magazines impacted their ideal of what the perfect female body should look like.[5]

Yet another study found that girls who spend time each week reading teen and fashion magazines are more likely to develop an eating disorder over the next 18 months than those girls who only occasionally read those kinds of magazines.[6]

Early adolescent girls are especially vulnerable to media images. They're constantly searching for information to guide them as to how they should look and behave in this new world. As concrete thinkers, they haven't yet developed the necessary skills for discerning the different messages the media is sending. It's not until they reach about middle adolescence that they begin to develop the ability to scrutinize media messages and evaluate the themes with a certain level of skepticism. By the time they reach 17 or 18, they've had enough experience with the media to be able to assess and reject the messages. They're also more selective as to which messages they consume. They better understand the marketing behind the images and can critically choose whether or not to ignore the marketing. They know that advertisers seek to create a level of dissatisfaction with a girl's body image so she'll buy their products to attain body-image satisfaction.

THE IMPACT OF ADVERTISING

"Girls of all ages get the message that they must be flawlessly beautiful and, above all these days, they must be thin. Even more destructively, they get the message that this is possible, that with enough effort and self-sacrifice, they can achieve this ideal. Thus many girls spend enormous amounts of time and energy attempting to achieve something that is not only trivial but also completely unattainable. The glossy images of flawlessly beautiful and extremely thin women that surround us would not have the impact they do if we did not live in a culture that encourages us to believe we can and should remake our bodies into perfect commodities. These images play into the American belief of transformation and ever-new possibilities, no longer via hard work but via the purchase of the right products."[7] —Dr. Jean Kilbourne, *Can't Buy My Love*

53

SELLING A MESSAGE

"Young people really do believe, 'Well, I smoke because I want to smoke, I drink because I want to drink, I buy Nike because I want to buy Nike...And, they don't have a clue that in the Super Bowl game a 60-second commercial will cost $1.5 million. Why would a company spend that kind of money if they weren't absolutely sure that in 60 seconds they could make young people and adults buy whatever they want [them to]?"[10] —Dr. Jawanza Kunjufu

One now-famous example of the potential impact of media on body image is Dr. Ann Becker's research in Fiji. Prior to 1995, television was relatively unknown in this Pacific Island nation, and if you were a thin girl in Fiji, you were viewed as being poor or sick. Their culture valued heaviness, and it was the sign of a good host to feed your guests as much food as possible, even to well past the point of being full. In this pre-television culture that valued a robust figure, only three percent of girls said they purged to control their weight. But then in 1995, TV was introduced on a broad scale. And by 1998, 15 percent of the girls reported purging to lose weight. One girl in the study talked about how tall and slender the girls were on TV, "We want our bodies to become like that...so we try to lose a lot of weight."[8] Becker commented on her findings, "They see they're much bigger than these rich, successful Americans. Add to that a culture attuned to weight changes and the results are disastrous."[9]

The advertisers do understand that beauty is a key component of female identity and market accordingly. Whereas looks used to be just one of many facets that made up a girl, it's now at the forefront of her identity development. Dr. Mary Pipher reflects on this in *Reviving Ophelia*, "Appearance was important when I was in junior high, but it's even more important today. Girls who lived in smaller communities were judged more holistically—for their character, family background, behavior and talents. Now, when more girls live in cities full of strangers, they're judged exclusively by their appearance. Often the only information teenagers have about each other is how they look."[11]

The unfortunate reality is that a girl's looks give her social capital. When a girl is judged by her peers to be physically attractive, she's also considered more feminine.[13] An attractive girl is considered friendlier, more successful, and more intelligent than peers viewed as plain or unattractive.[14] A girl who is seen as pretty has stronger self-esteem than her peers, and she believes she has better relationships with her parents and her peers.[15] So, in a way, it makes sense that she's so concerned with her appearance. On an intuitive level, she knows that in her world, sadly, it pays to be pretty.

Family Impact

Family members and the media can both communicate this message of a thin and attractive ideal. Family observations and critiques cut especially deep as a girl puts on the normal amount of adolescent weight or perhaps is slow to develop physically. While parents might believe an observation such as, "Are you sure you should eat that ice cream, honey? It looks as though you've put on a few pounds," is just helping their daughter to think more carefully about her food choices, it can send an adolescent girl into a tailspin of questioning her appearance.

It's important that families reassure a girl that she's accepted and loved for who she is, not for her appearance. She's in a phase where she's constantly forming and re-forming her concept of her self, and her family acts as a crucial mirror in giving her feedback on whether or not she's okay. Thus, well-meaning relatives can devastate a young adolescent girl with seemingly innocent comments about how much she resembles her father (or grandfather, uncle, and so on). Although she may appreciate that observation later in life—say, when she's in her 20s (because at that age she's finally able to frame it within the context in which it was meant)—an early adolescent can only interpret that remark to mean she looks like a guy.

But at the same time, it's important that family members give a young girl positive messages that she is beautiful and attractive. Mothers especially have a clear impact on their daughter's body image. Girls who have strong and healthy relationships with their mothers are more likely to have a higher sense of self-confidence. They also have a lower incidence of

DID YOU KNOW...?

- In order to be a runway model, you need to be tall (at least five feet nine), long-legged, have a long neck, small waist, and broad shoulders. Less than five percent of the population has this type of body.

- The probability of having a body with the same proportions as Barbie® is one in 100,000. The probability of having a body like Ken® is one in 50.

- That when given the choice, 80 percent of three-to-five-year-olds prefer playing with a thin doll because it's more fun than playing with a heavy doll.

- Before the '60s, female models and performers weighed only seven percent less than the average woman. By the '70s, they weighed 15 percent less.[12]

DID YOU KNOW...?

Research has found that families who spend time together, easily express their feelings with each other, and feel connected with one another have healthier attitudes about eating and weight.[19]

COSMETIC SURGERY ON THE RISE

With reality shows such as *Extreme Makeover* and *The Swan* showing how people can dramatically alter their appearance, the cosmetic procedure business is booming. Nose jobs, breast enhancements, liposuction, chemical peels—all of these elective medical techniques have added up to more than a 400 percent increase in cosmetic procedures since 1997.[16] According to the American Society for Aesthetic Plastic Surgery, Americans had almost 11.9 million cosmetic procedures in 2004, with 90 percent of those patients being female. This is an increase of 49 percent from the previous year. How much did all of this cost? Americans spent $12.5 billion on cosmetic procedures in 2004.[17]

And adolescents are in the midst of the trend. "All in all, teenagers underwent nearly a quarter million cosmetic procedures last year," according to an article in the May 2005 issue of *Boston Magazine.* The article goes on to quote Sharlene Hesse-Biber, professor of sociology at Boston College: "Teenagers are the new market. Magazines

CONTINUED >

eating disorders. It doesn't even matter if the mother has a poor view of her own body image; if a girl feels connected with her mother, the daughter doesn't pick up the mom's insecurity. However, if the girl doesn't feel connected with her mother, she does pick up her mom's view of her own body. It's interesting to note that mothers with a negative body image are much more critical of the way their daughters look.

Cultural Impact

While flipping through any of the top teen magazines, it's unusual to see a figure with curves, although it's not as rare as it used to be. As more and more females of color are gaining media recognition, there is a fight for a shift, albeit a subtle one, in what is portrayed as the ideal female body type. Girls of color seem to have an acceptance and even a celebration of their figures that many Caucasian girls are missing. For example, African American girls are less likely to diet than Caucasian girls. They feel less pressure to be skinny and typically have a more positive body image than Caucasian girls or Latinas.[20] In an interview with a group of African American and Latina girls, they were asked about body image and whether they struggle to be thin. The group burst into laughter.

"Oh, that's a suburban White girl thing," exclaimed one.

Another jumped up and ran her hands down her waist and hips, and with a toss of her hair, declared, "We like our curves, like Jennifer Lopez's. We don't like that thin, White-girl look like Paris Hilton." The other girls laughed and screamed in approval.

However, these girls' reactions may be in conflict with the larger population of women of color. There is research emerging that challenges the myth that women of color don't suffer from eating disorders. In fact, one study says they're just as prone to eating disorders as their Caucasian sisters.[22] There is some speculation that eating disorders are underreported among females of color because of the perception that they may be betraying their cultural roots (i.e., the myth that only white females have eating disorders).[23]

There are many factors that impact the development of eating disorders in girls of color, such as socioeconomic status, gender expectations, immigration status, racism and discrimination, and community context. For example, there is research that body satisfaction levels change when girls of color are in a community of peers where there's pressure to be thin. When that happens, they're just as likely as Caucasian girls to be dissatisfied with their body image and start to diet.[24]

Christina is a second-generation Latina who's a senior at an upper-middle class, predominantly Caucasian, college prep school where, by her own admission, body image is a huge deal. "The girls are like, 'I need a nice body to wear the nice clothes to drive the nice car,'" she observed. "It's like you can't have curves if you have a BMW. But I have Latin roots and that means having nice hips that are good for giving birth," she lightheartedly exclaims. She then goes on to reveal, "It used to be that I'd have a bag of Skittles and then not eat anything else for three hours. But now I'm healthier in what I eat. I go to the gym and work out; I work hard to have the body I have. Too many of the girls here survive on water and caffeine. It's like a rite of passage when you turn 13—you start to diet. We have a BSA [Black Student Association] and GLAS [a Gay and Lesbian support group]. Maybe we need a Weight Watchers Club at school, as long as everyone's going anyway," she laughs.

It's also been found that Caucasian girls who describe themselves as being overweight are more likely to attempt suicide. However, the opposite is true for African American and Latina girls. They're more likely to attempt suicide if they believe they're ex-

CONTINUED >

have pushed the envelope on what it means to be beautiful, and surgery is now a way to deal with body issues. We're a very visual and quick-fix society. Young people are now getting that quick fix, that instant body." [18]

In a study by *Teen People*, 1,500 girls from 13 to 18 years of age were asked how they felt about their bodies. Fifty-one percent of African American girls said they were almost completely satisfied with their bodies. Only 31 percent of Caucasian girls, 30 percent of Latinas, and 29 percent of girls who designated "other race" answered that question positively. Best feature? Twenty-four percent of girls said their breasts and their butts were their best features. Worst feature? Forty percent said their stomachs.[21]

tremely underweight.[26] And just because these girls *believe* they're over- or underweight, that doesn't mean they are. The same study found that about 72 percent of the girls who responded had a normal Body Mass Index (BMI), but 37 percent of the respondents considered themselves overweight and 12 percent thought they were underweight. It's no wonder our youth ministries are filled with girls who are struggling with body image problems.

EXTREME EXERCISE

With the rise in childhood obesity, many parents welcome an adolescent who's physically active. With the approval of Title IX in the 1970s, many more doors opened for girls to become involved in athletics that were previously off-limits to them due to limited resources or restricted access to programs and coaches. Many girls are involved in at least one sport per season, and the impact on their lives—both short-term and long-term—is extremely positive.

The danger comes when girls are focused on trying to mold their bodies through exercise that is excessive, even compulsive. When a girl becomes extremely anxious because she has to miss a workout or heads to the basement and runs on the treadmill for two to three hours at a time, or she gets up in the middle of the night at a sleepover and finds a secret place to jump rope or run in place, there's cause for concern. Even if she's involved in team sports, it's important to keep an eye on her activity level and make sure she's training in a way that's healthy.

OBESITY

Kaitlin was talking with her youth pastor about her parents' separation. Her dad had left several months before and was in the midst of a full-blown mid-life crisis—complete with six-pack abs, a muscle shirt, and a brand-new sports car. Her mom, a slightly overweight platinum blond, was left with three adolescents at home. She struggled to pay the bills with income from her basement beauty shop.

Kaitlin was very upset. The vitriol spewing from her mouth fit her new look—bleached white hair, heavily lined eyes, and a baggy black T-shirt that covered her snug black jeans. "Do you know how I'm getting back at him?" she hissed. "I'm eating like crazy. Everything in the fridge." Her eyes were filled with pain, but her voice was filled with revenge. "He hates it when women are fat." Kaitlin's youth pastor had noticed the sudden weight gain and wondered what was behind it. Now it all made sense.

Kaitlin was doing what a number of obese adolescent girls do—eating to hide painful or difficult emotions. It was still too early to determine if she was struggling with a binge eating disorder (see below), but her youth pastor knew she had always wrestled with her weight.

Unfortunately, adolescents who struggle with obesity in our society often get caught in a catch-22. They eat to hide the pain, causing them to put on more weight. Then they must face a world that makes fun of their weight and large size, and they eat again to hide the pain.

The media doesn't make it any easier on them. Too often the easy joke on TV is to make fun of overweight people. There were a number of *Friends* episodes that portrayed "fat Monica" as the butt of the sitcom joke. If a show does have a regular heavyset female character, rarely is she the lead role or the object of romantic interest.

And it also doesn't help that the average child is exposed to more than 40,000 television ads a year, and that the majority of them are food products directly targeted at young people (cereal, fast food, snacks, soft drinks, and so on). Add to that the increase in portion size and the decrease in physical activity, and it's easy to see why the number of overweight

BEAUTY IS SKIN DEEP *AND* IN THE EYES OF THE BEHOLDER

"I'll never marry a man who's darker than me," proclaimed Shareese, a fair-skinned African American. Her friends (all African Americans) reacted in disbelief; one even exclaimed that she was being racist. They prodded her for her rationale, but she just shook her head and stubbornly said, "I just won't."

For her, skin color was a defining characteristic. Skin color is often used as a determinant of beauty in certain ethnic groups. In the past it was believed that the lighter the skin, the more beautiful someone was considered to be (seemingly due to the White influence on cultures). Spike Lee dealt with this concept in his movie, *School Daze* (Columbia Pictures, 1988). This belief is now changing, although slowly.

Often skin color is an issue in Hispanic, Japanese, and Indian cultures as well (to name a few). There are Latinas who talk about being pale enough to "pass" as White. In Indian cultures, some men prefer to marry women who have a pale complexion.[27]

CONTINUED >

CONTINUED >

Some Japanese women have been seeking to whiten their skin since the late 1980s.[28]

Among certain adolescents of Asian descent, eye shape is a sign of beauty. There's increasing pressure to have eyelid surgery that adds the illusion of a crease, so a girl's eyes will resemble those from European backgrounds. Some girls who don't want to have the surgery have taken to using special glue to achieve a Western-type round eye. Other Asian cultures describe long necks (to show off their indigenous costumes) or hair length as symbols of beauty.

Questions to ask in your youth ministry:

- Take a look at the different cultures that are represented in your youth ministry. How does each culture define "beauty"?

- Has that definition changed in recent generations?

- When are definitions of "beauty" healthy and when are they unhealthy?

- What sacrifices are girls making to attain those standards of attractiveness?

adolescents in the United States has tripled since 1980, now at 14 percent of the population.[32] More than 43 percent of 12-to-15-year-old girls have been told by their physicians that they're overweight.[33] Among children and adolescents of color, the rates are even higher. Forty percent of Hispanic and African American children and adolescents (ages six to 19) are considered either overweight or in danger of becoming overweight.[34]

While the impact of poor diets and lack of exercise needs to be considered, there are other factors that indicate that an adolescent might be headed toward a lifetime of obesity. In a study published in 2005, researchers found that "having obese parents, suffering from depression, and engaging in radical dieting like forced vomiting, were all risk factors for future obesity in adulthood."[36] The more a girl follows extreme dieting habits, the more likely she'll struggle with her weight later in life. She's also more likely to suffer from type 2 diabetes.

EATING DISORDERS

For a normal person, eating is part of the typical rhythm of the day. Some days, we eat too many sour cream and onion potato chips or too much ice cream. Other days, we forget to eat altogether because our schedules are crazy. But in the end, we find a way to get the balance of nutrition our bodies need.

However, for some adolescent girls, eating has become the central focus of their lives. It has lost its pleasure and become an obsession. We can blame the media, the fashion industry, dysfunctional family systems, cultural expectations, or whatever we choose, but the reality is that our girls have become focused on food and their figures. Youth workers need to understand what's going on.

In the past, eating disorders were associated with upper- and middle-class girls, perhaps because some of the earliest examples of anorexia came from de-

how do dancers define?

scriptions of girls from wealthy families in Victorian England.[37] The thought was that a woman was viewed as much more feminine if she only ate a small amount of food. Her limited appetite was also a sign of her spiritual purity.[38] However, these days we know that eating disorders cut across all socio-economic, racial and ethnic boundaries. In Western culture, there is no adolescent female who is immune from the possibility of developing an eating disorder.

An eating disorder is an illness that includes abnormal behaviors and attitudes about weight, body image, and food. It's estimated that anywhere from three to 10 percent of teenage girls have either a full or partial eating disorder.[39] But many, many girls show signs of abnormal eating tendencies, whether it's an obsession with counting calories, bingeing, abusing laxatives or diet pills, or inducing vomiting.

Risk Factors for Eating Disorders

Researchers have looked at many possible risk factors that impact eating disorders: family, socioeconomic context, cultural context, hormone abnormalities, genetic susceptibility, body shape, emotional state, self-image, peer relationships, and media influence, to name a few. While there are some common factors that people with eating disorders have, much of the research is still inconclusive. For example, there is some evidence to suggest that a girl is more likely to develop an eating disorder if someone else in her family has one.[40] But researchers still aren't certain if this is genetically based or due to family patterns.

Some other factors that put an adolescent at risk are:

1. Being female. Ninety percent of teenagers who have an eating disorder are female.

2. Being a teenager. Girls who are most at risk for developing an eating disorder are between 14 and 18 years old.[42]

IT'S NOT JUST PROFESSIONAL BASEBALL PLAYERS

Researchers are finding that adolescent girls are turning to a more buffed and toned look in response to the drugged-out, emaciated look that has been popular for so long. But many of them are turning to supplements to do so. One study, sponsored in part by Kellogg's, found that out of 10,000 adolescents, 44 percent of the girl respondents reported to have participated in strength training. And eight percent of the girls said they used some kind of supplement in the past year to improve their appearance.

The adolescents cited using not only protein shakes, but also "steroids, growth hormone, amino acids and other potentially unhealthy products."[29] The Centers for Disease Control and Prevention now estimates that five percent of high school girls have abused steroids, and not all of them are athletes. They speculate that females are using steroids in much the same way they use diet pills and protein shakes, while at the same time they're ignoring the possible damage to their kidneys, livers, and hearts.[30]

3. Living in Western society. Although eating disorders are found throughout the world, they're much more prevalent in Western cultures.

4. Abusing substances. Girls who abuse chemicals such as alcohol or drugs are 11 times more likely to have an eating disorder than girls who don't abuse these substances, according to a 2004 report by the National Center on Addiction and Substance Abuse. They not only will use laxatives and diuretics, but alcohol, tobacco, caffeine, amphetamines, cocaine, and heroin to control their weight. Some girls are even using Adderall (an ADD/ADHD drug) to lose weight. Adderall, in the amphetamine category, was first developed as a drug for weight loss. The girls will mimic the symptoms of ADD or ADHD and get prescriptions for the drug or buy a pill from their friends because one of the side effects of the drug is a loss of appetite.

5. Being overweight. An overweight girl may be overly concerned about peer or familial expectations about body shape and put pressure on herself to lose weight using extreme measures.

6. Early maturing. A girl who has her period earlier than her peers has a tendency to befriend older boys. Consequently, she may become sexually active at an earlier age, increasing her sensitivity about her body image.

7. Perfectionist tendencies. A girl who tends toward perfectionism is a highly critical judge, not only of others, but also of herself in particular. If she believes she's failing in her peer relationships or her performance in school or her relationship with a family member, she can feel like a success if she takes control of what she eats and what she looks like. Since thinness is valued in much of Western culture, her

efforts are often encouraged until she reaches an extreme. Thus, in her mind, she's been successful in at least one area of her life.

8. High levels of stress and trauma. A traumatic event or internal struggle can sometimes increase the chance that an adolescent will develop an eating disorder. Situations such as grieving the loss of a loved one, living in a chaotic home situation, extreme academic pressure, concerns over sexual identity, bullying, or relational aggression can create environments where the adolescent will seek to cope in ways that are harmful to her.

9. Fear of growing up. She can suffer from severe anxiety about becoming an adult. In her mind, her world is quickly spinning out of control. Her body is changing, her school is changing, her friends are changing. Controlling her eating is one area of life where she can feel as though she still has power over her own destiny.

It's important to note that these risk factors don't necessarily cause an eating disorder. They're just indicators that a girl may be more at risk than a girl without any of those factors in place. And conversely, a girl with none of these risk factors can still develop an eating disorder.

Often, girls can show symptoms of unhealthy eating patterns, but those around her chalk it up to typical adolescent female behavior. A week of counting calories or eating nothing but salads may not raise suspicion. The problem is when these behaviors and attitudes go undetected for weeks and months and therefore it isn't until the adolescent begins to show physical manifestations of the illness that drastic steps are finally taken.

The two most commonly known eating disorders are *anorexia nervosa* and *bulimia nervosa*. However, binge eating is becoming more common. And even though obesity isn't classified as an eating disorder, it does impact the health of adolescent girls.

Anorexia Nervosa

Anorexia nervosa is a disorder marked by self-starvation, through severely restricting calorie intake, use of diuretics or laxatives, or excessive exercising, resulting in extreme weight loss. Often, the onset is during adolescence when a girl becomes more conscious of her body and compares it to her peers' and to what she sees in the media. (It should be noted that boys may also suffer from anorexia nervosa, although to a much lesser degree.)

Girls with anorexia nervosa suffer from a powerful determination to be thin that can result from an overwhelming fear of being overweight. They have strict control over what goes into their mouths. They know the calorie content of each morsel, and they know how much exercise it will take to burn off those calories.

One of the dangers of anorexia nervosa is that the onset can be so subtle. At first, girls will receive compliments on their weight loss. They might be admired for their willpower to say no to sweets and high-carbohydrate foods and encouraged to keep up their dieting. This can feed into the mindset that "thinner is better" and affirm their efforts. So they continue to lose weight in an effort to reach what is the "perfect figure" in their mind.

But what they don't realize is that they have a distorted mental picture of their body. When a girl with anorexia nervosa looks in the mirror, she sees a body that is still overweight and—in her eyes—ugly and undesirable. Whereas when anyone else looks at her, they see a skeleton. The descriptive phrase often used by family members is, "She looks as though she belongs in a concentration camp."

Behaviors

Several behaviors manifest themselves in girls dealing with anorexia nervosa. This is just a partial list and should in no way be construed as a tool for diagnosis. Use these only as a guide to raise your awareness:

- Obsession with calorie counting

- Weighing in several times a day

- Abusing laxatives, diuretics, or diet pills

- Frenzied need to exercise

- Vomiting after eating

- Avoiding eating in front of people

- Denying that she's hungry

- Cooking her own meal (e.g., when the family is having pizza, she makes a dinner of broccoli and salad with no dressing)

- Hiding her food at a meal (e.g., slipping bread into her jacket pocket so that watchful family members believe she's done eating)

- Cutting her food into small pieces and pushing the pieces around her plate

- Consistently going to the bathroom immediately after she eats

- Strict adherence to a diet or exercise plan; any "slip-up" is marked by abnormal guilt or shame

- Wearing baggy clothing to hide the weight loss (especially if she's been previously asked if she has an eating disorder)

- Wearing heavy clothing that's inappropriate for the weather (because of her loss of body fat, she may need the extra warmth)

- Increased isolation from friends

- Depression or extreme moodiness

"So many people have asked me, 'How did you become anorexic?' that I'm about ready to tape-record my life story and play it back the next time the question comes up. I try to explain using the analogy of a rainbow. The entire spectrum of colors comprises the rainbow, but no single color can be extracted—they all blend together to form a continuum. The same can be said of the illness. Anorexia wasn't something that just 'happened' to me—I didn't one day suddenly decide to stop eating. My problems ran much deeper than simply 'not eating.' The disorder was my desperate attempt to maintain some semblance of control in my life. It was a cry to establish who I was, to pick up the pieces of my shattered identity."[44] —Chhaya

"Another way to think about…anorexia is [as] a kind of social club (albeit a dangerous one), which has rules, norms, and certain membership debts and assets. Without trivializing the seriousness of an eating disorder, there are some similarities between an eating disorder and the 'club' metaphor. Members are actively recruited, often identify themselves with the club itself, have a sense of purpose and belonging when they join, and are provided, primarily through the media, with explicit rules for behavior. At the same time that members are recruited, they also have the capacity to give up their membership."[45] —Dr. Marie L. Hoskins

Physical Impact of Anorexia

Besides the extreme weight loss, there are other external changes to a girl's body: hair loss, dark circles under her eyes, brittle nails, cold hands and feet (due to poor circulation), and the development of soft hair on her back, stomach, or face. (This last one is in reaction to the fat loss. It's the body's attempt to keep her warm.) She can also develop an orange tint to her skin; it's especially evident on her palms. This is possibly evidence of eating a large amount of carrots, but also could be an indicator of starvation.

Anorexia takes a serious toll on a girl's body. Not only do her periods cease, but also her body temperature and her blood pressure drop. Her bones become more fragile due to low bone density. Her growth may be permanently stunted. There can be severe, and sometimes irreversible, damage to her brain, her kidneys, and her heart, resulting in death.

Bulimia Nervosa

Bulimia nervosa is similar to anorexia nervosa in that it's about a person's desire to control her weight. But where a girl with anorexia nervosa will starve herself, a girl with bulimia nervosa will "binge and purge." For example, she'll eat a large amount of food in a short period of time, such as a quart of ice cream or a box of Twinkies in one sitting (bingeing). But a binge is followed by a wave of shame because of her perceived lack of control over her eating habits or a fear of putting on weight. To manage the shame or the fear, she'll purge herself of the food, usually by self-induced vomiting, but sometimes through laxatives, Ipecac, diuretics, diet pills, or by excessive exercise or fasting.

Typically, a girl who struggles with bulimia is slightly older than a girl who is anorexic. Bulimia usually develops in middle adolescence (versus the onset of anorexia during early adolescence), and it's more likely to occur in girls who develop early. It's also possible that a girl may have both eating disorders, since about one-third of girls with anorexia go on to develop bulimia. It may take awhile for others to become aware that a girl is struggling with bulimia nervosa. Where anorexia nervosa is marked by extreme weight loss, bulimia nervosa can be present in girls who are thin, average weight, and even overweight. Their weight can vary quite a bit, due to their erratic eating habits.

Behaviors

As with anorexia, there are several behaviors that manifest themselves in girls dealing with bulimia. Again, this is just a partial list and should in no way be construed as a tool for diagnosis. Use these only as a guide to raise your awareness:

- Consumption of large quantities of food—usually high in calories—within anywhere from two hours to two minutes, followed by extreme guilt and shame

- Consistently heads to the bathroom after every meal

- Development of and adherence to a strict diet and exercise regime

- Evidence of vomiting or abuse of diet pills, laxatives, or diuretics (e.g., empty packages hidden in the garbage)

- Large and rapid variations in weight

- Hiding food for easy access

- Stealing or sneaking food

- Irregularity or cessation of her period

- Self-mutilation

- Depression and suicidal ideation

Physical Impact of Bulimia

Many of the physical signs of anorexia are also true for those suffering from bulimia. But because of the

CASE STUDY: CONFRONTING ANOREXIA

The small group of first-year college students was known for its binge parties. These young women would easily chow through several packages of Oreos, a tub of ice cream, and a couple dozen cookies in a night. Renee was always on the fringe of the group, laughing but trying not to be too obvious with her baggie of celery and carrots. While the other girls would take advantage of the all-you-can-eat cafeteria food, Renee cautiously planned out her meals. Once, when they went over to one of the girl's homes for a home-cooked meal, Renee panicked because she was served something for which she didn't know the calorie content. She thought she was thin and beautiful and in control, when compared with the other girls in the dorm who were packing on the "freshman 15."

But her friends realized there was a problem when, on a particularly windy day, Renee was too weak to open the door to one of the classroom buildings. So they tried an intervention—it failed miserably. It wasn't until summer break, when her mom dragged her to the family doctor, that Renee began to realize that her health was seriously in danger. When

CONTINUED >

CONTINUED >

she looked in the mirror, she saw a beautiful, thin woman who matched the models in the magazines. The reality was she resembled a survivor from a concentration camp. So her doctor recommended a residential treatment program.

Looking back, Renee realized there were many factors that contributed to the development of her eating disorder. But one incident in particular that stood out in her mind. During her junior year in high school, one of the popular guys in her high school youth group (whom she had a crush on) commented that it looked as though she was starting to put on a little weight. According to Renee, becoming anorexic was the one way she could control her life and try to win his approval.

Questions to ask in your youth ministry:

- Who should shoulder the responsibility in this situation: Renee, her roommates, her mother, her youth pastor, or the high school guy?

- What would you have done if you were Renee's youth pastor? If you were one of her friends?

CONTINUED >

purging, there are additional factors that need attention, for example, a loss of tooth enamel or a persistent sore throat (due to recurrent vomiting). A girl with bulimia may also look as though she's developing "chipmunk cheeks" due to enlarged salivary glands (also due to the vomiting). If she self-induces vomiting by putting her finger or hand down her throat, she may also develop calluses on her fingers or on the backs of her hands due to exposure to stomach acids.

Girls with bulimia will experience many of the same physical tolls as those with anorexia. In addition, girls with bulimia are more likely to suffer from low potassium and arrhythmias. As with anorexia, these complications can result in death.

Binge Eating Disorder

Binge eating is similar to bulimia, in that both disorders involve bingeing. However, in binge eating disorder (or BED), purging and laxative abuse is absent. This disorder is marked by episodes of eating extraordinarily large amounts of food, usually secretively. Afterwards, a girl is plagued by a sense of guilt and embarrassment over her behavior. This disorder isn't in response to a sensation of being hungry, nor is it due to feelings of deprivation due to dieting. In fact, a girl could have finished a full meal and still feel the need to binge. It usually comes about as a response to depression, boredom, worry, or anxiety.

Because BED is a relatively new disorder, compared to anorexia and bulimia, the research is still fairly limited. What is known so far is that it generally shows up in an older population (typically adults in their 40s), although there are also adolescents who suffer from it. Also, more males suffer from BED than from anorexia or bulimia.[47]

While African American and Latina girls aren't as likely to suffer from some of the more well-known eating disorders such as anorexia nervosa, there is some evidence that they're slightly more at risk than Caucasian females for developing a binge eating disorder, especially Latinas.[48]

Behaviors

Binge eating has many behaviors that are similar to those of a bulimic. When dealing with someone who may have a binge eating disorder, check to see if some of these behaviors or indicators are present:

- Depression or struggling with difficult emotions such as anger, guilt, or shame

- Large amounts of food missing (e.g., containers of ice cream go missing from the freezer, bags of chips disappear quickly)

- Lack of control over eating habits (i.e., an inability to stop eating after the average person would feel full) or lack of impulse control

- Sneaking or hiding food (e.g., a box of snack cakes are stuffed inside a glove compartment, a backpack contains several bars of chocolate)

- Eating as a reward

- Eating as a coping mechanism (e.g., eating large amounts of "comfort food" in response to a stressful situation, but on a regular basis)

- Increased weight gain (although many adolescents who binge are able to maintain a normal weight)

- Affected by a cultural expectation that being heavier is better than being thin

Physical Impact of Binge Eating Disorder

As with the previous disorders, the impact of binge eating can be life-altering if it's left untreated. However, because BED is still so new, there has been little research done on the long-term effects on a body. However, since the nature of the disorder relates to

CONTINUED >

- What is the prevailing attitude toward a person's weight in your youth ministry?

- How often do you hear comments made about a student's appearance, especially female students? Who's making the comments?

- Which students get more attention, the heavier or physically fit students?

- How often does the youth ministry curriculum cover the topic of healthy living?

FACTS ABOUT EATING DISORDERS

- Fewer than one in 10 adolescent girls with symptoms of eating disorders seek diagnosis.

- With treatment, 75 to 80 percent of adolescents recover from eating disorders.

- Anywhere from five to nine percent of adolescents with eating disorders eventually die, either directly because of the disorder, or they commit suicide.[46]

a considerable intake of calories, obesity is a strong possibility. Because an adolescent with BED is sometimes heavier than her peers, she can sometimes be viewed as lazy. The resulting feelings of shame and inadequacy only add to the problem.

RECOVERY AND TREATMENT FOR EATING DISORDERS

It can often take more than five years for a girl to recover from an eating disorder. The good news is that the earlier she gets help, the more likely she'll be to recover and regain a normal life. Treatments can range from full hospitalization to partial (day treatment) to residential programs. Treatment programs often use a variety of therapeutic approaches, such as interpersonal, familial, body image, relaxation, or even art, music, and dance therapies.

THE YOUTH WORKER'S ROLE

It's important to realize that unless someone is properly qualified, youth workers are not trained to diagnose an eating disorder. However, because of their roles, youth workers are often the first to notice abnormalities about a student's perception of her body. These are issues that family members might be oblivious to, perhaps because of inexperience or because of denial.

Eating disorders can be extremely difficult to recognize. Girls will go to great lengths to hide their behaviors, both from their youth pastors and their parents. Expect a girl to become antagonistic when confronted about the possibility of having an eating disorder. Expect denial, tears, rage, and accusations. Expect promises to do better from now on and promises to keep you abreast of her eating habits. Expect pleas not to tell her family members.

However, it's important that as soon as you have a strong hunch that a girl is suffering from an eating disorder you seek to draw the parents into the situation. As a youth pastor, you're also a pastor to the parents of adolescents. You may need to help parents understand that this will be a long road and they'll need to seek support for themselves during this time. They may also need assurance that they didn't cause the eating disorder. The reality is that eating disorders are caused by a complex combination of factors.

If this is the first time you've dealt with a student who has an eating disorder or if you have concerns about the parents' reaction, you may want to work with a licensed therapist who can help coach the process along. It's extremely helpful to have a list of referrals for the parents, should they need them. You can usually find out who specializes in eating disorders in your community by contacting the local hospital, a doctor or a counselor in the public school system or at a community resource agency.

As youth workers, body image and eating disorders are areas where we need to be extra alert and cautious. We need to promote healthy lifestyles and exercise, perhaps by offering healthier food choices at youth events. At the same time, it's critical not to draw attention to or shame girls who choose junk food over a piece of fruit. At lock-ins or retreats, bring cut-up veggies and fruit in addition to the usual junk food. And make sure they have plenty of time to run and play.

We need to represent a healthy, holistic theology that we don't just preach but practice in our own choices and lifestyle. Are we modeling healthy eating and lifestyle choices? Do we complain about our weight and compare ourselves to impossible media images? We need to help girls understand how God views them and his perspective of beauty and body image. We need to help them understand that they are indeed beautifully and wonderfully made (Psalm 139:14).

CHAPTER FOUR

ALTERED STATE:
ADOLESCENT GIRLS AND
SELF-INJURY

ANNA'S STORY

"My best friend got me into it. Her boyfriend broke up with her and she was over at my house and I watched her do it, I couldn't stop her. I wanted to help her but I didn't know what to do. I could relate exactly to her pain. I had a lot of the same issues, I just never thought of dealing with them the same way she did. She just wanted to be better; she wanted to succeed and to be different from her sisters, who were in jail. She wanted to make her dad proud, but she couldn't handle the stresses of life. She didn't want to die; she just wanted to let it out of her. I was dying to have a real best friend and I wanted to be there for her, to help her, so I started cutting too. It was more like scratches back then, nothing really, just enough to make a mark, to show her. But then she got better; she told her parents and got help. I was suddenly forgotten, and I stopped scratching.

"About a year later, life became hell. Work was crazy, school was insane, I wanted a boy to love me, colleges were calling, the bank account was empty, and I had no real friends…Then I became a real cutter…But I really didn't want to die. I just wanted to get away. Get this dream out of my head. Cutting was a release. Kind of like a hot shower when you're sick…When it bled, I felt like I was getting better. I had to cut deeper, to get it all out, to be truly fixed. I'd cut and cut, in the shower, in bed at night, watching TV…I couldn't feel myself hurting me. So I made it worse so that I could feel my sins. I poured rubbing alcohol on my cuts or even hydrogen peroxide…I'm okay now; I'll be all right. I've stopped for now, and I want to survive this. I don't want to die. I never did, but when I cut, life becomes way too close to death."

This is a letter from Anna, a 17-year-old girl on the threshold of her senior year in high school. She's what's known as a cutter, self-injurer, self-mutilator, or self-abuser. She's part of a growing phenomenon that's affecting our adolescent girls.

SELF-INJURY

The story of self-abuse and mutilation is at least as old as the Bible. Mark 5:5 talks about an encounter Jesus had with a cutter—a man from Gerasenes who cut himself with stones. Today, adolescent girls are mutilating themselves with paper clips, safety pins, pen caps, scissors, razor blades, or shards of glass or a broken mirror. Some choose to burn themselves with matches, cigarettes, hot metal, or chemicals. It goes by many names: self-injury, self-abuse, self-mutilation, parasuicide, the "new anorexia," to name a few. As Anna wrote, they aren't trying to kill themselves; they're seeking to release the pain within.

In a simple definition, it's when a girl inflicts physical harm on herself, usually with the intention of easing her emotional and mental state. The authors of *Bodily Harm* define self-injury as "the deliberate mutilation of the body or a body part, not with the intent to commit suicide but as a way of managing emotions that seem too painful for words to express. In can include cutting the skin or burning it, or bruising oneself through a premeditated accident. It can mean scratching the skin until it bleeds, or interfering with the healing of wounds. In more extreme cases, self-injurers break their own bones, amputate their own digits, eat harmful substances, or inject their bodies with toxins."[1]

Self-injury is different than tattooing or piercing. People have long sought to identify themselves through their skin, using markings and piercings to affiliate with tribes or identify with particular religions. In these cases the community accepts the symbols as signs of connection. But the trend of tattooing and piercing isn't the kind of self-mutilation we're talking about here. Psychotherapist and author Steven Levenkron describes it this way, "An analogy to conventional dieting versus anorexia nervosa is useful...When most of us diet, we feel deprived, annoyed. When the anorexic is starving herself, she

DIAGNOSTIC DEFINITION

Steven Levenkron, psychotherapist and author of the book *Cutting: Understanding and Overcoming Self-Mutilation* details the following criteria to help in the clinical diagnosis of self-abuse:

- Recurrent cutting or burning of one's skin.

- A sense of tension present immediately before the act is committed.

- Relaxation, gratification, pleasant feelings, and numbness experienced concomitant with the physical pain.

- A sense of shame and fear of social stigma, causing the individual to attempt to hide scars, blood, or other evidence of the acts of self-harm.[2]

feels satisfaction, even though she's suffering in pain and may be in danger of losing her life."[3]

Who's Abusing?

It's estimated that one percent of the population of the United States has tried to abuse themselves at one time or another.[4] It's a growing trend among adolescent girls (the majority of self-abusers are female), especially white, middle-class females who suffer from low self-esteem, depression, and a lack of close friendships where they can express themselves. Girls are learning how to cut and mutilate by watching others, as we learned in Anna's story. Some are moving from eating disorders to self-abuse, upping the ante, so to speak, feeling as though they need to take more drastic measures to either gain control or relieve the inner anguish they're facing. Often girls who are self-abusing have also had an eating disorder or abused chemicals.

In 1985 Karen Conterio, an addictions counselor, and Wendy Lader, a clinical psychologist, founded the first inpatient treatment program for self-abusers called S.A.F.E. Alternatives—"Self Abuse Finally Ends"—in suburban Chicago. In their years of working with self-abusers, they've developed a profile of common traits or histories. However, they warn that not all self-abusers will show all or even any of these characteristics. This is an abbreviated summary of some of the traits they've discovered in their work:

- Difficulties in various areas of impulse control, as manifested in problems with eating behaviors or substance abuse.

- A history of childhood illness or severe illness or disability in a family member. [This sense of loss or grief can add to the sadness and depression a self-injurer already feels.]

- Low capacity to form and sustain stable relationships.

- Fear of change.

- An inability or unwillingness to take adequate care of themselves.

- Low self-esteem, coupled with a powerful need for love and acceptance from others.

- Childhood histories replete with trauma or significant parenting deficits that led to difficulties internalizing positive nurturing.

- Rigid, all-or-nothing thinking.[5]

Why Are They Abusing Themselves?

At some time in our lives, all of us have been frustrated to the point where we want to lash out physically, whether that be punching a pillow, slamming a door, or flinging a glass across the room. There's an immediate release of pressure when that happens, but girls who self-injure will experience that release on a different scale. They often talk about being overwhelmed by situations or emotions and not knowing how to handle it. Whereas a healthy person would go for a run, paint, write, or talk with a trusted friend, cutting provides a quick release for a self-abuser. It's a coping mechanism, albeit a dangerous one.

Girls who self-mutilate talk about feeling numb while they're cutting. In a way, they become dissociated with their bodies, and their skin becomes a canvas or another surface on which to "paint" or express themselves, so to speak. They don't stop until they can see blood—until they feel the anxiousness has been replaced by a deep calm. Afterwards, they're often plagued by guilt and shame, starting the cycle all over again. Self-abusers don't want to kill themselves; rather, they're looking to release the inner anguish that seems to be crushing them.

Serious self-injurers cut in places that won't be easily noticed—upper arms and legs, breasts, genitals, and the stomach. They often wear long-sleeved

Dr. Lisa Machoian has spent years researching adolescent girls and depression. In her book, *The Disappearing Girl*, she said this about her findings: "Girls who are depressed and thus start acting out and hurting themselves are doing so in the desperate hope of being listened to and understood, getting help, finding real relationships, and being true to their real selves. In that effort, they discover they are taken more seriously when they endanger or hurt themselves with violence than when they communicate with words. As a society, we pay lot of attention to violence just watch the news."[6]

shirts and long pants—even on hot days—to cover up their work. Those who identify themselves as "cutters" talk about their frustration with "poseurs"—girls who fake cutting to get attention or to be part of a perceived trend. They'll scratch their bodies in places that are easily seen and rarely do any damage to tissue. However, even the cries of these girls trying to get attention need to be taken seriously. They're moving toward extreme measures to cry for help and we need to heed their cries, as well as the cries of those more serious self-abusers.

THE YOUTH WORKER'S ROLE

Youth workers are often among the first to know when a student is self-injuring. Sometimes we can identify a self-injurer before she's even willing to get help. We need to be alert to girls who aren't connecting with other girls in the ministry—they appear to be loners and have an aura of depression. We need to be watchful for girls who show a change in behavior—gradually withdrawing from group activities, suddenly becoming very secretive about their behavior. We also need to keep an eye out for the physical signs: girls who wear long sleeves at inappropriate times—a sign that they're covering up their injuries—scratches that don't appear to be healing or that seem to form a pattern or symbol, burns that have odd explanations, and frequent "accidents" that are explained with flimsy excuses that fall apart when pressed for details. When at camp or on a retreat, keep an eye out for caches of objects a girl may use for cutting: a group of opened safety pins, a cluster of bent paper clips, or shards of glass stored in a jewelry box.

When a youth worker discovers a girl is self-injuring, it's crucial that you get help quickly. She may be resistant to the idea, even denying she has a problem. It's important to express empathy, create a safe place for her to talk openly, and offer assistance. For example, "I'm concerned about what I see, and I want you to know I'm here to help you, not get you in trouble. I'll walk through this with you."

It's important to draw parents into the conversation as soon as it is feasible. Understand they may have a variety of reactions, ranging from denial ("It's just a passing trend at school. She'll get over it on her own") to revulsion ("How can you do that horrible thing to yourself?") to embarrassment ("How could our little girl do this to our family?") to anger directed toward their daughter or toward you for exposing the problem. Thankfully, many families are appreciative for the assistance because they had a hunch that something was wrong.

Because the issues associated with self-injury are so complex, it's crucial to get a girl connected with help. The local hospital, school counselor, or community health agency should have connections with local experts specializing in the area of self-injury.

Both the adolescent girl and her family will need support through this process. It's important to remember that as a youth pastor, you aren't her therapist. She needs to know she can still attend youth ministry events without feeling as though she'll only be identified by her problems. Hold onto a holistic view of her and realize that she's more than a "cutter." She is a child of God; and although he grieves with her in her suffering, he also celebrates her life and who she is—all of her.

RESOURCES

Here are several books and Web sites that may provide helpful information:

- S.A.F.E. Alternatives program:
  www.selfinjury.com

- Focus Adolescent Services:
  www.focusas.com/selfinjury.html

- Kids Health:
  www.kidshealth.org/teen/your_mind/mental_health/cutting.html

- *Bodily Harm: The Breakthrough Healing Program for Self-Injurers* written by the developers of the S.A.F.E. Alternatives program—Karen Conterio and Wendy Lader, with Jennifer Kingson Bloom (Hyperion Books, 1998)

- *Cutting: Understanding and Overcoming Self-Mutilation* by Steven Levenkron (W.W. Norton & Co., 1998)

(*Inclusion on this list in no way implies an endorsement of their sites, practices, or philosophies.*)

CHAPTER FIVE
DATING MATTERS

I'd just finished leading a class discussion with a group of energetic junior and senior girls at a small high school in a rural east Texas town. The topic was how to say no without feeling guilty. The subject had touched some kind of nerve as the girls opened up regarding their school culture—about the expectation that you should be engaged at least once by the time you graduate, about the many girls who get pregnant before graduation, and about the girls who don't make it to graduation.

Afterward a young woman pulled me aside. I'd noticed her in the class—partly because she was so quiet while the rest of the girls chattered and ranted. Her gaze was intense as she lowered her voice to a confidential tone, "Do you really mean that it's okay for me to tell a guy no?" It was obvious she had a painful story. As I nodded my head, she exhaled slowly. "This is the first time someone's ever told me that I can tell him no. Thank you." Her face showed a mix of relief and regret.

In just one question, that young woman expressed the common angst of adolescent girls. As they wade into this emerging world of love, romance, and dating, they're constantly conjecturing about what's right, what's wrong, what's normal, what's safe, and what's dangerous. They're weighing what their parents and big brothers and sisters have taught them against what they've learned at church and from their friends.

Questions such as, "Does he like me?" "How far is too far?" and "Should I go all the way?" seem archaic in the current culture. Girls who are just years removed from the playground are now dealing with issues such as hooking up, oral or anal sex, same-sex attraction, and "friends with benefits"—issues women usually haven't had to deal with until their 20s and 30s, if then.

A LITTLE DATING HISTORY

Dating is a relatively recent concept. Prior to the twentieth century, "calling" was more the norm. A young man asked for permission to call on a young woman at her family's home. They would sit and visit while her family constantly kept a watchful eye on them. It was well known that if a young man was calling, he was interested in marriage. By the 1920s the culture had changed. Young men had access to cars, thus mobility and soon "dating" replaced calling. A couple (usually in their 20s) would go somewhere together, such as a dance or a movie, but away from the scrutiny of her family. However, adolescents were still closely monitored. It wasn't until the middle of the twentieth century that teenagers started dating without adult chaperones.

Today, 12 or 13 is the average age when a girl starts to date (depending on her family and cultural expectations).[1] Because teenagers meet each other in places outside the home—such as the mall, a club, or even church—her family is sometimes among the last to know that she's in a relationship.

STAGES OF DATING: EARLY ADOLESCENCE

When it comes to romance, girls and guys have an amazingly intricate relational dance that constantly changes as they grow older. It starts with chasing each other around the playground or choosing each other as square-dance partners in gym class. From there it progresses to bumping into each other by a locker and passing tightly folded notes or coded text messages. The dance can fluctuate between the mildly amusing to the painfully awkward, as early adolescents emerge from the cooties and "boy germ" phase and awaken to the wonders of the other gender.

During her early teens, a girl tries to discern the necessary social skills for relating to boys. She becomes an acute observer of human behavior as she fervently seeks to polish those skills by reading

"Obviously attraction is the first thing you see. You can see someone (this is going to sound really bad), but if you see someone with one arm or something silly like that, or something wrong with her face, people aren't going to go up to that person to get to know them. I've liked Jeremy forever, since like grade school. I've always liked him. I thought he was cute. He has a really good personality. At first he was kind of quiet. But I think I brought out the goofy side of him because I do that to everyone. He is genuine, and he is a nice guy. He does nice things for people and is sweet."[2] —Taylor, a 16-year-old girl, talking about her boyfriend

every available article in *Cosmo Girl* and *Seventeen* and by scrutinizing her peers' interactions. Simply put, she's trying to figure out how to talk to boys, and how to get the boys to talk back to her. Part of her strategy will include hanging out in places where she and her friends will probably run into guys. For example, a group of girls will head to the mall after school and purposefully loop by the arcade or the sports gear store, all with the intent of running into a group of boys from school. (Who says females aren't hunters?)

If any pairing up does occur, it's usually accomplished through the plotting of friends (e.g., "Do you like Tonya? She wants to know.") After the interrogation, the results are passed—within minutes—to the other party, either face to face or via text message, IM, or cell: "Tonya, Sammy says you're cute, and he'll be at Subway this afternoon with his friends. We'll come with you." And so goes the group communication. It's hard to imagine any relationship forming at this age without a network of friends involved in the process.

In early adolescence, physical features play a large role in the girl-boy attraction. At times, it feels as if they're playing an ad-libs game:

"He is so adorable!

"He has such _____

[*insert adjective*: cute, gorgeous, hot, tight]

_____._____

[*insert body part*: eyes, smile, abs]!"

Phrases such as "incredible six-pack," "soulful eyes," "a great smile," or "amazing dreads" are just a few examples of the physical-feature-of-the-week, which constantly changes and largely depends on what a girl's peer group says is desirable this season.

Attraction to external traits starts changing by the time a girl begins middle adolescence. At age 15 or 16, she's less likely to focus only on a guy's externals (although they're still important) and more likely to consider his personality and character qualities. While she may still be attracted to his spectacular smile, a middle-adolescent girl also wants to know: Is he kind? Does he have a good sense of humor? Does he understand me? Can I trust him? (Note: Guys take a little longer to get to this point. They focus on physical traits until late adolescence when they finally start looking more at a girl's interpersonal qualities.)

An early adolescent girl will find that her status increases by being the first girl in her peer group to date or "go with" someone. "Go with" is one of those ambiguous terms that fluctuates from culture to culture. Generally, it means there's been some sort of mutual agreement that a boy and a girl like each other, and they've made some kind of commitment. The length and depth of that commitment is debatable, as these relationships typically have a relatively short shelf life, at least in adult terms.

Romantic relationships in early adolescence are very transitory, lasting anywhere from a few hours to a few weeks. Although the relationships are short, they're still significant and the break-ups can be very painful, as well as very public. The good news (although it probably doesn't sound good to a girl who's going through it) is that these shorter relationships are much better for a young girl. Research has shown that girls who get involved in a serious relationship too early in adolescence often struggle with depression and problems in school.[4]

STAGES OF DATING: MIDDLE ADOLESCENCE

In middle adolescence (about 14 to 16 years of age), girls and guys still enjoy hanging out in mixed-gender groups, but their activity is much more deliberate. They'll make plans to meet as a group at the movies on a Friday night or gather to play touch football at the park on a Saturday afternoon. They don't hide in

DID YOU KNOW...?

Researchers in Ontario, Canada, studied male university students' reactions to beautiful women. They showed them a series of pictures of attractive females and found that after looking at the pictures, a guy's ability to think about consequences was hindered.[3]

their same-sex groups anymore. Remember middle school dances with bastions of boys on one side of the gym and a fortress of girls on the other, with only a courageous few venturing alone into no-man's land? Today the unspoken purpose of these social gatherings is to form cross-gender friendships, as well as to check out potential romantic partners.

Within these social groups, couples begin to pair off. However, they usually don't isolate themselves from the group for long periods of time, but are constantly drawn back to the group setting. If you've ever gone on a church retreat, you've seen this pattern. A couple connects on the first night of the retreat (usually they've already checked each other out during the bus ride), and they'll sit with each other at dinner or during a session. But while they're beginning to couple up, they're still very much in the midst of the group. They might separate from the group temporarily by going for long walks or by sneaking out of their cabins late at night, but they're persistently attracted back to the larger group (and not just because a counselor said so).

One advantage of this pattern is that it can help a girl as she learns how to handle the intimacies and dynamics of a romantic relationship. As a mid-adolescent, she may feel as though she's lacking the necessary skills to handle herself in a one-on-one setting with a guy she's attracted to, and who's strongly attracted to her. Group settings offer a certain degree of security. She can always check in with her friends (or with an older female, if it's in a ministry setting), if she believes things are getting beyond her, either emotionally or physically. (Granted, this is the ideal. There's always the danger that her "friends" will escalate a risky situation. And if they're sexually active, it's more likely that she'll become sexually active as well.[5])

Romantic relationships in mid-adolescence are very emotional and very intense as teenage couples spend hours talking on the phone or online. Although a girl's family might not be thrilled about it, this investment of her time is necessary. Not only is she learning about the other person, but she's also in the midst of learning about herself. Up until now, the voices that have influenced a girl's identity have primarily come from her family, her friends, and her community (including school and church). For the first time, she has an influential voice speaking into her life that's coming from someone to whom she's romantically or sexually attracted.

Because a girl is so relationally attuned, she's constantly taking in clues from this significant person and discerning what parts of her identity she wants to keep, change, or get rid of. If her sense of identity is relatively strong before she begins dating, she isn't as likely to morph to meet the expectations of the person she's attracted to. It's easier for a girl with a solid sense of self to extricate herself from a relationship that's running contrary to her values and to what she knows to be true about herself.

If her sense of self is fragile and she's hungry for affirmation and affection, she's more likely to alter her values and even her personality in order to gain acceptance by a guy she's attracted to. That's why it's so important that adolescent girls are taught discernment about whom they enter into a romantic relationship with—will this person positively influence her identity, or will he damage her? One potential bright side is that, because middle adolescents are still in such a changeable state when it comes to identity formation, their relationships are still relatively short-lived and usually last only a few weeks to a few months.

Girls at this age date for a variety of reasons. They often date just for recreation—they're looking for someone to do something fun with, whether that's hanging out at her house, going to a movie, or grabbing a coffee drink. However, sometimes a girl will date for status—she identifies someone who is socially desirable at school (or at church) and dates him in order to increase her social capital. This is where the phrases "trophy boyfriend" or "arm candy" come into play.

Besides recreation and status, a girl might also date for self-esteem reasons. Whether she dates one guy on a steady basis or a lot of different guys, it signifies to her (and to others too, she hopes) that she's desirable and worthy of love and acceptance. There is some research to back up her beliefs. Girls who are frequent daters are perceived to be more popular, have a stronger self-esteem, and have greater social capital than girls who date infrequently.[7]

It's usually not until a girl reaches late adolescence (age 17 to 20-something) that dating becomes more exclusive and long-term. It used to be that by the time a girl graduated from high school, she was dating to find her future spouse. However, with more women waiting to get married until they're in their mid-to-late 20s, dating in late adolescence is much more about companionship than searching for a life partner.

EMERGING PATTERNS AND ISSUES

Emerging Pattern—Female Aggression

An emerging pattern in girl-guy behavior is an increase in aggressiveness on the girl's part. Although the research is still predominantly anecdotal, educators, counselors, trend watchers, and even other teenagers are noticing the difference. In the not-too-distant past, it used to be that girls were the responders in the dating script—they'd wait until a boy initiated contact, either by phone call or a face-to-face conversation, and then they'd either respond to that invitation and go out or decline. If a girl were to initiate a romantically inclined conversation (i.e., calling a boy or asking him out), unless she invited him to a Sadie Hawkins dance (a girl-ask-guy event), then she'd be considered social anathema.

Girls today have learned—from messages in the media and elsewhere—that they can go after whatever they want in every area of their lives, including their sexual lives. Some credit the popularity of *Sex and the City* as having a large influence on adolescent girls, where girls will now imitate those characters' aggressive sexual behavior, especially Samantha's (played by Kim Cattrall).

In the movie *Sisterhood of the Traveling Pants* (based on a book by the same name that's popular among early teenage girls), the character Bridget is a star soccer player who aggressively pursues one of her coaches (a young college guy) at soccer camp. Even though he makes it clear to her—several times—that he's uncomfortable with her pursuit, they eventually have sex.

In a *New York Times* article on this topic, Tabi Upton, an adolescent counselor, said, "The teenage boys I see often say the girls push them for sex and expect them to ask them for sex and will bring it up if the boys don't ask…There has been a shift where girls now see themselves as sexualized and approach men with pretty much the attitude, 'This is all I have to offer.'"[9]

Laura Sessions Stepp, a reporter with the *Washington Post* who often writes about adolescent issues, has this observation, "As the one being pursued, a woman used to be able to set the course and pace of a relationship. As the pursuer, she relinquishes control, not to mention the fun of being chased." She goes on to quote a senior woman at Stanford University, "I see that aggressiveness all the time. Girls say I'm just as casual in this relationship as the guy, but deep down they're hoping for something more real and longer lasting."[10]

DATING HAS CHANGED

"Whereas dating used to say…'We're interested in each other.' Now sex says, 'You're mine.' That's a very scary concept, because what we see is increased incidences of physical battering, jealousy, stalking, all kinds of inappropriate behavior for young people who can't figure out why they can't 'hold onto somebody.' Well, they're trying to hold onto them through their bodies, through physical contact."[8]
—Dr. Gail Wyatt, licensed clinical psychologist and professor of psychiatry at Drew University and UCLA

Emerging Pattern—"Friends With Benefits" and "Hooking Up"

Another recent change in dating patterns is the prevalence of sex without a romantic relationship. Although teenagers still date, it's becoming much more common to hear phrases such as "friends with benefits" and "hooking up."

The meaning of the term "hooking up" varies from community to community, but it's much more casual than dating, where there's usually a specific invitation and an explicit plan. Not so with hooking up. Typically, a group of students will gather somewhere, say at a house party or a game, they'll find someone they're vaguely attracted to (or not), and they pair off, usually with the expectation of something sexual, but not necessarily intercourse. This almost always takes place without any emotional attachment or expectation for a future commitment.

"Friends with benefits" (FWB) is a concept that's been floating around the adolescent sphere for the last several years. Writer Benoit Denizet-Lewis describes it as, "A friend that you can also have sex with."[14] "Sex" in this case can mean anything from intercourse to oral sex to old-fashioned kissing. In an article in *The New York Times Magazine*, Denizet-Lewis quotes 16-year-old "Brian": "Being in a real relationship just complicates everything. You feel obligated to be all, like, couply. And that gets really boring after a while. When you're friends with benefits, you go over, hook up, then play video games or something. It rocks."[15]

The new dating patterns have interesting implications for adolescent females. Most girls value emotional intimacy, support, and communication in their relationships. So when there's sexual intimacy, girls desire for that to occur within a romantic relationship. Hook ups, on the other hand, are the antithesis of those values. The very purpose of a FWB relationship or hook up is not to have any kind of romantic commitment or relationship afterward. Therefore, it's feasible that a pattern of casual hook ups may have long-term consequences on a girl's future relationships.

Emerging Pattern—Dating Violence

One of the most difficult days for a youth worker is getting a call from one of the girls in the ministry, and she says in a quiet voice that she needs to talk. Then, through her anguished emotions, she shares that she's the victim of a date rape, and she's trying to figure out how to cope with it all.

What is date rape? It's when someone is forced to have sexual relations against her will by someone with whom she has some type of romantic connection. It could be a steady boyfriend, a first-time date, a friend, or an acquaintance—someone she's just met at a party or youth group. Unfortunately, about 15 percent of adolescent girls have been the victims of date rape.[17]

Rape, as painful and life-altering as it is, is just one painful facet of the larger problem of dating violence. Statistics say that one out of every 10 teenage couples has experienced some element of violence.[18] A Harvard study of 4,000 high school girls in Massachusetts found that one in five has experienced some type of abuse on a date, either physical or sexual. When compared with girls who haven't been abused, girls who've been in abusive relationships are four times more likely to use drugs or alcohol, six times more likely to become pregnant, and eight times more likely to attempt suicide.[19]

It's not just girls who are experiencing the violence, although the kind of violence they deal with is very different than what boys encounter. In a study of over 900 high school students, 45 percent of both males and females said that they'd experienced some kind of physical violence while on a date.[20] The guys reported being shoved or kicked, usually by a girl

They're jaded."[12] —Dr. Marsha Levy-Warren, psychologist

• "I was in a hookup with this guy Zachary. I tried to kiss him, and he wouldn't let me. That was weird. I mean, we were doing stuff way beyond kissing, but he didn't want to kiss. I asked him why he didn't want to kiss me and he was like—'I don't kiss girls on the mouth because if I'm not in a relationship why should I kiss.'"[13] —A 16-year-old girl

BREAKING UP IS HARD TO DO

It's the topic of mediocre songs and tepid poetry, but it can rip a girl apart. It's difficult to watch a girl go from the heights of love to the depths of despair, just because "things didn't work out between us." However, contrary to common perception, girls end dating relationships more often than guys do. Girls also bounce back from rejection much faster, and they find it easier to stay friends with their ex than do guys who've been rejected.[16]

But for some girls, a break-up isn't just emotionally difficult; it can be downright scary. These girls experience what's known as "romantic harassment"—after they've broken up with a guy, he refuses to accept the fact that they're no longer a couple. He may call her late at night, follow her around school, visit the church she attends, drive by her workplace, constantly send e-mails or text messages, threaten her potential dates, and he may even physically threaten her.

Understandably, this can be an extremely disturbing experience for an

CONTINUED >

who was angry or wanted revenge. The girls, however, reported that the boys were motivated by jealousy or anger and the resulting violence included forcing them to participate in unsolicited sexual behaviors.

A girl's age impacts her risk level when it comes to dating violence. The younger she is, the greater her risk of unwanted sex. Dating violence rates are highest for girls who've had sex early on. Research says that anywhere from 70 percent of girls who've had intercourse before 13 years of age report that they've had intercourse against their will.[21] In a survey of sixth-graders, researchers found that those who were romantically involved with someone older than they were more likely to have experienced sexual activity that was unwanted.[22]

Wanting an active social life is normal for an adolescent girl; however, if she isn't careful, that desire can place her in high-risk situations. It's not unusual for adolescents to attend a party where they may not know everyone or at least not know them well. And if alcohol is served, her odds of becoming a victim of abuse increase. For example, if she's been drinking, she may go into a bedroom with a boy she just met at the party—a risk she wouldn't take if she were sober. With alcohol as a factor, she'll be less effective when communicating her desires. Meanwhile, he'll be less likely to listen to her and more likely to overpower her.

Another difficulty arises when alcohol is combined with chemicals known as "date rape drugs," such as Rohypnol ("roofies"), GHB (gamma hydroxybutyric acid, also known as "grievous bodily harm" or "Liquid X"), and Ketamine ("Special K" or "K"). One possible side effect of these drugs is memory impairment. And if a girl can't recall the exact details of what happened, then she'll be more hesitant to report the rape.

Plus, if she knows the person who raped her, as is common in date rape situations, she may believe that she's partly responsible for what happened—perhaps she "led him on." Or she might believe she's at fault for putting herself in a risky situation or by not saying no sooner or because she slept with him before. All of these erroneous beliefs make her more hesitant to report the rape to the authorities or to anyone else. She may be afraid that people will refuse to believe her, will say she's a "whore," or will believe the guy if he says it was actually consensual sex.

However, even if alcohol or other chemicals were involved, it's critical for a girl to understand that *she is not at fault* for incidents of sexual violence, and she needs to report it to the proper authorities and seek counseling.

When working with a victim of date rape, understand that there will be deep repercussions. A victim of dating violence or rape may experience post-trauma symptoms, such as flashbacks, rage, or depression. She may also be terrified of returning to the place where the rape occurred or experiencing a situation that bears any similarities to when she was raped. According to Dr. Mary Pipher, "41 percent of rape victims expect to be raped again; 30 percent contemplate suicide; 31 percent go into therapy; 22 percent take self-defense courses and 82 percent say that they are permanently changed."[29]

THE YOUTH WORKER'S ROLE

It's important that youth workers remain aware of their female students' dating relationships, especially if they're dating people several years older. We need to check to see how they're handling the pressure they may be receiving from (or giving to) their partners. Ideally these are issues that should be dealt with by their parents, but sometimes parents are disconnected from their daughter's love lives, perhaps distracted by other concerns within the family system.

Often youth workers provide the safe place that adolescent girls need in order to begin talking about

---

CONTINUED >

adolescent girl, producing an atmosphere of anxiety and fear. Ignoring, threatening, confronting, or getting others to confront the harasser often doesn't work. Usually, in time, a harasser gives up and she's able to move on.

As youth workers, it's important that any time a girl feels as though her life or well-being is at risk, we must notify the proper authorities as well as her parents or guardians.

SOME STATISTICS ON DATING VIOLENCE

- In one study of over 700 male adolescents: "52 percent reported engaging in sexually aggressive behavior; 24 percent engaged in the unwanted sexual touch of another teenager; 15 percent engaged in sexual coercion (such as lying) to initiate sexual activity; [and] 14 percent engaged in assaultive behavior (use of physical force, threats of physical force, or using alcohol to gain sexual activity)."[23]

CONTINUED >

CONTINUED >

- According to the United States Justice Department, more than 1.5 million women encounter sexual or physical violence from a romantic partner each year.[24]

- Adolescent girls who are the victims of dating violence are at an increased risk of eating disorders and substance abuse.[25]

- Girls who have experienced either physical or sexual violence from a dating partner are six to nine times more likely to struggle with both thoughts of suicide and suicide attempts than other girls.[26]

- In one survey of adolescents under 14 years of age, 34 percent of boys thought it was acceptable to pressure a girl to have sex if they had had sex before.[27]

- Nearly a third of adolescents report being either physically or psychologically abused by their dating partners.[28]

tough relationship problems. After she's opened up with another caring adult, she'll probably feel more ready to talk with her parents about those same issues. We need to be careful that we don't become either passive listeners or aggressive judges. By listening passively to a girl's dating decisions, we're implicitly communicating that we agree with her choices. And by aggressively judging her (especially before we hear the whole story), we alienate her so she feels the need to defend her choices. Thus we've effectively shut down the open communication we were trying to establish. Youth workers need to practice being caring listeners who also offer loving guidance.

Jesus exemplifies this for us. In John 8 he encounters a woman who was caught having sex with another man. The religious leaders want Jesus to judge her. Yet he responds not by passing judgment, but by coming alongside of her and challenging her to make different choices.

Our role is crucial when dealing with victims of sexual violence. Girls may go to their pastors before they'll go to their parents, perhaps out of fear of a volatile, judgmental, or blame-filled response. In the short-term, it's important to create a safe environment, to listen with care, and to support her as she pursues help from the proper authorities. Strongly encourage her to report any attack and offer to walk through the reporting process with her, including talking with her parents.

In the long-term, we need to think about educating our girls on the potential hazards of dating. Youth ministries often work "dating" into the curriculum on an annual basis. But we need to add several sessions that teach not only the boundaries of sex and dating, but also the possibility of dating violence. For instance, teach the girls that no one has a right to touch their bodies without their permission and that they have the right to stop any sexual activity at any time. It's important that girls know that "No" means

"No," and "Stop" means "Now!" And just because she's said "Yes" before, that doesn't mean she has to say "Yes" again.

Teach girls how their dress and nonverbal cues can be interpreted by the other gender. Girls are often clueless when it comes to understanding how guys interpret their signals. A girl's flirtatious behavior on a date might be interpreted as seductive. This isn't to say that she's at fault for any dating violence that may occur. But she needs to understand how guys are wired. For women, sex is tightly tied to a relationship. This isn't true for most guys.

Offer a class on self-defense principles so girls are less likely to feel powerless in a risky situation. Teach them how to set and enforce boundaries in their dating relationships. Help your female students to discern when an environment is unsafe and to have a plan of action. Also help them to discern when a relationship is unsafe, and be willing to walk with any girl as she severs a relationship.

And last, but certainly not least, help boys to understand these same principles. Teach them through word and example what it means to treat a woman with respect. And make sure that the male and female volunteers in the youth ministry are modeling God-honoring behavior toward one another.

"Young men need to be socialized in such a way that rape is as unthinkable to them as cannibalism."[30]
—Dr. Mary Pipher, *Reviving Ophelia*

CHAPTER SIX
SEX MATTERS

IMPACT OF ABSTINENCE PLEDGES

- One study found a difference between those who pledged abstinence and those who didn't. In the study's sample group, almost 100 percent (99 percent) of the teenagers who *didn't* make the pledge had sex before marriage, compared to 88 percent of those who *did* pledge abstinence.[1]

- Pledging virginity until marriage can help some teenagers delay sex for up to 18 months.[2]

- Adolescents who break their pledge are less likely to use contraception or condoms.[3]

Standing on the edge of a parkway in Washington, D.C., I looked out over hundreds, if not thousands, of small acrylic easels driven into the ground like spikes. It looked like a miniature version of Arlington National Cemetery. And each easel held a virginity pledge card signed by someone who wanted to tell the world that he or she would wait until marriage to have sex.

Like many youth pastors, I was filled with a mix of hope and skepticism. I knew students would need to make a strong commitment if we're to have any hope of slowing down the growing numbers of sexually active teenagers. But I also knew the reality of adolescence.

GIRLS' SEXUAL ACTIVITY—BY THE NUMBERS

The good news is that recent years have shown a decline in sexual intercourse, pregnancy, and abortion rates among teenagers. However, the reasons behind this drop in numbers are up for debate. Researchers hypothesize whether this decrease is in direct relationship to the virginity pledge cards, a fear of pregnancy and STDs, or the rise in oral and anal sex (which many adolescents don't consider "real" sex). And just because certain behaviors and results have changed, can we interpret the numbers to mean our girls aren't as sexually active as they used to be?

In answer to that last question, one government survey found that more girls (47 percent) than guys (46 percent) are reporting that they're sexually active.[4] (It's interesting to note that the report cites that sexual activity among young men has dropped nine percentage points since 1995, down from 55 percent.)

The level of sexual activity does depend quite a bit on a girl's age. Among early adolescent girls, sexual intercourse is still fairly rare. Only about five to 10 percent of girls have had coital sex by the time they're 13. That figure rises to about 20 percent by the time they're 15.[5] By the time they're 17, about half of all adolescent girls have had intercourse. Typically, most of the girls who are having sex are involved with guys who are within two to three years of their own age (usually older).[6]

When it comes to having intercourse for the first time, about 50 percent of women say it happened because they felt affection toward their partners (only 25 percent of men gave this response). About 25 percent of women indicated that it wasn't so much about being in love; rather, they felt they were ready for sex and were curious to know what it would be like.[7] Some girls have sex in order to please their partners, feeling as though it's the only way to maintain a relationship with them.

Others have sex because of the increase in status they'll gain among their peers. Some girls just don't want to be the last ones to get their periods, and they don't want to be the last ones to have sex. But unlike getting periods, which they can't control, girls can control whether or not they have sex.

Girls are well aware that there's a fine line between having "status sex" (the kind that raises their social capital) and "slut sex" (i.e., having too much sex with too many partners and ultimately lowering their social capital). When the latter happens, they may be branded "slut," "skank," "bitch," or "'ho," which is in marked contrast to a guy who exhibits the same behavior and gets endowed with the title "player."

When it comes to a first sexual experience, there are many girls who feel pressured into it, especially if they're early adolescents and their partner is over two years older than they are.[9] For girls who had sex for the first time before they turned 15, 40 percent said they were forced.[10] When a girl is forced or coerced into a sexual relationship, it can have a lifelong impact on her relationship with men and with herself. She may find it difficult to trust men in the future. She may also act out in anger, aggressively

THE "SLUT" LABEL

On the dark side of "girl world," a phrase popularized by the movie *Mean Girls* (Paramount Pictures, 2004), adolescent girls realize the social impact of a label like "whore." Thus, they don't hesitate to use it to brand an undeserving girl whom they want to ostracize from high school or middle school society.

In the book *Fast Girl: Teenage Tribes and the Myth of the Slut*, author Emily White explores the dynamics of how the "slut" role is different than the other roles girls play in high school, such as "cheerleader" or "prom queen." White writes,

> To become the slut is not to be associated with a group or a tribe; rather, it is to be singled out...By turning one girl into the slut among them, the kids try to reassure themselves that they are on the right side of fate: They're good while she is evil. They're safe while she is unsafe. They have the right kind of desire while she has the wrong kind.[8]

In White's research, she found that most of the girls

CONTINUED >

CONTINUED >

who'd been labeled a slut in their high school fit a pattern: they were usually outgoing Caucasian girls from the suburbs who had a history of being sexually abused. For some of these girls, the pressure of an undeserved reputation was too much. It almost took on a prophetic nature where they chose to live into the reputation because they were tired of fighting against it.

If you ask a group of high school or middle school girls, they'll be able to tell you right away who the "slut" is in their school. During my junior high years, I would have said "Jennifer." She was an early developer who had curves long before the rest of us did. Her tight clothes made it seem as though she reveled in the power of her body (at least that's what the rest of us awkward seventh-grade girls assumed).

I first encountered "Jennifer" during math class. She had a bubbly personality. She wore makeup when the rest of us felt lucky if our moms allowed us to wear Lip Smackers. Her shiny brown hair bounced playfully, and her dark brown eyes flirted with the boys easily. All

CONTINUED >

and vengefully pursuing guys in order to right the wrong that was done to her.

In the book *Adolescents in Crisis,* author G. Wade Rowatt, Jr., quoted one girl as saying, "Since I was raped, I have nailed seven virgin guys and taken theirs."[11] An adolescent girl who's been the victim of unwanted sexual activity may slide into a depression or shut down emotionally. She may choose to escape the memory by using chemicals or may try to regain control of her life through an eating disorder. It is crucial for youth workers to be alert to any sudden or drastic changes in a girl's behavior that might indicate sexual abuse, *especially* if she's dating as an early adolescent.

For those girls who choose not to have sex, their reasons are varied. Some don't want to get pregnant or get an STD. Still others say they haven't found the right person. And a large majority of girls who aren't sexually active cite their religious beliefs as being the key reason as to why they refrain.[12] It should encourage youth workers to know their teaching isn't falling on deaf ears; rather, it's influencing girls as they make decisions about their sexual lives.

ORAL SEX: THE NEW GAME IN TOWN

Blame it on Bill Clinton. Blame it on *Sex and the City.* Blame it on MTV. Blame it on—the list goes on. The reality is that the last few years have brought a rise in the number of adolescents who are participating in oral sex. One national survey found that 10 percent of females ages 15 to 19 have had oral sex.[15] Since it's not penile-vaginal intercourse, many teenagers don't consider it real sex. After interviewing high school students in Boston, reporter Alexandra Hall remarked, "Oral sex is the new second base…Things are very, very different in high school from the way they used to be. Not different from two or three generations ago, but different from just five or ten years ago."[16]

I posed the question to a group of African American and Latina girls about how common oral sex was in their schools. They didn't hesitate to talk about how many were doing it (a lot of the school, it seemed) and where they were doing it (locker rooms, band rooms). One girl talked about how the boys on the football team all wore T-shirts for their senior class picture that read, "We love bust downs." The girls informed me that it wasn't until the end of the day that teachers learned that "bust down" was another term for *fellatio*.

Many adolescents believe that by having oral (or anal) sex, they remain virgins. In one study of first- and second-year college students, they described abstinent behavior as including oral sex (37 percent) and anal sex (24 percent).[17] As one female youth said during the HBO documentary special, *Middle School Confessions*, "I'm still a virgin, except for my mouth."[18] Some younger adolescent girls choose it because it's a way to avoid embarrassing physical intimacy; according to one girl—you can keep your clothes on and the boys don't have to touch your body.[19] This fits with the self-consciousness of an early adolescent. And yet other girls choose to have oral sex as a method of birth control.

What many don't realize is that although the risk of pregnancy drops, they're still at risk for getting an orally transmitted STD such as HPV, hepatitis B, genital herpes or warts, gonorrhea, syphilis, or chlamydia, just to name a few.

While a sexually active girl is always at risk for physical consequences, what she may not realize is that the shift from coital sex to oral or anal sex puts her at even greater emotional risk. Usually when there is coital sex, there is some type of relationship present. With the emerging patterns of increased oral sex and hookups, intercourse now has the potential to become extremely impersonal and thus emotionally damaging for an adolescent girl. As one girl said, "I know it was a hookup. But it felt so right, I was

CONTINUED >

of that, plus the fact that her figure was light-years beyond even the eighth-grade girls, drew all the guys to her—even the eighth-graders. So, naturally, her confidence with the older guys posed an immediate threat to the other girls.

Soon into the fall semester, there were whispered rumors about what she did with the eighth-grade guys and how she beat up girls in bathroom fights. Even as a seventh-grader, I could see that the sparkle in Jennifer's eyes was dimming as the school year progressed. The rumors grew worse, her makeup got heavier, and her clothes got skimpier. Explanations about her parents divorcing were offered as a reason why she was acting "that way." But the slut label persisted.

Thankfully, a youth pastor in the community saw beyond Jennifer's reputation and was able to help her. By the end of high school, she had the reputation of being a strong Christian. But the bubbly personality I saw in Jennifer during that September of our seventh-grade year never emerged again.

YOUTH AND YOUNG ADULT SEX STATISTICS

Part I[13]

Number of females reporting they've had vaginal intercourse:

- 26% of 15-year-olds
- 40% of 16-year-olds
- 49% of 17-year-olds
- 70% of 18-year-olds
- 77% of 19-year-olds
- 92% of 22-to-24-year-olds

Number of females reporting they've had oral sex:

- 30% of 15-to-17-year-olds had given oral sex to a male
- 38% of 15-to-17-year-olds had received oral sex from a male
- For 15-to-19-year-old females: 5.8% of African American, 9.9% of Hispanic, and 12% of Caucasian females have had oral sex but not vaginal intercourse

Number of females reporting they've had anal sex:

- 2.4% of 15-year-old females
- 32% of 22-to-24-year-old females

Part II[14]

Number of females (listed by grade level) who report having four or more sex partners:

- Ninth grade—6.4%
- Tenth grade—8.8%
- Eleventh grade—13.4%
- Twelfth grade—17.9%

CONTINUED >

sure he would call. I just couldn't believe it when he never called. Then two weeks later, after I hadn't heard from him at all, I saw him at a party and he wanted to hook up again. It made me feel dirty. Like he just wanted to, like, use me, *use* my body. Like I wasn't really even there. Like he was just j--king off, using me instead of some porn magazine."[20]

INCEST AND SEXUAL ABUSE

Maya, an eighth-grader, was new to the youth ministry. She connected easily with the youth leader and enjoyed their conversations, revealing a little more about herself during each talk. On one of their student retreats, she was talking about her relationship with boys. "Oh yeah, I've had sex with a bunch of different guys," she stated matter-of-factly and tossed her hair back to emphasize her blasé attitude. She went on to explain how she'd discovered that the best place to have sex was under the bleachers at the local community hockey arena.

Surprised at the level of sexual experience Maya claimed to have, her youth leader followed a hunch and began asking questions about her family life. It turned out Maya was being sexually abused by her high school-aged brother and had been for a number of years. Knowing she was in over her head, the youth leader went to her supervisor to ask what she should do. The response she received was, "Tell her to pray about it and that she needs to tell him to stop it." Thankfully, Maya's leader was able to connect with another youth worker in the community who was also familiar with Maya. Together, they got her help and got her brother out of the house.

While we might cringe at such simplistic and damaging advice, incest and sexual abuse is still a topic that many youth pastors and pastors hesitate to discuss. It's estimated that 20 percent of all women have been sexually abused by the time they are 18. Sexual abuse increases significantly for girls between the ages of 10 and 14.[23] Much of the sexual abuse that occurs with early adolescents is incestuous in nature, and the abuser is usually a close relative. The most common perpetrators of incest are brothers, cousins, or stepfathers; not biological fathers, as is sometimes thought. When the perpetrator *is* the biological father, there are usually other signs of trouble; for instance, he is often abusive to his wife, as well as to other family members.

When a family member abuses a girl, there is a strong sense of betrayal. This is intensified if her mother (or another caregiver) doesn't believe her story and sides with the abuser. This can also be the case in church settings where the perpetrator is a respected member of the congregation. There are too many stories about times when a girl finally and courageously steps forward to confront her abuser, but the church refuses to act and sometimes labels her as the problem. She's then forced or pressured to leave the church while the abuser remains in good standing. Not only does she feel betrayed by her church family, but she may also transfer those feelings of betrayal onto God.

The results of sexual abuse are long lasting. A girl's ability to trust others is impaired, as is her self-esteem. She's more likely to become depressed and to develop an eating disorder or a substance addiction. A girl who has been sexually abused also tend to be more aggressive and hostile, showing problems at school, as well as at home. She may have a pattern of absenteeism from school, or she may drop out before graduation. If she's been abused, she's also more likely to run away from home. In research done among teenage female prostitutes, it's been found that many of them were victims of childhood sexual abuse.[24]

The Youth Worker's Role

The youth worker's role in this is NOT to tell a girl just to pray and tell the abuser to stop. Many states

CONTINUED >

Females (listed by grade level) who've had intercourse before age 13:

- Ninth grade—5.3%
- Tenth grade—5.7%
- Eleventh grade—3.2%
- Twelfth grade—1.9%

YOUTH WORKER IDEA

Create forums where both parents and students are invited to discuss these emerging trends. (It's probably a good idea to get the senior pastor's approval on this one!) Many parents and children have divergent ideas on what it means to abstain from sex. Parents might believe that by saying, "Don't have sex!" they're telling their daughters to abstain from all sexual activity beyond kissing or petting. Meanwhile, their daughters believe they're obeying by abstaining from penile-vaginal sex, but they're still engaging in mutual masturbation, anal sex, or oral sex. By creating discussion forums, you can give families a safe place to talk about awkward subjects that might otherwise go unaddressed.

PARENTAL INFLUENCE ON SEXUAL BEHAVIOR

Do parents have any influence on their children's sexual behaviors? Absolutely. In fact, they wield more influence than they realize. In a survey of 1,014 adults and 1,000 adolescents,[21] the National Campaign to Prevent Teen Pregnancy found that:

- 37 percent of adolescents say their parents have more influence on their decisions about sex than their friends (33 percent) or their sisters and brothers (six percent). (Another study found that older brothers have more influence over their younger sisters' sexual behavior than do older sisters.[22])

- Parents, however, believe that friends (47 percent) have more influence on their adolescent children than they do (28 percent).

- Parents (91 percent) and teenagers (87 percent) agree that a conversation would help teenagers delay their sexual activity.

CONTINUED >

are now mandating that a youth worker or pastor must report any signs of abuse to the proper officials. And even if they're not legally required to report the abuse, it's the stance of many pastors that they're ethically required.

In making a report about suspected sexual abuse, it's helpful to go through the process with the support of a licensed therapist or social worker who knows the ins and outs of the reporting system. The youth worker can then take on a more supportive role as she pastors the girl throughout the process. The adolescent's view of God may be affected, as well as her trust of others in positions of authority or influence. She needs to know that God loves her and that the abuse was not in his plan for her life. It's important that the youth worker create an environment where the girl feels safe to talk. For example, the youth worker should set up proper boundaries with the girl, including asking permission to give her a hug or any other kind of physical touch.

Eventually, in the later stages of the process, the idea of forgiveness must be addressed. It's critical that a youth worker be careful not to push that idea too soon, but only do so with a great deal of discernment and guidance from a knowledgeable counselor.

As difficult as this idea might be, someone (other than the youth worker) also needs to be a pastor of the abuser during this time, especially if the abuser is part of the faith community. What form that particular type of pastoring takes is best discussed in consultation with an experienced therapist.

PREGNANCY AND ABORTION

Standing in the pharmacy section in Target one day, I noticed two high school girls debating the pros and cons of home pregnancy tests. The casualness of their conversation made one think they were actually standing in another aisle discussing what shampoo to buy. When you consider the fact that the average

age of a girl's first period, or *menarche*, is around 12 years old, the fact that the average age of marriage today is some time in the mid-20s, and the statistic that 70 percent of 17-year-old girls have already had intercourse, then you can understand why pregnancy is a very real issue in today's teenage culture.

Each year, about 500,000 children are born to adolescent girls. The good news is that unplanned pregnancy rates dropped by 30 percent in the 1990s, and they're expected to keep dropping.[25]

Part of the reason there has been a drop in these numbers may be due to a rise in contraception use, as well as the increased focus on abstinence training—both in school and in faith communities. For those girls who do become pregnant, about half do so within six months of their first experiences with intercourse.[26] Anywhere from 35 to 40 percent will end their pregnancies by abortion, and another 10 to 14 percent will have miscarriages. About five percent of girls put their babies up for adoption, and the other 45 percent raise their children alone or within their extended family systems.[27]

The social stigma attached to pregnancy "out of wedlock" certainly has faded, although not completely—and especially not in the church community. Adolescents aren't as likely to use contraception if they come from an environment where any sexual activity is strongly disapproved of and there's a powerful atmosphere of guilt.[28] The reason for this is because if they use contraception, it means that sex was anticipated and planned for, versus being a spontaneous act of passion. Many would prefer to deal with the guilt rather than admit that they're sexually active. However, then they also have to deal with the possibility of pregnancy.

When an adolescent girl discovers she's pregnant, she can typically expect to receive one of these four reactions from her church:

CONTINUED >

- 90 percent of parents believe they should have conversations with their teenagers about sex, but they don't know what to say or how to initiate the conversation.

- 37 percent of adolescents say they've never talked to their parents about sex.

1) Ostracism from the faith community. Parishioners may believe that having a pregnant teenager around will negatively influence the other adolescents. They may also believe that social ostracism is a way of showing their disapproval of her sin, assigning her to wear the scarlet A, so to speak. If she's not ostracized from the larger church, she may be excluded from any contact with the youth or the youth ministry.

2) Pressure to get married, especially if she's an older adolescent. In recent years, this is less popular, especially because of the low success rates of these marriages. In the late 1950s, it was estimated that half the teenage girls who got married were pregnant on their wedding day.[29]

3) Ignored. This usually comes from a belief that "this situation" is a matter to be dealt with in the home and the church has no say about it. This approach is much easier in a large church than in a smaller one.

4) Embraced. Although some churches avoid this approach because they're concerned that they might be viewed as condoning her sin, other churches realize that although the act of sex outside of marriage is sin, the life resulting from that act is not, and the child should not be punished. These churches also realize that there are a variety of sins that each parishioner is guilty of, and although many of them don't have consequences as visible as a swollen belly, they are equally serious in God's eyes. These churches seek to have a redemptive approach and to support the new mother through her pregnancy and beyond.

A pregnant teenager faces a myriad of problems. For instance, she is twice as likely as her peers not to finish school, and she probably won't go on to college, either.[30] Her peers are more likely to get married, but if she does marry someday, then it's more likely that her marriage will end in divorce.[31]

Because of the discouraging impact of pregnancy on teenage mothers, churches and schools have developed programs to help girls get back on their feet financially, finish their educations, and learn how to be good mothers. For example, one Chicago church is located right next to an inner-city high school and provides a daycare program for the children so their mothers can finish their schooling. They also provide an experienced mother to mentor each teenage mother, giving her emotional and spiritual support, as well as helping her with some of her physical necessities. An extended family or faith community can do much to help a pregnant girl. Their support is crucial in the long-term goal of a successful and healthy life, both for the mother and for the child.

Anywhere from 35 to 40 percent of pregnant girls choose to abort their child. The abortion rate dropped significantly in the '90s, along with the teenage pregnancy rate. Part of the reason was that more girls chose to give birth. Another reason is due to the increase in contraceptive use, especially emergency contraception, such as the morning-after pill. Researchers have found that a girl who chooses to abort will typically talk with at least one of her parents about her decision beforehand, and that parent usually supports her in it.[32]

Youth workers need to realize that even if abortion is not an option in their minds, it almost always is in the mind of the pregnant teenager. The panic of finding out she's pregnant, especially if she's from an unsupportive family, can override her moral and theological views. It can be extremely difficult to figure out how to pastor a girl who chooses to abort when that decision is antithetical to the youth worker's personal theological beliefs.

The discovery of her pregnancy can send a girl into a crisis mode, and she may experience a multitude of emotions ranging from fear and disbelief to joy. Youth pastors often assume that guilt and shame may be her chief emotions. However, for some girls, getting pregnant is an achievement. She may believe that she'll finally have someone who will love her unconditionally, or that she can now escape a tough home situation, or that she's become a "real" woman and is no longer a child.

When she becomes pregnant, a girl's identity is suddenly called into question. No longer a little girl, she wonders if she's ready to embrace motherhood. She's faced with numerous adult decisions—will she continue the pregnancy? Will she keep the child? If she does, how will she care for herself and for her child? What will her parents' reaction be? The church's reaction? Will she be able to finish school? Does this mean that her dream of becoming a doctor (or lawyer or CEO) is no longer a possibility? Does this mean she'll never achieve economic success?

Depending on her church culture, she may also question her identity as a Christian, wondering whether or not God will forgive her. This is one of the reasons why the church's response to a pregnant teenager is so crucial. It's sending a message not only to this girl, but also to the other teenagers struggling with issues that could be frowned upon by the church. They're watching to see if the church is a safe place for them to deal with difficult issues. It's important that we create a place that is.

SEXUALLY TRANSMITTED DISEASES

Pregnancy isn't the only concern for sexually active girls. According to Dr. Meg Meeker, a physician specializing in child and adolescent health, sexually transmitted diseases, or STDs, are impacting the lives of sexually active teenage girls on an epidemic level. "Every day, 8,000 teens will become infected with a new STD. The number of teenagers who have STDs but don't know it (because they have no symptoms) probably exceeds those whose diseases have been diagnosed."[33]

The adolescent urban myth is that a girl has to be sexually active for a long period of time—and with many partners—before she'll get an STD. That myth falls apart in light of one British study of adolescent females. The researchers discovered that 46 percent of adolescent girls were infected with HPV (human papillomavirus) after only their first experience of intercourse.[34] There are anywhere from 15 to 19 million new cases of STDs reported each year, and anywhere from 25 to 48 percent of those were in adolescents (15 to 24 years of age).[35] Rates are extremely high for adolescents; for example, one out of four sexually active adolescents is likely to have an STD[36] and 2.5 percent of all young women ages 15 to 19 have a sexually transmitted disease.[37]

Forty years ago, there were primarily two sexually transmitted diseases—syphilis and gonorrhea. Now, there are scores of STDs; the most common for adolescents are chlamydia, HPV, herpes, HIV/AIDS, gonorrhea, and syphilis.

As a rule, STDs fall into two categories: viral and bacterial, plus one (Trichomoniasis) that's caused by a parasite.

Viral STDs

Viral STDS are particularly dangerous because they cannot be cured with medication. The symptoms can be managed through care and medication, but once someone gets a viral STD, it remains in her body for life. This can be extremely difficult news for an adolescent girl to hear. What might have been a one-time "slip up" can have a life-long impact, and not just for her, but for her future children as well. Some of the most well-known viral STDs impacting the lives of teenage girls are HPV, genital and oral herpes, and HIV/AIDS.

HPV—Human Papillomavirus

HPV infects the body through a mucous membrane, such as the vagina, cervix, or mouth. Young girls are especially susceptible to the virus. "Their young bodies have receptive vaginal mucous that easily hold the virus, and their cervical cells are more receptive to viral infections, allowing the viruses to reproduce easily," says Dr. Meeker.[38] What many young women don't understand is that HPV is responsible for almost all cases of cervical cancer. That's right, a girl can get cancer from having sex. What used to be a cancer found mostly in women over the age of 55 is now being seen in more and more women under the age of 25.[39]

Genital and Oral Herpes

Nearly 20 percent of people over the age of 12 have tested positive for herpes simplex type 2 or genital herpes.[40] Genital herpes is spread only through sexual contact, either through vaginal or oral sex. With the increase in the occurrence of oral sex, clinicians are finding that oral herpes now causes 75 percent of genital herpes versus 24 percent just a few years ago.[41] Herpes has no cure. Once you get it, it's yours for life. It appears as ulcers in the genital area and can erupt again and again. Some herpes sufferers have painful sores, while others have no idea they even have the disease. This means they can continue to pass it on without knowing it. Herpes can also be passed from a mother to her baby.

HIV/AIDS

Although the myth that HIV/AIDS is only a gay man's disease has faded during the last decade, many adolescent girls still don't believe they're at risk for contracting it. They believe you can only get it through exchanging needles or a blood transfusion. And they don't realize that they put themselves at risk not just through penile-vaginal sex, but also by participating in any activity where there might be an exchange of sexual fluids, including oral sex. Because there have been such well-publicized leaps in the research of

HIV/AIDS, many teenagers believe they're immune to it. But as of 2003, 4.7 percent of all people diagnosed with AIDS were from 13 to 24 years of age.[42] From 1999 to 2003, females diagnosed with AIDS increased by 15 percent.[43] Females between 16 and 21 years of age have a 50 percent higher rate of HIV than males in that age group.[44]

If an adolescent girl has unprotected sex—just once—with an infected partner, she has a chance of getting an STD: a one percent risk of getting HIV/AIDS, a 30 percent risk of getting genital herpes, and a 50 percent chance of getting gonorrhea.[45] A teenage girl needs to understand that the more often she has sex, and the more partners she has, the more at risk she is for getting some kind of STD.

Bacterial STDs

The bacterial STDs are those such as chlamydia and gonorrhea. The key difference between bacterial and viral STDs is that a bacterial STD can be cured with antibiotics; a viral STD can't. However, that isn't meant to discount the damage that a bacterial STD can cause. If left untreated, it can be devastating.

Chlamydia

Chlamydia is the most common STD in America. Nearly one in 10 teenage girls has chlamydia. Of the three million new chlamydia cases diagnosed each year, about half are diagnosed in girls 15 to 19 years old.[46] A girl who has chlamydia may not know it unless she's tested. If she does have any symptoms, she'll most likely notice it in the form of vaginal discharge, since the bacteria enter her body through the vagina. If they stay near her cervix, chlamydia may run its course in about 15 months. But there is the chance that the disease will travel toward her uterus, and then on to her fallopian tubes and ovaries. If those organs become infected, she can develop scar tissue and possibly become infertile. Chlamydia can

**PID—PELVIC
INFLAMMATORY
DISEASE**

When a girl gets PID, it can
leave her fallopian tubes and
ovaries severely scarred and
possibly make her infertile.
Almost 250,000 adolescent
girls are diagnosed with PID
every year, usually as a result
of chlamydia or gonorrhea.
As an adolescent, she has
a much greater chance of
developing a PID (one in
eight) than a 30-year-old who
has the same infection (one
in 80).[48]

also lead to pelvic inflammatory disease (PID), infertility, and possibly ectopic pregnancies.

Gonorrhea

Gonorrhea is very common, especially among high school girls. The highest rate for gonorrhea is among girls between the ages of 15 and 19.[46] It can lead to PID, infertility, and ectopic pregnancies. The good news is that when it's caught in time, gonorrhea can almost always be treated with antibiotics. The bad news is the "almost always." Health officials in recent years are finding new cases emerging that are resistant to traditional antibiotic treatment.

Syphilis

Syphilis is one of the oldest STDs known to humans. It progresses in stages, usually starting with a single sore. If caught early, syphilis is treatable with antibiotics. But it's possible that a girl may not realize she has syphilis since its symptoms mimic those of other diseases. If left untreated, it impacts her nervous system, heart, and other major organs, and if she's pregnant, her fetus. It may eventually result in death.

Trichomoniasis

Trichomoniasis, also known as "trick," is a common and curable STD that often appears in young women. It is caused by a single-cell parasite and is usually contracted through intercourse. But because the parasite can live for 45 minutes outside the body, trichomoniasis can be acquired through genital contact with a damp or moist object (e.g., a towel or toilet seat) carrying the parasite. Usually she can be successfully treated with medication.

The Youth Worker's Role

The diagnosis of an STD can be devastating to an adolescent girl. Suddenly, issues such as pimples and a bad hair day seem trivial to her. Especially if she has a viral STD—she now has to deal with it for the rest of her life. She has to think about how she'll tell her future partner and consider whether or not she should have children, since there's a chance she can put them at risk. There's an emotional impact to getting an STD—a girl can feel grief and depression as well as feeling "dirty" and "untouchable." She can feel guilt for violating one of her morals and think that an STD is God's vengeance on her for messing up.

Youth workers must work with a girl to help her understand and experience God's forgiveness and redemption. This will be an ongoing process, as issues and insecurities can arise every time she has a new outbreak or enters into a serious relationship.

It's also important that local youth workers from the same area network together to address the larger epidemic of STDs in their communities. Too often we leave the sexual education of adolescents to the public school teachers. We need to examine the attitudes of both adolescents and parents toward STDs, and educate them on the possible repercussions.

Beyond education, it's crucial that youth workers also address community systems and influences that put our adolescents' lives at risk.

SAME-SEX ATTRACTION

Scenario One: Stacey had been in youth ministry for several years. She thought she was beyond the point where she could be shocked—that is, until she rode the bus heading to winter retreat. It was dark and the students were pretty noisy in anticipation of the weekend. She was chatting her way down the aisle of the bus, doing the typical "meet and greet," when one of the volunteers walked up from the back of the bus and whispered, "We need you to break up a couple in the back."

Already? During registration Stacey could smell the hormones in the air and had watched all the flirting with a wary eye. She just wanted to make sure it

WHAT IS SAFE SEX?[49]

According to a survey of adolescents, *safe* sex can be anything from "knowing how to put on a condom; getting your partner to go to the doctor with you; getting tested together; no sex at all; and even discussing sex."

To an adolescent, *risky sex* includes: "being homosexual; not knowing your partner's background; having anal sex, oral sex, or sex with more than one partner; and using the 'pull out' method."

didn't go any farther than flirting while the students were on this retreat.

She'd broken up many bus make-out sessions in her time, so she wasn't worried as she headed back. But what she wasn't prepared for was that the couple making out was two girls—one she didn't recognize, but the other was on the ministry's leadership team. Stacey realized in an instant that it was no longer youth ministry as usual; she had entered a new era.

Scenario Two: The university where I teach is located in an urban area. We have three high schools and one middle school within easy walking distance, which means we constantly have high schoolers and middle schoolers crossing through our campus. It also helps that we have a fast-food restaurant across the street, which is a major congregating area for the local adolescents. One afternoon, two of our youth ministry students headed over to the restaurant to meet some high schoolers for an assignment. While they were discussing adolescent life over fries and sodas, there was a commotion going on in the playground area. A large group of high school students had taken it over for some type of celebration. When asked what was going on, the interviewees casually said that two lesbians from one of the high schools were having a mock wedding.

These two scenarios speak about many adolescent issues. One of them is the casual attitude toward sexuality that seems pervasive among adolescents. They see same-sex attraction as yet another emerging trend in adolescent culture. One high school girl commented about her school culture, "Gays and lesbians hang around together listening to experimental music. They're accepted to a certain extent. There was a lesbian couple that was making out—a lot of PDA [public display of affection]. It seemed like they wanted to make a point, and people didn't like that. But we have a huge queer student association."[50]

Although same-sex attraction is far from being the norm, it's increasing. In one survey of nearly 10,000 adolescent women (15 to 19 years old), almost 11 percent reported that they had some kind of same-sex contact in their lifetimes, and almost eight percent reported that they had contact within the last year.[51] In young women (18 to 29 years old), same-sex contact used to be about five percent, but it has recently soared to 14 percent.[52]

There are a variety of reasons for the rise in these statistics. One possible reason is that our culture is much more comfortable with homosexuality. The popularity of an increasing number of TV shows such as *Will and Grace* and *Queer Eye for the Straight Guy* have added to an environment where homosexuality is no longer a "special event" (e.g., Ellen DeGeneres coming out on TV), but part of mainstream TV culture.

It could also be true that media is impacting teenage behavior in a different way—females are turning to same-sex relationships as a way of revolting against the media images that exploit females. They feel that a female will value another female for more than just her physical appearance.

Another possible reason for the rise in lesbianism and bisexuality is that it's a protective measure. Girls turn to other girls because they're afraid of getting pregnant or contracting STDs, they think they're less likely to be abused, or they're reacting to guys who jump from girl to girl (i.e., the player mentality). Some girls prefer female intimacy to male intimacy. They believe females know how to communicate with other females and are better able to give them what they need. One boy from New Orleans commented about a classmate who had "turned gay": "She feels like she can trust a girl more than a boy."[53] And still others see it as a way to both irritate and stimulate the guys.

THE NEW GAY TEENAGER

Ritch Savin-Williams has been studying gay teenagers for years. In his book, *The New Gay Teenager,* he makes the observation, "They [adolescents] might consider having sex with someone of their own sex, if they were asked or if the other person was really good looking or popular. They may even find themselves falling in love with someone of their own sex. They find same-sex encounters, alliances, and crushes appealing. They may be ordinary, boring teens, and yet they have so distorted 'gay' to mean something more than sexuality and something less, something that has nothing to do with sexuality. For these new teens, 'gay' carries too much baggage. One young woman told me in no uncertain terms, 'If you want to know about me, don't ask about my sexual labels like my mother did.'"[54]

CASS SEXUAL IDENTITY MODEL

Dr. Vivienne Cass developed this model that can assist in the understanding of the development of sexual identity:[56]

Stage 1: Identity Confusion—a girl recognizes that her feelings, thoughts, and behaviors could be identified as homosexual. It's a stage marked by anxiety, fear, tension, and uncertainty. At this stage, she labels herself as either gay or not gay.

Stage 2: Identity Comparison—here she evaluates her feelings against the feelings of others to see if she is or isn't gay, while thinking there might be a chance that she is. She checks with family, friends, and others. She weighs the pros and cons of a homosexual identity.

Stage 3: Identity Tolerance— this stage begins tenuously ("I might be gay") and ends with certainty, but with a degree of hesitation ("I am gay, but I'm not thrilled about it"). At this point, she'll begin to network with other homosexuals to research behaviors and her identity. She may also "come out" to close friends and family.

CONTINUED >

Some say it's a trend, a way to get attention; it's the new edge for adolescents to dance on. Since adolescents listen to the same music as their parents, and since their parents approve and even join them in getting tattoos and piercings—homosexuality is the new way to rebel and shake up their parents. Those who have this view allude to the number of women who are "try-sexuals," females who say they'll try anything and anyone. But once they graduate from college, they settle down and marry…a male.

Adolescence is a time when identities are going through a transformation and there are all sorts of questions surrounding gender issues. Gender is actually made up of three different facets: 1) sexual orientation (same sex, other sex, or bisexual), 2) gender identity (female, male, transgendered), and 3) sex typing (feminine, masculine, androgynous).55 During their adolescence, girls are trying to understand their gender and their sexuality. This raises a series of questions: *How feminine does her social group require her to be? What does it mean if she can attract the other gender? Does that attraction give her power or take away her power, making her more likely to become a victim? How masculine can she be before she's no longer sexually attractive to the other gender? Should that be an issue?* Trying to find the answers to these questions can be a frustrating process.

An adolescent girl may also be dealing with questions about whether having a same-sex experience or behavior means she has a same-sex orientation. Just because she's had a passionate or affectionate relationship with another girl (i.e., sexual behavior) doesn't necessarily mean she's homosexual (i.e., sexual orientation), much in the same way that just because she prefers to play sports and hates wearing dresses (i.e., sex typing) doesn't mean she's a lesbian.

Often women who consider themselves lesbians talk about knowing early on that they were not like other girls who were attracted to boys. They talk about "feeling different," but they may not have gotten clarity on their feelings of "different-ness" until well into adolescence or beyond. However, just because a girl perceives that she feels differently than other girls, it doesn't mean she's homosexual. Researcher Lisa Diamond has studied young women for years. She found that, "60 percent changed their lesbian or bisexual label at least once, and nearly 50 percent gave up their lesbian or bisexual label at some point."[57]

Perhaps that's the reason why many adolescents avoid using the tag of "lesbian" or "gay." Often adolescents will use descriptors like, "I'm gay-ish," "I'm experimenting," "I'm attracted to girls," or "I'm a bi-anything girl." Part of that may be due to seeing their sexual orientation as being only one part of who they are. But an adolescent girl also knows that there's a risk involved for those who choose to label themselves homosexual. They risk losing friends who may not understand or may be threatened by their identities. They risk losing a church community or family if they come from more conservative cultures. They risk being the target of physical, emotional, or social abuse.

The Youth Worker's Role

Homosexuality is one of the Christian hot topics of the twenty-first century. Although adolescents may have a cavalier attitude about it, churches, parents, and community members do not. It's often a polarizing topic; either you accept homosexuality or you don't. But the reality is that there are many shades to the topic. And if you're dealing with adolescents, you'll need to have an attitude of open dialogue rather than rigid dogmatism.

Remember, they are just now developing the capacity to think abstractly; therefore, they're drawn to argumentation and debate. Sexuality, especially same-sex attraction, is a topic already being discussed in school hallways. Adolescents want to

CONTINUED >

Stage 4: Identity Acceptance—at this point, she has come to full acceptance of her identity and is optimistic about her identity. She freely connects with other homosexuals, although she may sometimes seek to "pass" as straight.

Stage 5: Identity Pride—being vocal in her identity will inevitably produce conflict. This will lead her to prefer spending time with peers who feel similar pride in their identities.

Stage 6: Identity Synthesis—she begins to integrate the different facets of herself. She no longer seeks to identify herself solely as a lesbian, but will seek to draw in other parts of her identity.

HOW SAFE IS YOUR GROUP?

What's the atmosphere like in your youth group when it comes to homosexuality? How often is the term "fag" used as an insult? Do you ever hear students (or leaders) use the phrase, "That's so gay" when they're putting something down? Do you shrug it off thinking, "There are bigger hills to die on," or do you confront it? Is your ministry a place where students who are struggling with their gender identity feel safe or threatened? What do you need to change in the ministry? In yourself?

CASE STUDY: PLAYING "VAGINA TAG"

"We have some middle school girls who play what they call 'vagina tag.' It's where they run around and you can only be 'tagged' on the vagina. We have two girls, in particular, who play this game constantly. They are extremely close, and one girl walked alongside the other through her mom's cancer. She became a cutter and developed an eating disorder while her mother was going through chemotherapy, and her friend was the only person who knew, outside of the youth pastor, therapist, and her family. These two girls began going to each other for comfort. I would often walk up on them during trips or youth group lying on top of each other, touching each other's breasts and vaginas. They also peck lips in front of other people. During game times, they would often sneak away so they could be alone together." —Felicity, volunteer youth worker

Questions to ask in your youth ministry:

- What are the possible issues that you can identify?

CONTINUED >

know if the church is a place where they can discuss the topic as well.

While as youth workers we may have strong theological and personal views on the topics of homosexuality and sexual experimentation, it's important to remember that we are called to pastor young people, no matter where they come from or what issues they've got packed in their baggage. Jesus didn't turn people away because he didn't like the issues they were dealing with or because the topics made him feel uncomfortable. We can't turn students away, either.

This means trying to understand an adolescent's worldview and what's bringing her to that view, even if we wouldn't necessarily choose it for ourselves nor believe she should choose it. We also need to help a girl in the development of her identity, understanding that it needs to be grounded in Scripture and in accordance with who God says he is, and who he says *we* are.

On a practical level, it means we need to act lovingly toward a girl who's struggling with her sexuality. Understand that interacting with her on this topic may trigger some of our own issues to the point where we may need to refer her to a licensed counselor who specializes in adolescent issues. It's important that we create a safe place for her to process what she's thinking and feeling and not rush to judgment. When we judge, we cease learning about her and communication stops.

Don't push her to conclusions about her sexuality (e.g., "You're either gay or you're not.") but understand that the development of her sexual identity is as much in process as the other areas of her life. Explain to her what your faith community believes and why they have chosen to take that stance. Talk to her about the implications of her decisions. Also, help her to set behavioral and emotional boundaries, both for herself and for others. If she's wrestling with her sexuality, she may choose to act out or be more vulnerable with someone who's aggressively pursuing her. For her sake, it's important to her well-being that she knows how to say no and not feel guilty about it, whether it's someone from the same gender or not.

CONTINUED >

- How would you prioritize the issues?

- What immediate steps would you take? What long-term steps?

- Who would you involve in the decision-making process?

CHAPTER SEVEN
EMOTIONAL MATTERS

Growing up in the Minneapolis area, our family would often head to Lake Superior for vacations. The "North Shore," as it's known in Minnesota, is ruggedly scenic and known for its quickly changing weather patterns. As the saying goes, "If you don't like the weather, wait 10 minutes."

Recently I experienced the North Shore once again. For one week in August, I felt as though I was in a case study for a meteorological class. One morning I woke to a cloudless blue sky and a lake infused with tiny ripples of sunshine; it was a day where the weather wore like velvet, the kind of day you try to relive during the frozen gray of January. When I awoke the next morning, the sky was studded with ominous steel-colored clouds and the lake was a slate gray, wild with white-capped waves that pounded the rocks outside our cabin. And yet another day during that same week, a deep, unmoving fog traced the trees and created the sensation of being in a Japanese etching.

My experience of the North Shore is much like the emotional life of an adolescent girl. Every day yields a change in her emotional weather; sometimes you'll get a bright, sunny disposition that's a joy to be around. The next day (or hour or even minute), the thick fog of the blues enshrouds her; or she's a tumultuous storm, blasting everything in her path and sending passers-by heading for cover. Unfortunately, there's no such thing as a weather forecaster to help you deal with adolescent girls.

Now, to be fair, some girls are consistently San Diego—they're almost always sunny and warm. Other girls seem to be caught in Seattle—shrouded with clouds and rain, with only brief glimpses of sunshine. But most adolescent girls experience a gamut of emotions, so as youth workers, we need to learn how to weather the storms as well as the sun.

THE TURMOIL OF THE ADOLESCENT GIRL'S EMOTIONS

"I just don't understand it," said Andrea. The dark-haired, outgoing seventh-grader was bemoaning her morning. "Here I was having an intelligent, adult conversation with my mom and seconds later—I'm screaming at my little sister like I'm six again. What's up with that?" Andrea was getting in touch with the fact that she was heading full speed into the most emotionally volatile season of her life.

During adolescence, a girl's emotions are intense and varied. Even she doesn't always understand what's going on. As an early adolescent, her emotions can resemble a rubber ball after it's thrown against a wall in a tiny room—they're all over the place and change directions quickly. Sometimes it may feel easier to duck than to try and regain control of them.

Part of an early adolescent's emotional turmoil is due to her shift from childhood to adulthood. Most little girls are relatively happy creatures. Difficult things may happen to them that elicit strong emotional responses (e.g., grieving the death of a pet, or experiencing disappointment and anger over not being chosen for a particular team). But their emotions bounce back to a state of equilibrium fairly quickly.

However, once a girl starts moving toward adolescence, there's an increasing awareness that her emotional reactions are becoming more intense and the mood shifts are more extreme. She might find herself grieving the loss of the emotional stability of her childhood and longing for a time when life seemed much simpler and more manageable. Usually these erratic emotions are chalked up to "raging hormones," especially during early adolescence; but that's only one piece of her emotional mosaic. Her emotions are also influenced by her context and her cognitive abilities.

"A friend once told me that the best way to understand teenagers was to think of them as constantly on LSD. It was good advice. People on acid are intense, changeable, internal, often cryptic or uncommunicative and, of course, dealing with a different reality. That's all true for adolescent girls."[1]
—Dr. Mary Pipher, *Reviving Ophelia*

"Emotions show up uninvited." —Dr. John Weborg, theologian and pastor

Changes on the Home Front

Contextually, her life is constantly in a state of disequilibria during adolescence. In her family, she realizes her parents are responding to her differently than before. She may feel she's no longer "daddy's little girl." Dad may be more hesitant to pull her close to comfort her when she's had a bad day, or he may suddenly become more vocal in his opinions about what clothes she wears, what boys she hangs out with, and what time she's coming home. From his uncomfortable distancing, she infers, "He no longer loves me," rather than realizing that Dad is also struggling to know how to handle the fact that she's growing up.

Meanwhile, Mom is no longer seen as a close confidant but is often viewed as "the destroyer of joy"—being overprotective, telling her she's wearing too much make-up, asking too many questions, and then questioning her answers. And so she finds herself discombobulated by these new parental interactions that are unfamiliar to her, unsure of how to react to them and confused by her emotional reactions. As emotionally messy as she is, she fully expects that during adolescence her parents will stay committed to her. Her parents hope for the same.

As an adolescent, part of her longs to go back to the days when everything was safe and predictable. But another part of her longs for adulthood that seems just beyond reach. She's often unclear about what she's feeling. So the adults around her shouldn't expect her to know, either.

Friend or Foe?

Not only is her family context changing, but her social context is changing as well. This can be incredibly unnerving. Try to imagine going to work every day and wondering if your coworkers will accept you, or if they'll tease you because you wore the wrong style of pants. Imagine having everyone you work with suddenly ostracize you because one of your coworkers spreads a rumor about your love life. Imagine receiving anonymous e-mails telling you what a loser you are and how you should quit. And then you find out they're from a colleague you thought was a trusted friend—you even invited her to your house for dinner!

Now, imagine heading into that volatile—and sometimes hostile—environment day after day without the coping skills you've learned over the years. That's just a tiny taste of an adolescent girl's changing context, particularly if she's an early adolescent. It's no wonder her emotions are unpredictable. She knows she can't let her guard down; she must constantly be aware of what her surroundings might throw at her that day.

Reading Between the Lines

In addition to her shifting contexts, an adolescent girl also experiences a shift in her cognitive abilities. She's moving from being a concrete thinker to wrestling with abstract thoughts. The result is that she understands the nuances of human communication better than ever before. She picks up on a tone of voice or a fleeting facial expression and can read volumes into it. And while some of her perceptions are accurate, some are not. Either way, her observation is reality to her. She grasps that there are hidden messages and ideologies lying beneath the surface of her conversations and interactions. And in grasping this, she also realizes that she may not agree with the other party. But if she voices her opinion, a conflict may occur that could cause a rift in the relationship.

For instance, she may find herself disagreeing with a teaching of her church or its stance on a certain issue. As she thinks through her position, she begins to realize that in order to be true to her own beliefs, she may need to renegotiate a relationship that has been dear to her since her childhood. She may even have to find another church that is in agreement with her position. This renegotiation results in both external and internal conflict and can stir up a mass of difficult emotions for her to sort through. What will it cost her if she follows her beliefs? What will it cost her if she doesn't? She may find herself wishing for the time when questioning her faith meant asking simpler questions such as, "If God is everywhere, does he live in beer bottles?"

Leveling Out

By the time a girl reaches mid-adolescence, her moods aren't quite as unpredictable and explosive as they were during her early teens. She's getting more depth of understanding to her emotions and she's better able to articulate what she's feeling. She realizes that "I'm bored" means anything from "I'm tired" to "I'm lonely, but I'm afraid to call someone" to "I really have nothing to do that interests me right now."

It's important to note that while emotions are more predictable in mid-adolescence, it doesn't mean she's out of the woods just yet. Middle adolescence is the time when depression peaks in girls, something we'll discuss further later in this chapter.

By the time a girl reaches late adolescence (age 17 or so), her emotions will have eased in their intensity and evened out quite a bit. Not only is she now able to identify her emotions, but also she's self-reflective enough to understand what's at the root of many of them. However, while emotions may not be as extreme as before, she can still experience a lot of anxiety surrounding her decisions about the future: "Should I go to college or get a job? Can I afford to go to college? Where will I go to college? Should I live close to home? At home? Across the country? What career should I choose? What kind of man do I want to marry? Do I even want to be married? What about kids?" Decisions such as these can create a knot of angst in a high school girl's mind and impact her emotional state.

STRESS AND ANXIETY

Adolescent girls typically deal with more stress than adolescent boys.[2] That can be due to a variety of reasons. If she's an early adolescent, she's at a point in her life when her body is rapidly changing. In the midst of trying to deal with that, she has to leave her safe elementary school, where there were wonderful things such as recess and teachers who knew her and kept an eye on students who struggled. She leaves that environment to head to a middle school where she has to change teachers every hour. In the end, this means the faculty members have less time to build relationships with individual students. New peers from other grade schools are now added to the social mix and friendships are morphing on a regular basis. Sometimes a girl's anxiety about being in middle school increases to the extent where she begins avoiding school altogether, citing cramps or headaches. This can cause the problem to escalate, as the longer she stays out of school, the harder it is for her to enter back into that world.

Academic Stress

Besides the social stress of school, there is also academic stress. Beginning in about sixth or seventh grade, students start worrying about whether or not their grades are good enough to get into college. By ninth or tenth grade, they're thinking about what college they want to go to. They choose to be involved in activities that will look good on their applications rather than seeking involvement in activities they enjoy or that will make a difference in their world.[3]

For example, a girl can feel pressured to focus on a sport such as soccer or basketball because it might give her an edge when it comes to college scholarships. However, she might come to hate the sport because of the inordinate stress that comes with the sacrifices required by an intense athletic schedule—practicing all day and still facing three hours of homework when she comes home, or having to choose between being on a traveling squad or going to homecoming.

There can be stress from parents to succeed academically as well. This seems especially an issue for girls whose parents immigrated to the United States. For example, a high school girl whose parents were raised in Latin America talks about the difference between her parents and the parents of her white friends:

> My parents are worried about grades, but having drinks in the house is okay because of how they were raised. It's okay to go out at night, as long as you get an education. My friends—their parents would freak if they had a beer at some party somewhere some night. But if they come home with a C they're like, "That's okay. You tried." My parents would be irate if I didn't get good grades. They want me to make a better life for myself. My dad came to the U.S. in his early 20s. He cleaned toilets, he was a bellboy, and then he built his own company. "I worked hard to give you a better opportunity so you better take advantage of all the opportunities."[4] —Marisa, age 17

A young woman whose parents are from Taiwan put it this way, "'If I get a 99 percent on a test, they ask me where the last one percent went. Anything less than an A- is considered flunking…My parents remind me that if I don't get 'good' grades, *Li xi-ya*—I'm dead.'"[5]

When parents put a strong value on a daughter's academic performance (or athletic, musical, or even spiritual performance), she begins to think that perhaps her parents love her more for what she can do than for who she is. She begins to wonder what would happen if she failed—would they still love and accept her? Rather than taking that risk, she'll put more emphasis on how she performs. And that, in turn, becomes the way she defines herself—"an excellent student," "a strong athlete," or a "perfect Christian." Maintaining these labels can bring about even more stress.

how do dancers define themselves?

The Family Feud

A girl can also experience stress and anxiety because of family circumstances. Parents who fight or are going through a divorce can become a substantial source of stress. She may be in the midst of deciding who she'll live with: Mom, Dad, or Grandma. She might be carrying an additional load because she's expected to help care for her younger siblings.

Because of the isolative nature of current American life, there are few extended family members or people in her community or church with whom she can talk about her anxious feelings. And when her anxiety becomes extreme, she may panic whenever she's separated from her parents for any length of time and worry that they might not come back, especially if a family member has recently died. (Note: If this goes on for longer than a month, she may be experiencing what's known as a "separation disorder," and it's important that she seeks professional help.)

Excessive Anxiety

Anxiety is a very normal emotion, especially during adolescence. It appears when changes in life feel threatening to a girl. Anxiety is a vague sense of uneasiness, agitation, and restlessness. Often it's felt in relation to an upcoming event or conversation (e.g., a solo performance during a concert, giving a speech in class, or confronting a friend who hurt her). But there is cause for concern when the anxiety doesn't seem to be attached to any particular set of circumstances, yet it's still pervasive throughout her day. If she seems excessively worried and wary, has stomachaches or headaches with no physical explanation, frequently hyperventilates, or is overly jumpy—especially for any length of time (six months or so)—then it's time to connect her with a therapist or counselor.

It's possible that her anxiety can turn into a disorder where it overwhelms her life, such as an obsessive-compulsive disorder (recurring rituals and uncontrollable anxious thoughts) or a post-traumatic stress disorder (PTSD). PTSD is associated with a trauma, such as a car accident or rape, and it's more than just a disturbing memory of the experience. The girl actually feels as though she's reliving the event.

Her anxiety may escalate into a phobia (irrational fear) about an interaction or object (e.g., a phobia of leaving home or of public speaking). Or it could lead to panic attacks, when she feels overwhelmed by fear. Some people even describe it as feeling like a heart attack. Panic attacks are much more common in girls than in boys, and usually show up in girls between the ages of 15 and 19.[6] If a girl is experiencing any of these signs of excessive anxiety, it's a good idea to get her help from a professional counselor or therapist.

Strategies for Help

As youth workers, we sometimes pick up on clues that a behavior or reaction may be out of the ordinary because we have the opportunity to observe a wide variety of adolescents' reactions to similar situations. When a girl appears to be overly anxious or stressed about life, the solution may be as simple as providing a listening ear. She might be hesitant to talk with her parents—perhaps she doesn't want to add to their already heavy load. This is when a caring youth worker can focus on a girl for a period of time and listen to her concerns.

It's important not to discount her feelings (e.g., "You have no reason to feel anxious.") or dole out a Bible verse as an antidote (e.g., "Just memorize Philippians 4:6-7 and you'll be fine"). Rather, listen with focused care and concern. What seems to be at the root of her anxiety? Reassure her that certain levels of anxiety are normal when she's heading into new or risky territories. If she's willing, help her develop a plan of action to reduce her anxiety and stress. Maybe help her map out her different options and develop her decision-making skills. Encourage her to search through Scripture (especially the Psalms) in order to discover the many promises God gives to those who are anxious.

Guide her in reframing her view of God so she sees him caring about her anxiety rather than sitting in judgment of her (e.g., 1 Peter 5:7). Help her to discern when her anxiety and stress levels seem abnormal and appear to be overtaking her daily activities. Because high levels of anxiety and stress can feel paralyzing, she may need you to talk with her parents and to assist her in seeking therapy and possibly medication.

DEPRESSION

Another issue that adolescent girls face at higher rates than boys is depression. In fact, one of the highest risk factors for depression is being female. By the time they reach 15, girls are twice as likely as boys to be depressed.[8] This is a switch from childhood, where typically boys are more depressed than girls.[9] In one study of adolescent girls, 23 percent of the girls reported that within the past two weeks, they had experienced at least a few symptoms of depression. Ten percent of the girls reported that their symptoms were severe.[10] Not only is being female a risk factor, so is her location. If a girl lives in the suburbs, she's three times more likely to experience significant symptoms of depression (22 percent versus seven percent of others).[11]

Depression is more than just an occasional sad day or bad mood. In mild depression, a girl can enter a "blue" phase where she's sad, irritable, bored, or

GIRLS FROM AFFLUENT FAMILIES NEED HELP TOO

It's assumed that affluent teenagers have access to more resources for help. However, research finds that even though there are increasing signs of depression and substance abuse among these students, they aren't getting help from either their teachers or their parents. The teachers assume that because these teenagers come from privileged backgrounds, they're getting the help they need. The parents seem to believe that because they're successful, they should be better than most people at handling their own problems. They value a façade of strength, so they don't look for outside assistance. Add to that the isolative nature of wealthy suburban life (i.e., distance from neighbors, few if any family meal times, and lack of supervision from adults—not due to money but because parents believe it promotes self-sufficiency), and these teenagers are often left on their own to survive adolescence.[7]

has explosive outbursts that can last for several days or weeks or even years (at this point, depression is usually diagnosed as a "dysthymic disorder"—when milder symptoms of depression are present for over a year). She can also have nagging feelings of self-condemnation or worthlessness. Often these mildly depressive symptoms are credited to general teenage angst.

However there's a fine line between angst and depression, and it's important to note the difference. Unfortunately an insidious image of adolescent girls permeates our culture. They're portrayed as being sullen, despondent, melancholy, and surly. So when a girl behaves like that image, she's thought to be "just a typical teenager" and her depressive symptoms are ignored. This can be dangerous because when these minor depressive risk factors are disregarded for too long, a girl could possibly spin into a major depression.

But the good news is that if she has someone to talk to and cry with—someone who will encourage and support her—it's more likely that she'll come through mild depression just fine.

Symptoms of Major Depression

Major depression is when a deep sadness or a sense of despair or hopelessness is persistently present (for two weeks or longer). When a girl is experiencing a major depression, these are just some of the signs she might exhibit:

- Frequent bouts of crying

- A change in sleep patterns (too much or too little), or constantly being tired and not having the energy to participate in activities that previously excited her or brought her joy

- A change in appetite (not eating or bingeing)—the development of an eating disorder

- A change in grades or school attendance

- Constant feelings of self-doubt, shame, guilt, or worthlessness

- Struggling to focus (e.g., on school work or family chores or even in conversations) or make decisions

- Seemingly obsessed with death or thoughts about suicide, even to the extent of having a plan for suicide or stating her preferences for how she'd like to die

- Increased sexual activity or use of chemical substances (although some researchers now say that these are precursors for depression rather than the result of depression[12])

- A change in social relationships—withdrawing from friendships, isolating herself in her bedroom or her bathroom for long periods of time

- A pattern of self-abuse, such as cutting or burning herself

Sometimes it's important to remind her (or her parents) that when she's struggling with any of these symptoms, it's not simply a matter of having a better attitude or willing herself to be happy. She needs qualified help, whether that help comes in the form of regular therapy, medication, or both.

When she's in a bout of depression, she may not have the internal strength to get help. This is when a trusted youth worker can intervene and discuss her observations with the girl's parents and talk about options for getting her support.

Causes

What causes depression? That depends on whether it's a blue mood or a full-blown depression. If a girl is having a down *mood*, it's usually caused by an experience where there's some kind of interpersonal

A MALE YOUTH WORKER'S PERSPECTIVE...

Q: "What do you wish you'd have known about teenage girls before you started in ministry?"

A: "How girls love, care, and listen so wholeheartedly. I also wish I knew the depth of arrested development in their lives; what happens when, in our formative years, something traumatic happens that scars us for the rest of our lives. In some cases, boys who feel the pain release it through anger, bad grades, and fights. Girls have to be cute, loveable, and respectful. So they continue to achieve at high levels, although they begin to wither inwardly with bad choices about places, people, and things."
—Gerald

conflict, such as a poor grade that she believes will result in her parent's disapproval. Or it could be a break-up with her boyfriend, or rejection by a friend or even a group of friends.

If it's major *depression*, there are several possible causes. It could be biochemical in nature or related to an illness, either hers or someone in her family (e.g., Mom's just been diagnosed with breast cancer). Or it could be related to her early maturation. If she matures earlier than her friends, she can feel out of step with them and may begin to connect with older boys instead. All of this can make her feel as though she's in over her head emotionally and can result in depression.

Some researchers speculate that it runs in families: If one family member is depressed, a child is more likely to be depressed.[13] It could be that circumstances in the family add to a depressive environment—concerns about money, the health or the destructive behavior of a family member, parents who are either emotionally or physically unavailable, or the breakdown of the parents' marriage. It's understandable that if a girl is exposed to stress in the family home, it would have a ripple effect on her emotional state, as well as her other relationships. She may withdraw from friends who have more positive family dynamics.

Still others hypothesize that depression in girls may be due to gender role expectations. A girl is in a state of conflict between wanting to continue to achieve academically, as she did in grade school, and now perceiving that desire for achievement as not being feminine. She's concerned with wanting to vocalize her beliefs and opinions, yet fearing she'll be rejected. She worries about her developing body and whether or not she's attractive. She wonders if she'll ever have a close friend to share her heart and thoughts with; then worries that if she does find such a friend, she might be thought a lesbian.

As a Christian, she might fret about her dreams that come in conflict with church expectations. For example, she may want to have a preaching ministry, but her church says that only males are allowed to do that. Or as a future mother, she may be expected to stay at home and home-school her kids. Theorist Carol Gilligan describes how adolescent girls learn that, in order to meet what they perceive as society's expectations, they must submerge their own voice and enter into an acceptable silence. They look as though they're obeying cultural and ethnic role expectations, but they're only doing so in order to protect their inner voices from being criticized or ignored. This conflict turned inward can result in depression.

All of these are possible causes or factors in a girl's depression. These may also indicate the presence of other disorders and problems. All the more reason for her to seek help from a professional counselor.

Gender Differences

Depression in girls is different than depression in boys. For one, relational problems seem to trigger a girl's depression more often. Whether it's a breakup with a guy or a misunderstanding with a friend, either one can impact her emotions. And it's not just the breakdown of individual relationships. If a girl thinks she's unpopular, then she's more likely to be depressed. This isn't the case with boys.[14]

Another way depression manifests itself differently in girls and boys is how they respond to the first signs that it's approaching. When a boy feels a depressed mood coming on, he'll try to distract himself so he doesn't have to think about it. He'll direct his feelings externally or away from himself. He'll likely become more aggressive in his behavior, taking more risks and possibly causing harm to himself or to others. Girls, on the other hand, are more likely to turn their emotions inward. They're more likely to mull over a problem and focus on what they're feeling, expressing themselves by writing poetry,

DEPRESSION AND THE INTERNET

An adolescent who spends a lot of time online might be depressed. In a study of 425 middle school students, researchers found that less than a third *weren't* at risk for depression. There were 11 percent who were found to be highly addicted to the Internet; they also scored highest for depression. This was true for girls as well as boys. The Internet addicts tended to have low attention spans, as well as nominal goals. And all that time spent alone looking at a computer screen doesn't help; isolation contributes to depression.[16]

listening to sad music, or journaling. They become hypercritical of themselves and tend to spin into a depression. If they internalize their emotions in an increasingly unhealthy way, it can take the form of self-mutilation, an eating disorder, or even suicide.[15]

Strategies for Help

Dr. Lisa Machoian has worked with adolescent girls for over 20 years. She says, "I made a wonderful discovery in my research of and psychotherapy with teenage girls struggling with depression: No matter how despairing they may feel, there is always a spark of hope within them, and the energy to make their troubles visible to themselves and others. In doing so, they can feel better about what is troubling them."[17]

Someone who's depressed will tend to isolate herself, so youth workers need to be alert whenever an adolescent girl is ready to open up. It's important that we don't just hear the words but watch and listen for her nonverbal clues as well. What is her body language saying? Is she slumped down in the chair? Does she speak in a flat voice that's devoid of emotion? As you listen, lean forward to express interest. She's taking a risk by talking with you, and she'll shut down if she thinks you don't care. Make eye contact, even if she avoids your eyes. Ask open-ended questions—something that demands more than a yes or no answer. And make sure not to judge or criticize her responses.

Because relationships are so important to an adolescent girl, we need to try to get her connected with healthy relationships. Try to get her plugged into a caring small group of girls. There's something about belonging that can bring hope to a girl. We can preach about God's love for her until her ears bleed, but it won't become real until she feels it through the touch of those around her.

And, as stated earlier, don't hesitate to get her specialized help. Depression is more than just a bad day—it can lead to suicide. A good therapist or counselor can help a girl find her way out of depression. But don't abandon her once she agrees to get professional help. She still needs a youth pastor to walk alongside her and care for her.

SUICIDE

It was after youth group when one of the small group leaders, Laura, came up to the youth pastor with a distressed look on her face. "I don't know what to do," she whispered. The youth pastor pulled her out of earshot of the rest of the group and asked the obvious question, "What happened?" Her eyes brimming with tears, Laura revealed that, during their small group, one of the girls talked about wanting to kill herself. (They had a pretty tight group that was known for being vulnerable with each other.) The girl had broken a mirror the night before and tried to slice her wrists with the shards of glass. She showed Laura the bloody bandages covering the scars and told her, "I stopped because I got scared." Apparently, this wasn't the first time she'd tried to end her life. What made the interaction even more disturbing was the conversation Laura had with the girl's mother after youth group. The mom just brushed off the incident with a "girls will be girls" attitude.

Laura knew she needed to report the incident to the youth pastor, but the mom's response (or lack of it) made it even more imperative. The youth pastor called a therapist, whom he had consulted with before, and she coached him on how to deal with the situation. When the youth pastor called the girl's home, her mother answered. Her response about her daughter's suicidal behavior was flippant, "She's always seeking attention. This is just one more way." The youth pastor then assured her that her daughter was indeed crying for attention, but she was doing it in a way that could cost her life. He then gave her two options: 1) call the number of a psychiatrist who could walk her through what to do next, or 2) take her daughter directly to the emergency room. If she didn't do one of the two within the next hour, the youth pastor said he would call 911 on behalf of the daughter. There was an echoing stillness on the other end of the phone.

Then, in a subdued voice, the mother asked, "It's really that serious?"

"It really is *that* serious," emphasized the youth pastor. When they touched base later that day, the mother gratefully acknowledged that she had taken the daughter to see the psychiatrist and was finally getting her the help she needed.

The Numbers

Suicide is the third leading cause of death among 15-to-19-year-olds (after car accidents and homicide), and the fourth leading cause of death for 10-to-14-year-olds.[18] For girls, their suicidal behavior reaches its peak at about age 13 or 14.[19] According to the 2004 National Survey on Drug Use and Health, about 900,000 American adolescents reported that they planned to commit suicide during their worst bout with depression. Of those 900,000 teenagers, 712,000 actually attempted the plan.[20] And of those attempts, about 5,000 a year result in death.[21] However, a third of those who survive their attempt end up with serious injuries that need medical care.[22] The good news is that in the last decade, the suicide rate appears to have dropped.[23] Some credit this to an increase in the use of antidepressant medication. Others say it's due to stricter gun laws or a reduction in substance abuse. Whatever the reason, the news is encouraging.

Gender Differences

Like many areas we've looked at so far, there's also a difference between adolescent females and males when it comes to suicide. More guys than girls actually kill themselves by committing suicide. However, it's estimated that girls are anywhere from two to four times as likely to *try* committing suicide.[26] Part of the reason is that males typically use more violent methods in their attempts (e.g., shooting, stabbing, hanging, standing in front of a train, crashing a car, leaping from a height). These methods are more deadly than the methods girls usually use—overdosing on pills or taking poison. One youth worker tells the story of a girl who attempted suicide by swallowing perfume. Thankfully, it wasn't fatal, and it acted as a wake-up call to her family that she needed help.

The friendships girls have also impact their thoughts of suicide. If a girl has a strong sense of self, is well connected with friends, or goes to a school where there is a lot of social support, then she's less likely to consider suicide. On the other hand, if she's socially isolated or has friendships that are relatively unstable, she's more likely to have suicidal thoughts.[27] Other factors that increase a girl's thoughts of suicide are if she's been forced to have sex, she's inclined to fights, she frequently gets drunk, or if she's heavier than others in her peer group.[28]

The Threat of Suicide

Girls are more likely than guys to threaten suicide without actively moving on their threats.[29] That isn't to say that girls shouldn't be taken seriously when they threaten suicide. When a girl is suicidal, she's crying out for something—a deeper relationship, a plea to be loved, a demand to be noticed. This could be the reason why so many girls tell someone after they attempt suicide.[30] By attempting suicide, she doesn't necessarily want to die; she may be screaming to be heard. The trap that some youth workers (and parents) fall into is dismissing a suicidal threat as a girl just being manipulative, and then they ignore her threats.

In response to this perception, Dr. Lisa Machoian, in her book *The Disappearing Girl*, writes:

> My research with girls shows that dismissing teenage girls' suicide-behavior as manipulation overlooks what may have been the meaning of the suicidal act in the first place. They may have learned to manipulate but are doing so in the spirit of hope, of getting needs met that have not been met otherwise. The original meaning of the word "manipulative" is "to lead by the hand." When suicidal acts enable girls to get help, it is inaccurate to see these acts as merely "manipulative." Treating them as such can lead girls to give up hope. And then, psychologically or literally, they are more likely to kill themselves.[31]

THE YOUTH WORKER'S ROLE

Youth workers need to take a threat of a suicide very seriously, whether they hear it directly from a girl or from one of her friends. Once a warning flag has been raised, they need to respond immediately, involving the right authorities, including her parents. If a youth worker senses that a girl is threatening to commit suicide, she needs to be taken at once to the emergency room at a hospital. If in doubt, consult with a licensed therapist.

Besides the signs that are present during depression, some of the other indicators of potential suicide that youth workers must be aware of are

- When a girl starts giving away items that are precious to her

- When she makes comments such as, "I wonder how many people would come to my funeral?" or "I wonder if anyone would miss me if I were gone?"

- When she asks specific questions about suicide, such as, "If people commit suicide, does God send them to hell?"

- When she draws up a will

- When a close friend, family member, or someone from school attempts to commit suicide (whether it's deadly or not)

When a girl shows any of these signs, it's critical to have a conversation with her right away to assess how she's doing. Listen closely to her as she talks, and communicate your concern for her. Let her know that you take her words and behavior seriously. If she asks, don't promise her that you'll keep the conversation confidential, but do assure her that you care deeply for her and will take the necessary steps to get her help and will treat the conversation with respect (i.e., you're not going to publish it in the church prayer letter).

You also need to determine whether or not she has a plan to end her life. The more specific the plan, the more at risk she is. For example, "I'm planning on taking my mom's sleeping pills," versus "I don't know; I think I'm just having a bad day." You also need to find out if she's attempted suicide in the past or knows of someone else who has (she might try to copy their behavior).

Because a girl's social network is crucial when it comes to thoughts of suicide, youth workers can try to get a girl who's showing signs of depression involved in a strong, healthy small group. Also, try to get her actively engaged in the youth ministry or other extracurricular activities. Teenage girls are remarkably resilient and usually aren't as hopeless as adult women who contemplate suicide. There is almost always a small spark of hope in the most depressed of girls; we need to fan that spark into a fire with love, concern, prayer, and support.

CHAPTER EIGHT

BRAIN MATTERS: COGNITIVE AND EDUCATIONAL ISSUES

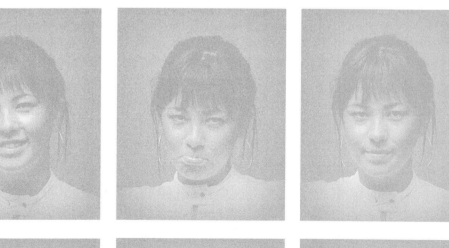

When a girl hits adolescence, it can sometimes feel as though this sweet little girl, who's always believed exactly what she's been told, has been overtaken by one of the lawyers from *Law and Order*. Basic premises that she has abided by for years are now up for questioning. "Why do we have to dress up to go to church? Isn't it a sin to be concerned about impressing people instead of God?" "Why should I stay a virgin? It doesn't say premarital sex is wrong in the Bible." "I've decided to become a _____ (insert: vegan, atheist, Republican, etc., here) and you're not going to change my mind."

Not only are they inquisitive and argumentative, but they're also extremely creative. Just ask a girl why she sneaked out of the cabin at 2 a.m. during the retreat and you'll hear a wonderfully intricate and ingenious excuse. Although these questions and statements may feel antagonistic and even far-fetched at times, they're indicators that she's developing her cognitive skills.

For a long time, it was believed that by the time a person reached adolescence, her brain was fully grown. But research done in the last several years has proven that there's another growth spurt that occurs in an adolescent's brain. Through brain scanning machines, such as MRIs and PET scans, neuroscientists are discovering that this development of the brain is almost as dramatic as in infancy.[1]

Dr. Jay Giedd is a neuroscientist at the National Institutes of Health. He has been scanning adolescent brains for more than a decade as part of a long-term research study of brain development in normal adolescents and children. According to Giedd, the frontal lobes are one of the last areas of the brain to finish developing, sometimes not until well after age 20.[2] The frontal lobes (or prefrontal cortex) are the areas of the brain that direct our moods. They also assist us in planning ahead. This might explain why so many adolescents forget to sign up for an event until the day it's happening.

The frontal lobes also help us control our impulses. There were a couple of our older high school girls who helped us with a junior high event at church. At the end of the day, they were commiserating about how squirrelly the junior high girls were. They looked at me with serious faces and proclaimed, "We were never like that!" The look on my face told them a different story. They were observing the lack of impulse control firsthand.

The frontal lobe area is also the part of the brain where consequences are thought through. With this part still under development, it's easier to understand why an adolescent can make quick decisions without thinking through the consequences.[3] So when a high school girl decides to take her friends for a joy ride to another state—in her parents' car—and later you ask her what she was thinking, her reply might be, "I didn't think about it. My friends wanted to go, and it seemed like fun at the time." Perhaps her frontal lobes haven't fully developed yet. As Giedd puts it, "They have the passion and the strength but no brakes and they may not get good brakes until they are twenty-five."[4]

Dr. George Realmuto, professor of child and adolescent psychiatry at the University of Minnesota, says that it's during this time that an adolescent's mind has heightened creativity but poor control of those new ideas.[5] This might explain a girl's decision to spray paint the school with her friends, or to dye her hair a brilliant green the night before her grandparents' wedding anniversary party. Realmuto stresses the importance of outside guidance to help adolescents manage these new ideas and help them discern the wisdom of them.

The results of this brain activity are evident as we watch middle schoolers begin to move from concrete thinking to abstract, usually during their sixth- or seventh-grade year. I saw this portrayed very clearly one summer when I was speaking at a camp that had a huge rope swing that swung out high over the river. It was a badge of courage among the girls if they were able to hold on tight and then fly off, spinning into the dark, cold water. At one of the evening sessions, I made the analogy of how becoming a Christian is like jumping off the rope swing. You can climb up to the base of it, you can touch the rope, and you can even watch other girls jump off; but you still haven't really experienced the rope swing. It's not until you actually take that step of faith and grab onto it and ride it over the water that you truly experience the rope swing. No one else can do it for you.

Later, one of the counselors told me that a sixth-grade girl in her cabin asked her if that meant she had to jump off the rope swing in order to become a Christian. This sixth-grader was still operating in concrete terms—what they see and hear they take literally. Think of how you learned addition—the teacher had one apple and then she put another apple next to it to show you that $1+1 = 2$. Concrete thought. You don't teach algebra and calculus to small children because those disciplines require abstract thought.

There are glimmers of abstract thought in sixth- and seventh-graders, and it progresses throughout adolescence. Abstract thought means that adolescents begin to make sense of symbols and ideas. Adolescents who are able to think abstractly are more attuned to the finer nuances of communication and thought. They understand irony and analogies. They pick up on the emotions and worldviews of others. They start putting the pieces together and coming to conclusions.

Sarah, a 16-year-old, talks about her move to abstract thinking, "I remember walking by a building and I looked at its 'For Rent' sign and, for the first time, I had all these weird thoughts...I didn't just think of it as a building, but I thought, gee, someone had to paint that sign and someone had to make that building—probably there were dozens of people who worked on the building to get it there. And, to me, it was the first time that I really realized what a big world it was and that it has a lot of people in it, and I began to think: Where do I fit in?"[6]

It's this capacity for abstract thinking that allows youth workers to guide students into deeper thought about their faith. As early teens they still see things in black-and-white—either it's a sin or it isn't. But as they grow, they're able to wrestle with the gray areas of life. They begin to struggle with concepts of justice and honesty and fairness. At this age, they need to be able to both question and to experience so they can understand.

For example, at our seminary we run a program in the summer where youth workers can bring one or two of their leadership students for a weeklong immersion into seminary life. Each day has a different theme; students sit with a professor in the morning, do a related activity in the afternoon, and then play at night. On the day when we focus on "justice" the students spend the morning in a lively discussion about racism and inequity. The participants are of many different ethnicities, and for some this is the first time they've met peers who've experienced racism and injustice firsthand. After they've been challenged in the classroom, we head to the Cook County Jail for a tour. This is the first time some of them have ever been inside a jail, while others nod to relatives as they walk by. Students who have only learned about justice at their desks are now able to see, smell, and feel it. They notice that most of the people have a certain skin color or are just a few years (or even months) older than they are, and this raises questions about why them and not others? They observe that three or four people are crammed into a cell meant for two; that lunch is a flattened bologna sandwich served on a Styrofoam tray; that showers are out in the public area; and that some people have been waiting to go to trial for months and even years, and the only reason they're not out yet is because of finances—they can't afford bond, or they can't afford an adequate lawyer.

Immediately after leaving the jail, with questions and emotions swirling, we pack them in vans and they head to a huge amusement park in the northern suburbs of Chicago. The contrast of a jail in the afternoon with the park at night throws them into a state of disequilibria. Suddenly, their quick answers about justice, which seemed to suffice that morning in class, are no longer adequate. They often stay up until two or three in the morning talking about Christianity and justice, their worlds and their futures. They're thinking abstractly, trying to make sense of it all, and trying to understand their roles—both now and in the future.

As youth workers, we need to create experiences where students aren't coddled in their thinking and given simplistic answers, but stretched to become critical thinkers who are thoughtful about their faith and their lives.

GENDER DIFFERENCES

When it comes to academics, there are some differences between boys and girls. Girls typically receive higher grades in almost every subject, no matter what their ages.[7] However, even though girls receive higher grades overall, they tend to feel less confident in their academic abilities and are inclined to critique their performance much more harshly than boys will.[8] Girls do better than boys on most standardized achievement tests, an accomplishment credited to everything from the way the sexes learn to the way the tests are designed to brain development. And even though girls typically receive higher grades on their report cards, when it comes to the competitive SAT, boys receive higher scores in both the math and verbal sections of the test.[9]

The noticeable lack of females in the fields of math and technology has been a topic of discussion for many years. Interestingly, girls and boys enjoy math and science equally during the grade school years. In fact, when girls are in grade school, they actually have the edge when it comes to math because it involves more memorization of math facts and calculations.

As they get older, girls are still as likely as boys to take advanced math classes by tenth grade.[10] And they do better than guys in algebra when they're dealing with problems that tap into the same cognitive skills needed for language processing.[11] Although there's a common myth that boys do better than girls in math, the National Center for Education Statistics found that in the United States girls and boys score very similarly on math tests and have since the 1990s.[12] However, girls don't look forward to math class the way boys do, and they're more likely to be anxious about asking questions in math class.[13] Girls are also less likely to participate in science or math fairs.[14]

There could be any number of reasons behind girls' perceived dislike of math: cultural or peer pressure on girls not to do well in math because that's a "boy's" subject; an internal fear of looking smarter than boys and thus intimidating them; a teacher's sexist bias; or brain development.[15] And the existence of a talking Barbie that whines, "Math is hard!" doesn't help little girls believe they can succeed in this area.

When it comes to computers, even though both girls and boys have equal access, girls tend to use their computers for sending and receiving e-mails and doing homework assignments.[16] Unfortunately, girls believe they're much less gifted in areas of technology.[17] Perhaps this is why boys are five times more likely than girls to consider a career in technology.[18] In fact, of the students who took the AP exam in computer science in 2002, only 22 percent were female. And the males had higher average scores than the females.[19]

On the other hand, when it comes to reading and writing, girls tend to have the higher test scores.[20] Girls also do better with long-term memory exercis-

SELF-ESTEEM AND GIRLS

The American Association of University Women (AAUW) undertook a major research study of girls' attitudes and identities.[29] As they researched 3,000 kids who were between fourth and tenth grades nationwide, they found that the self-esteem of both boys and girls drops during their adolescent years, but the girls' decline is more significant. Girls who are eight and nine years of age are confident and assertive. However, by the time they enter high school, their confidence in themselves and in their abilities has dropped significantly.

Not only does gender impact a girl's self-esteem, so does her racial or ethnic background. When a girl feels good about being part of a racial or ethnic group, her self-esteem is higher. For example, the AAUW study found that African American girls are more confident than Caucasian girls. However, they also discovered that while Latinas begin school with the highest level of self-esteem, they also show the most drastic change; by the end of school, they had plunged to the lowest level.

es and when it comes to articulating their thoughts and ideas. Boys, however, score higher when doing visuospatial exercises.[21] They also tend to be more knowledgeable about geography and politics.[22]

Girls tend to have higher educational goals than boys.[23] In one study, 80 percent of girls said they were likely to attend a four-year college compared to 72 percent of boys.[24] In 2001, only 44 percent of the first-year college students were men; 56 percent were women.[25] Not only are girls more likely to go to college, but they are also more likely to graduate with a degree.[26] The U.S. Department of Education speculates that by the year 2011, there will be 140 women graduating from college for every 100 men who graduate.[27] This has been the trend in the United States since 1982.[28] The only exception is if a girl gets pregnant during high school; those circumstances put her at a greater risk for dropping out of school.

A GIRL'S MENTAL DEVELOPMENT: ISSUES

As encouraging as the test numbers and statistics are, there are still many barriers that girls must overcome in their mental development. Research has shown that even though girls are excited about academics during grade school, once they hit middle school, their interest in academia declines. In fact, middle school girls report that they're more interested in popularity than in academics.[30]

Dr. Mary Pipher offers up a possible explanation: "Junior high is when girls begin to fade academically. Partly this comes from the very structure of the schools that tend to be large and impersonal. Girls, who tend to do better in relationship-based, cooperative learning situations, get lost academically in these settings. Partly it comes from a shift girls make at this time from a focus on achievement to a focus on affiliation. In junior high, girls feel enormous pressure to be popular. They learn that good grades can even interfere with popularity."[31]

Issue: Learned Helplessness

Unfortunately, some adolescent girls have learned to sacrifice their development for the sake of popularity and likeability. They quit trying to achieve and take on a position of powerlessness or what researcher Martin Seligman calls, "learned helplessness." This describes a situation in which "people have come to believe that success and failure depend on circumstances beyond their control. Because they think their fate depends on luck, they give up their goals too easily, offering a variety of excuses for failure."[32] Girls, more so than boys, fall prey to this issue of learned helplessness.

Dr. Leonard Sax in his book *Why Gender Matters* explains Mr. Seligman's premise with the following illustration. Take one mouse and let it freely explore an exciting new environment complete with tunnels and tubes. Call this mouse the "master" mouse. Take another mouse and instead of letting it roam freely, hold it tightly, even squeezing it when it tries to escape. Do this for several hours a day. Call this mouse the "helpless" mouse. Then take the two mice and put them in a tub of water. The "master" mouse will immediately start swimming to the edge. The "helpless" mouse, on the other hand, will make futile attempts to swim, and then start to go under. If not scooped up and rescued, this mouse will eventually drown.

I saw the concept of "learned helplessness" illustrated one day at a camp while I was helping another leader, Jason, at the climbing wall. But first, a little background: Jason had spent the previous year studying feminism at a highly regarded university. Now he wanted to see if the theories he'd learned would prove true with adolescent girls. We'd just finished a week of eighth grade girls-only camp, and it was amazing to watch the girls in action when there weren't any guys around. They seemed to play more, and they encouraged each other to take more risks, whether on the ropes course, swinging off the rope swing, or tackling the climbing wall. It was incredible to watch the girls challenge, coax, and sometimes downright threaten each other—good-naturedly, of course—to get another girl from their group to the top. These girls would push through their fear and, even though it might take numerous tries, the group would cheer each time a girl broke through to a new height on the wall.

Now back to Jason and the wall: Some of these same girls decided to stay on for the next week of camp when it was co-ed. The first day, the girls rushed to the climbing wall, eager to climb. Two of the girls, both strong climbers, were about halfway up the wall when a cabin of boys walked into the clearing. Suddenly, almost in unison, both of the girls on the wall let go of the rocks they were clinging to and leaned back in their harnesses. With a slight whine in their voices, they both claimed they couldn't climb any higher. "Let us down!" they complained. They were done. No amount of cajoling from the staff or the other girls could get them to move any higher up the wall. When they reached the ground, they clipped off their helmets and fluffed their hair as they started chatting with the boys. Jason looked at me in stunned disbelief. "I can't believe I just saw what I did," he said in dismay. He was observing "learned helplessness" firsthand.

Whether it's a teacher, a parent, peers, or even the president of an Ivy League university that applies the pressure, girls quickly learn where it's socially acceptable to succeed and where it's not. If a culture affirms helplessness in a female, it's often easier for her to conform than to push back against the pressure and take risks.

Sometimes the pressure toward helplessness is internal. In a study of girls in the United States, Britain, and Germany, they were found to self-handicap.

"They arc more likely than boys to offer excuses, such as inherent handicaps, test anxiety, or recent traumatic events prior to beginning a task, especially if the task is personally threatening."[33] Girls are also more likely to self-handicap by taking less active, up-front roles in presentations. For example, one research study observed the roles that girls and boys took in a student-led science demonstration. While the boys actively participated in the demonstration, girls took much less of an up-front role. They were much more likely to take notes for the group than to be in front of the group and active.[34] This is a great example of a phenomenon called the Horner Effect, otherwise known as the "Fear of Success Syndrome." Psychologist Matina Horner discovered this behavior in the 1970s when she observed that when men and women compete against each other in experiments, women would consistently lose, despite having the greater skills and abilities.

The 1990s saw a lessening of this effect (perhaps due to Title IX and an emphasis on equal rights), but girls still tend to concede when they feel a friendship or a relationship is at stake. As youth workers, we must foster a mentality of mastery (going back to Sax's mouse illustration) rather than learned helplessness. We need to teach girls that even though internal and external forces may be placing pressure on them to fail, that they indeed have the God-given skills and abilities to succeed. We need to sometimes challenge girls to take risks, whether that's climbing a wall or leading a group. We need to create environments where girls are free to experience the power and the gifts that God has given them.

Issue: Relationships with Teachers

The teacher-student relationship is especially important to an adolescent girl. She has a strong desire to connect with her teachers on a relational level. This means she's more likely to seek help from them much sooner and more often than a boy will.[36] Girls

TEACHING GIRLS TO TAKE RISKS

Margrét Pála Ólafsdóttir is an Icelandic educator who developed a program to thwart learned helplessness. She calls it "Dare Training" and she developed it after taking kindergarten girls on a hike. When the girls began to whimper that their feet hurt, she asked them what they should do instead of complaining. One replied, "Sing," and so they sang all the way back to their home base. Out of that experience, she developed a series of risk-taking exercises to challenge the girls. She would have them jump off a table onto mattresses, inviting them to yell as they jumped (fighting the stereotype that girls are supposed to be quiet). When the girls understood that risks were expected, they began to create their own challenges.[35]

also tend to respond better to a teacher who doesn't confront but encourages. They thrive in environments where they're allowed time to think deeply about their responses. This appears to be just the opposite with boys, who learn much better when there is stress and competition present.[37]

Teachers apparently respond to girls' relational approach as they continually rate girls as being better "in-class citizens" than boys.[38] And it doesn't seem to matter what the subject is; both math and English teachers rate boys as being more disruptive than girls, and that the girls try harder than boys.[39] Part of the reason girls are rated so highly by teachers may be due to the fact that girls are more likely to finish their homework on time, even if they don't understand the purpose of the assignment.[40] On the other hand, guys tend to risk waiting until the last minute to do their homework, and they expect to get better results.[41]

Girls also take their grades much more personally. Educational psychologist Eva Pomerantz observes, "Girls generalize the meaning of their failures because they interpret them as indicating that they have disappointed adults, and thus feel they're of little worth. Boys, in contrast, appear to see their failures as relevant only to the specific subject in which they have failed; this may be due to their relative lack of concern with pleasing adults."[42]

Issue: Attention Deficit Disorder without Hyperactivity (ADD)

When someone says a student has ADD, the instant mental picture is likely to be of a junior high boy bouncing off the walls, refusing to pay attention during Bible study, and generally causing trouble. Usually, one doesn't think of the quiet girl sitting in the back corner of the room, staring out the window as the rest of the group is memorizing Bible verses. But ADD shows up in many different forms.

The boy described above might be experiencing what's known as ADHD—attention deficit disorder with hyperactivity. The people who are diagnosed with ADHD operate at high speeds, are easily distracted, can't stop moving around, and act on impulses without considering the consequences. Typically, a boy is more likely to be diagnosed with ADHD than a girl.

However, girls are more likely to have ADD *without* hyperactivity. According to Sari Solden, adult ADD therapist and author, "ADD is a neurochemical disorder (not a psychological one) that affects three areas of people's behavior in various ways—their *attention* level, their *activity* level, and their *impulsivity* level."[43] Because the behaviors of ADD are less noticeable than those present in ADHD, girls are more likely to go undiagnosed.[44] A girl with ADD is likely to daydream or get lost in her fantasies. She has a hard time doing too many things at once because she's easily distracted. She can suffer academically because it's difficult for her to get started working on a project. Once she does, she'll need plenty of time as she progressively works on one thing before she can move to another. Parents and teachers who are only familiar with ADHD might not realize she has a disorder. They may challenge her to focus more, to become better organized, to quit being lazy, and stop dreaming all the time. These responses can be very discouraging and will only add to a girl's confusion as she wonders what's wrong with her.

Although the majority are diagnosed with ADD, some girls have ADHD. They're usually diagnosed later than boys with ADHD because they typically don't act out or misbehave as much. The hyperactivity in girls with ADHD usually manifests in their talking, socializing, and the expression of their emotions. Girls who have ADD or ADHD may turn to chemicals (drugs and alcohol), including caffeine, to self-medicate in order to regain some control in their lives. They may feel it makes them more focused and better able to operate socially. They're susceptible to addictive behaviors, sexual promiscuity, and eating disorders, partially because of the rigid structure that comes with an eating disorder.

How do you know what are normal teenage highs and lows, forgetfulness, and distractedness versus a teenager dealing with ADD? Consulting with a therapist who specializes in ADD/ADHD is crucial. Also, look for patterns that continue over time (i.e., not just during the finals crunch at the end of the semester) and impair her ability to function in life (e.g., she's constantly forgetting, forever being distracted, and so on).

When it comes to treating ADD/ADHD, medication is often very effective. Ritalin is perhaps the best known of the medications, although there are several others, each with different side effects. Behavior therapy, in combination with medication, is also very effective. If a girl shows consistent signs of either ADD or ADHD, it might be helpful to encourage her parents to schedule an appointment with a learning specialist or someone specializing in ADD/ADHD. This trained professional can coach a student with ADD and give her helpful strategies that will assist her in the management of her ADD.

Issue: Gifted Girls

My friends had just moved and were in the process of enrolling their daughter, Anna, in the local kindergarten. As they chatted with the principal in her office, she leaned over and asked Anna to count to 10. Anna replied earnestly, "In Swedish, Spanish, Greek, or English?" This is a girl who, the week before she turned five, began to read *The Hobbit* to me as we sat at her kitchen table. Anna is clearly a gifted little girl. Although there are some girls who struggle when it comes to learning, there are many who are gifted academically.

"Gifted" usually meant that a child had an IQ of around 125 or 130.[45] However, as more and more schools are acknowledging this often overlooked segment of the population, the definition of "gifted" is expanding. Entrance into gifted programs is no longer just based on IQ scores, but on examples of giftedness in all areas, such as art, music, writing, and leadership. According to Ellen Winner, there are four characteristics that a gifted student displays:

1. Precocity: This means that as a child, she displayed the ability to read, write, figure, and perform musically or athletically much earlier than her peers.

2. Independence: a gifted child has a high degree of autonomy. When given the choice to work alone or in a group, she'll work alone. She needs little instruction and little supervision to keep her on task.

3. Drive for mastery: a gifted child will spend inordinate amounts of time and energy perfecting her skill or abilities in a certain area of focus.

4. Excellence in information processing: a gifted child is able to absorb and process information at a much faster and more in-depth level than her peers. She's able to teach herself skills to learn the information faster and to increase her retention rate.[46]

Contrary to the "geek" myth—that all academically gifted people are socially inept—gifted adolescents are generally more well-adjusted socially than other kids, and they're also more athletically inclined. Gifted girls tend to be the "good girls"—well-behaved, obedient, helpful, sweet. They can also be slightly more depressed than gifted boys, often because of the struggle between academic success and what Western culture has defined as "feminine."[47] However, girls who are highly gifted (versus moder-

GIFTED GIRLS IN MINORITY POPULATIONS

Gifted girls from minority populations can have an especially difficult time achieving their dreams. Gifted programs in urban and rural areas are much harder to find. These girls may also face other barriers, such as a lack of information about how to apply to colleges, how to obtain financial aid, or dealing with school counselors who discourage them from applying to elite schools. In addition, they may experience pressure from their peers and their family not to stand out academically. Teachers, youth workers, and peers need to be alert to the gifted girls around them. They need to look for the spark of intellect and creativity that marks a girl as gifted and seek to nurture this girl and connect her with resources to help her thrive.

In Great Britain gifted girls are now surpassing boys not only in the areas of art, English, and history, but also in the sciences (physics and chemistry) and mathematics.[49]

ately gifted) seemingly don't care what others think of them. This attitude shows up in their preference for solitude over joining a group.

This profile is evident in Dr. Barbara Kerr's book about gifted girls and women, *Smart Girls*.[48] Kerr profiles several gifted women, among them Maya Angelou, writer, Rigoberta Menchú, Guatemalan Indian Rights activist, and Marie Curie, scientist. In the process of analyzing their stories, Kerr discovered that most of these gifted women had mentors in their lives to guide their talents and nurture their gifts. The mentors cared for them as people and used their connections to open doors for these women.

Kerr also discovered that almost all of these women had difficult adolescent years. They were socially awkward, yet, according to Kerr, the lessons that were learned during those awkward years led them to their future callings. For example, Rigoberta Menchú grew up working on the plantations in Guatemala. At 13, she started working in the city as a housemaid for a wealthy family. During her service she was made to sleep in a closet, constantly called names, and faced near starvation. After a few years, and still a teenager, she went back to help her father fight the exploitation of Guatemalan Indians. Her past, as well as her study of the Bible, provided a foundation for her articulate defense of her oppressed people and the ultimate exposure of the injustices of the government.

Gifted girls do face the typical adolescent pressures that ordinary girls face. It's interesting to note that several studies of gifted girls found that once they hit adolescence, they move from being very achievement oriented to being relationally oriented. When the girls were 10, they would talk about careers as astronauts or as scientists, but by the time they reached 14, they would talk about their friends and their boyfriends. Gifted girls are just as likely to respond to the culture's pressure to focus on their looks and to figure out their place in their social culture. Their parents might also encourage them to relax and play, not put so much emphasis on academic achievement. Sometimes friends and even the church communicate to a gifted girl that it's better to be pretty, popular, and have a boyfriend than to be smart and have high academic and career goals. Just as Kerr discovered with the gifted women she profiled, our gifted adolescent girls need mentors to come alongside them to counter some of the other messages they might be receiving. We need to identify the gifted girls in our ministries and seek to connect them with others who can help develop their gifts and talents.

THE YOUTH WORKER'S ROLE

"I feel that, as a woman, when I walk into a church I have to check my brain at the door. They think all I'm good for is baking cookies." She wasn't bitter, just reflective. The woman who spoke was dressed in a smart suit, and she had been successful in the corporate world for years. Now she was volunteering in a youth ministry and trying to offer girls an experience that differed from hers.

As youth workers, we're concerned about our students' souls, but are we also concerned about their brains? Do we ask them to check them at the door, or do we challenge them to grow and develop? One strategy is to make sure we include examples of strong women—not just in Scripture, but also in history and current life.

For example, did you know that the first African American to go to Colorado during the Gold Rush in 1859 was a woman? Her name was Clara Brown (1800-1882), and she founded many Sunday school programs in the Denver area. And according to a plaque hanging in the St. James Methodist Church in Central City, her home was the location of the first church in that area.[50] The students on your leadership team should study not only Jesus' style of leadership,

YOUTH WORKER TIP

If you have a gifted girl in your youth ministry, keep in mind that although she may be advanced intellectually, she may still be age-appropriate when it comes to her emotions. The youth group may be one of the few places in her life where she can feel "normal." However, if she's easily bored with the Bible studies and other curricula you're offering, it may be time to consider creating a small group made up of some of the more intellectually gifted students. This may be a good time to pull out those Greek and theology textbooks from your seminary days.

but also those of women and of people outside their own ethnicities.

Another strategy is to challenge girls to take an up-front role in leadership, even if they prefer to stay in the background. Give them opportunities to lead.

Connect girls with adult mentors who are active in their fields of interest. Invite female scientists, mathematicians, and computer engineers to speak to the group, as well as writers, artists, and musicians. In addition to offering information about their careers, have them talk about how *they* handled the pressures of adolescence. Our girls need to understand that God doesn't just care about their souls. He cares about their brains as well.

CHAPTER NINE

FAMILY MATTERS

Every year around Valentine's Day, the students in our youth ministry invited their parents to a "Love Your Parents" banquet.

It was a dress-up affair and the students paid for their parents' tickets out of their own pockets. Church volunteers and staff would transform the gym into a banquet hall with candlelight, white-linen tablecloths, and the church's good china. Steaming plates of chicken and potatoes were prepared by empty nesters and served by anyone who didn't have a kid in the youth ministry. It was as if the rest of the church body understood the importance of getting adolescents and their parents together in the same room, and they pulled out all the stops to make it happen. The night was filled with skits and stories and presentations and videos underlining the importance of family, in whatever forms that took.

But the real highlights were the note cards on every table. At the top of each card, "I love you…" was written in red script. Parents and kids were encouraged to fill out the cards and exchange them at the table. There were tears as parents and kids who hadn't exchanged a civil word in weeks hugged each other and said the all-important words, "I love you."

Manipulative? Absolutely. Sometimes you need to create environments where families remember why they love each other, especially when the kids are going through adolescence. It's not an easy thing for parents—or daughters—to witness the transition from being the little girl who loved running errands with Dad or going with Mom to the mall to being a moody teenager who walks 15 steps behind her parents and denies any family connection unless threatened.

WHEN PUBERTY HITS…

Puberty affects not only the girl but her family as well. Anyone who's experienced an adolescent going through puberty knows it's not only a physiological process but also a systemic one that impacts all who come in contact with her. Picture a mobile—the kind that's suspended over a baby's crib. Most of the time it's spinning happily, jiggling a little as it turns. But when the baby pulls on one of the dangling objects that hang down from an arm, the whole mobile is thrown off-kilter. Similarly, when adolescence hits, it's like pulling on the family system mobile—it can be a slow tug or a quick yank, but now the mobile is moving in a different way and the rest of the family has to adjust to the new orbit.

Some families welcome this change, thrilled about the new things this developing creature has brought to the family mix. They find her interesting and engaging. They weather the bumps well, realizing it's all part of the growing up process. But other families are terrified of this change. They long for the little girl of the past and hang onto that image, even as the "little girl" is fighting to grow up. For these kinds of families, adolescence is a kind of purgatory, a season to be tolerated rather than embraced.

Breaking Away Is Hard to Do

The reality is that when a child hits adolescence, the intimacy level in a family begins to decrease, while at the same time the level of conflict and argument increases. (And if a girl heads into puberty earlier than normal, then the conflict level rises even higher.) The very person that mom and dad have been trying to develop—a child who eventually becomes an independent adult—can sometimes have a messy growth process. One moment she's daddy's little girl and the next he's a vile beast resolute on destroying her social life.

A family will experience a certain amount of awkwardness as they adapt to this person who's quickly transforming in their midst. Although it can be distressing, it's a normal part of development as an adolescent enters into a phase where she's trying to become more independent—even from her own family. She's testing her opinions and her emotions

All adolescents are ultimately alone in their search for identity whether at the top of a mountain or in a crowded room, flopped on their bed listening to music alone or strolling the mall in a pack...Today's teens have grown up in the midst of enormous social changes that have shaped, reshaped, distorted and sometimes decimated the basic parameters for healthy development. They have grown up with parents who are still seeking answers about what it means to be an adult man or woman. They have lived in families that seldom coincide with the old ideal, and in a culture where the traditional wisdom of how to raise children has been replaced by a kind of daily improvisation as parents try to fit child-rearing into their busy lives. At a time when adolescents need to emulate role models, the adults around them are moving targets. Nobody seems to know what is "normal" anymore.[1]
—Patricia Hersch, *A Tribe Apart*

in a safe place. She knows (hopefully) that her family won't leave her, despite the fact that they'll often see her at her worst. So on a fundamental level, she knows she can be awful; but she needs to keep trying on the clothes of adulthood, even if they don't always fit quite right.

During early adolescence, it's common for both girls and boys to have more conflict with their mothers than with their fathers. Historically in Western culture, mothers have taken on the roles of nurturers and protectors, whereas dads have typically encouraged their children to take risks and thus have launched them out into the world. (Caveat: these roles can be adopted by either parent and can change according to culture and family systems.) Much like a toddler who pushes away from a hovering parent as she gains confidence in her ability to walk on her own, an adolescent seeking to gain her independence will push away from the more nurturing parent. Parents may understand perfectly well *in their heads* that it's necessary for their children to push them away, but it's still difficult for many to accept, especially in tight-knit families that equate love with time spent together.

Say What?

Besides increased levels of conflict, a family with an adolescent will also notice a change in their communication patterns. Communication begins to shift away from touching (for example, grasping a child's hand as you cross the street together, holding her on your lap as you read a story, spanking her when she disobeys) to talking (explaining why it's not okay to stay out past midnight on a school night, engaging in dialogue about dating policies).

Fathers may especially find that physical touch becomes more awkward when their daughters hit adolescence. Where they used to pull pigtailed little girls onto their laps to cuddle or wrestle on the floor before bedtime, they now see young women whose emerging sexuality can be difficult for dads to understand and handle. It can be just as confusing for a girl to have her father pull away. She knows her body is changing, and she's very self-conscious about touch. But the sudden lack of touch may communicate to her that she's unattractive and therefore even her family wants to avoid contact. While she doesn't want to be viewed as a little girl anymore, she still needs the affirming hugs and caresses of her family.

There's No Getting Around It—We Are Family

Despite the increased stress and conflict during the teenage years, the family still remains the primary influence on an adolescent. It's where she first learns how to develop bonds to other people and establishes patterns of pursuing either healthy or unhealthy relationships. It's where she learns how to operate in the greater world and what values and character qualities she'll adopt. It's the earliest and perhaps most important influence in the formation of her identity.

As youth workers, it's vital that we support the family throughout an adolescent's development, sometimes intervening when the system breaks down or when frustration runs high. Often our role is to simply translate. When it comes to adolescents and their families, we sometimes have to step in and help parents interpret the behaviors and language of their teenagers, and understand what's "normal" during this tumultuous period of time. We do so not to replace family members, but to support and encourage them.

THE ROLE OF MOTHERS

It was during one of our annual junior high parents' potlucks that one of the moms began talking with me as we spooned up globs of green bean casserole with that crispy onion ring topping. We were chatting about her youngest daughter when she said, "I don't understand what's going on. She used to love to come

DID YOU KNOW…?
Eating supper together as a family helps reduce drug use. "The more often teens have dinner with their parents, the less likely they are to smoke, drink, or use drugs."[2] This is true more so of girls than of boys.[3]

STRATEGIES FOR ENCOURAGING THE MOTHER-DAUGHTER RELATIONSHIP

- Help mothers understand the process their daughters are going through. Churches have developed programs to help new moms of infants. Perhaps a program for "new moms" of adolescents is also needed? This could be a mentoring program where some of the older women in the church act as sounding boards for these first-time moms of adolescents, helping them to discern what's normal and what's not.

- Create environments where moms and daughters can connect. For example, a mother-daughter retreat where daughters can learn about their mothers' stories and learn to appreciate all the facets of their identity—not just the "mom" one. At the same time, mothers can learn about the pressures their daughters are facing as adolescents and realize their daughters' worlds are different than the ones they faced when they were teenagers.

CONTINUED >

and sit with me after school and tell me about her day. Now she doesn't even acknowledge my presence as she rushes in and grabs something from the fridge before she heads to her room. Some days, the only way I know she's home is when I hear her bedroom door slam." Several nearby moms nodded their heads in agreement, and she continued on, "I don't remember Amy [her oldest daughter] being this way." She paused and then asked the question every parent of an adolescent asks, "Is this normal?"

The relationship a teenage girl has with her mother during adolescence is as rocky as it is beautiful. It's active and dynamic—with the daughter pulling away one minute and drawing close the next. A mother often agonizes over her daughter's journey through adolescence. Some of her daughter's pain will trigger memories and dig up issues from her own teenage years. Yet, when she seeks to comfort her daughter, she may find it's like trying to hug a porcupine.

Her daughter, although desperately needing comfort, equally needs to feel as though she's at least making some forward movement toward adulthood. Her mother's attempts to connect with her can feel like overprotective suffocation. For example, "Why do you always ask so many questions? Why do you need to know where I am and who I'm with? Why can't you just trust me?" Mom's attempts at communication are interpreted as prying judgments.

It's important for mothers to realize that although their daughters may seem to be distancing themselves, they aren't seeking total autonomy. Dr. Terri Apter of the University of Cambridge has studied mothers and daughters for more than 20 years. Her research refutes the commonly held idea that adolescence is a time to reject parents and embrace one's peers. She found that daughters aren't seeking a "divorce" from their mothers; rather, they're seeking to redefine the relationship in the midst of their changing world. Apter states, "The 'task' of adolescence is not to sever the closeness, but to alter it."[4]

Part of that altering means that Mom often goes from being the "Savior" to being the "Enemy." During childhood, a typical mother has been a constant source of comfort and stability. As an infant, a girl relied on the belief that Mom could be counted on to feed, nurture, and provide a safe place for her to start her life. As a child, she would run to Mom when monsters showed up in her dreams or when she was excluded from a friend's birthday party. Mom was the one who provided the same-gender role model that her daughter needed while she was growing up. In watching her mom, a girl began to learn the roles and responsibilities of being an adult woman.

However, as she reaches adolescence, a daughter becomes hypercritical of her self and turns that appraising eye toward her mother as well. She sees the "flaws" in her mother reflecting on her. The way her mom dresses, the way she eats, even the way she breathes can be seen as sources of embarrassment and irritation for a teenage girl. And since a girl will do whatever it takes to be perceived as "normal" among her peers, that sometimes means trying to control how her mother comes across. It's only after the daughter develops her own sense of self and realizes the world isn't watching her with a magnifying glass that she's able to embrace her mother as an individual and move from seeing her as the "Enemy" to valuing her as a "Friend."

During this prickly time, it's important for a mom to understand that this too shall pass. It's critical that the relationship stay strong and active. Often if a girl has a vital relationship with her mother, she'll do much better in life. Research has shown that adult women who consider themselves in good relationships with their mothers have higher self-esteem and are less depressed than those who don't get along with their mothers.[5] In the words of researcher Carol Gilligan, "The anger between mothers and daughters is legendary; the love is often held in silence."[6]

CONTINUED >

- Have women from a variety of backgrounds talk to the girls about their futures: whether or not to have children, to work outside or inside the home, their careers, and other life choices so the girls have contact with a wide range of role models.

- Broaden the ministry's definition of "mother." Sometimes it's a grandmother, aunt, or even a dad who occupies that role. Have the girls in the ministry celebrate those who have filled "mother" roles in their lives through writing notes of appreciation or making phone calls to say thank you.

THE ROLE OF FATHERS

I asked a group of high school girls if they ever talked with their dads about dating and sex. They shrieked with laughter, claiming that if they talked to their dads about anything like that, he'd be embarrassed or would shut down and go mow the lawn. Despite all the unpredictability, a girl typically feels closer to her mother than she does to her father during adolescence.

When she gets her first period, understandably she runs to Mom, not to Dad. When a boy breaks her heart for the first time, it's Mom who grabs the box of tissues and pulls up a chair to listen. Where she used to seek out Dad to bandage her scraped knee, he realizes he's now being dismissed from dealing with her wounded heart. Where he used to be the number one male in her life, he now has to make way for the boys who call and ask her out. He's left wondering what role he can play in her life.

The dynamics of the father-daughter relationship change when girls become adolescents. Dads appreciate the fact that their daughters are growing up, and that they're able to communicate with them more as adults than as children. Daughters strongly desire to have a relationship with their fathers, but they often feel that in order to connect with their dads, they have to be the initiators. The daughters are the ones who have to adapt their rhythms to his. For example, if a girl wants to spend time with her dad on the weekend, then she has to develop an interest in the same sports that he likes, such as watching football together on a Sunday afternoon.

When daughters talk about spending time with their dads, it usually refers to being in the house at the same time, but not necessarily talking with each other. They might participate in an activity they enjoy together, but there won't be a lot of verbal communication going on. Dads need to be encouraged to pursue communication with their daughters. The more relational a dad is, asking questions and keeping the lines of communication open, the less likely it is that his daughter will become involved in risky behavior in her later teen years.[7] One study showed a clear connection that the more involved a father was with his daughter during adolescence, the more likely it was that she'd have better psychological health later in her life.[8]

Dads (perhaps because males model more risk-taking in their behaviors[9]) typically take on more of a "launcher" role in the family system—pushing their children into society and urging them to take calculated risks and not be afraid to try new things. In my own family experience, I recall coming home from my ninth-grade U.S. Government class and announcing at dinner that I was going to be the first female president of the United States. Rather than responding with laughter and skepticism, my father said, "Well, perhaps we should go to Washington, D.C. for spring break so you can see what you're getting yourself into." Fathers, ideally, know when to encourage their daughters' dreams and to push them ahead when internal or external pressures seem to pull them back. They're critical in the development of future career success and the sense of being comfortable while operating in the larger world.[10] And, if a girl has a close relationship with her father, she's more likely to have a positive attitude toward academics.[11]

There are jokes about how daughters have dads wrapped around their little fingers, but the reality is that dads typically are more unbending when it comes to conflict.[12] Girls tend to perceive their fathers as rigid and stubborn, believing that dads think they know what's right and aren't willing to negotiate. When fathers do talk, they seem to lecture—at least in their daughters' eyes. These girls feel as though there's more preaching than listening going on. When a dad and daughter fight, it can be infuriating for a girl. Sometimes the dad will see her anger as amusing and her feistiness as cute. Naturally, the daughter interprets this response as condescending.

Other times during a conflict, a father will "power up" over her and pull rank, so to speak. "I'm your father, and you'll listen because I'm telling you to listen." That reaction usually generates a response of sullenness or a slammed bedroom door. Whereas moms might typically go after a daughter to reconcile the relationship, dads tend to be more willing to let the rift continue because they're thankful for the absence of verbal conflict.

The absence of a father has a serious impact on a girl's life. Not having that significant person to interact with can make it more difficult for her to connect with the opposite gender later on in life.[13] Her primary role model for male-female relationships is missing and it can be difficult for her to figure out how to build healthy relationships with men. In a landmark research study, Mavis Hetherington looked at how girls who were raised in a variety of family contexts related to their fathers, especially situations where the father was absent. Her study examined girls who were raised by married mothers, widowed mothers, and divorced mothers. She found that in comparison to girls raised by both parents in the home, girls whose mothers were widowed were more guarded and reserved in their dealings with men. They set high standards for potential mates. And the girls who were raised by divorced mothers flirted more and began dating at a much earlier age than the girls from the other two groups.[14]

Although daughters may not communicate with their dads either as frequently or with as much depth as they'd like to, and even if they don't see their dad on a regular basis, they still admit that they love their dads deeply. Youth workers need to help develop the relationships between dads and daughters. In the past it was assumed that mothers bore the brunt of parenting responsibility. But in recent generations, dads have been seeking to take an active role in the parenting of adolescents, and it's important that the youth ministry supports them. For example, one youth ministry started a ministry group just for dads that met at the same time the youth group did. It was led by a former youth group volunteer who helped this small group of dads discuss what it's like to parent an adolescent. A high school administrator who wanted to give dads a safe place to discuss the challenges of parenting teenagers led another similar group in the community.

Ministries need to provide opportunities for dads and daughters to connect. One church sponsored a parent-child canoe trip that provided an opportunity for dads to connect with daughters and mothers with sons. Some of the parents were married, and some were single. Another church hosted a dads-and-daughters retreat, providing several days where the father-daughter pairs could do activities together and talk. Besides creating great memories, it helped these dads connect with their daughters at a crucial time in both of their lives.

THE IMPACT OF DIVORCE

A college student in a research course I was teaching gave a presentation on the impact of divorce on adolescents. He passed out doughnuts beforehand, and I took his gesture to be nothing more than a great way to warm up the audience. As he presented his findings, he mentioned that the reason he served the doughnuts was that's what a lot of kids from divorced families end up eating for breakfast, along with pizza or fast food for dinner. He explained that one of the implications of divorce is that the custodial parent is now more likely to have to work longer hours to make ends meet. Sit-down dinners of home-cooked food soon becomes a thing of the past. Plus, less household income also means that the quality of the food decreases.

YOUTH WORKER TIP

The absence of fathers in adolescent girls' lives is just one of the many reasons why it's crucial to have both men and women volunteering together in the youth ministry. Some girls have rarely seen men treat women with respect. By being surrounded by both female and male volunteers, they can observe how the two genders work through conflict in a healthy manner. Some adolescents have never seen a situation where men and women argue, but both parties stayed engaged in relationship with each other. They're used to either mom or dad packing up and leaving after a fight. A strong community of volunteer staff can model the ups and downs of cross-gender relationships for these girls and can help fill in the gaps of absent fathers or mothers.

ADVICE FROM VETERAN YOUTH WORKERS...

- "I would recommend having a parent team for guidance, made up of a variety of parents: moms, dads, single, married, divorced, empty nesters, etc." —Kevin

- "The parents are really important to being a youth worker. Partnering and having the ability to come alongside and befriend parents is huge. It's not all about the volunteers and training them; it's developing relationships with the parents." —Julie

- "Most girls need authentic quality/quantity time. They need you there listening intently, caring passionately, and keeping your word consistently. Once these traits are in place, fight with all your might to keep them strong. Because if you stumble in these areas, whether by accident or on purpose, the wall that you chipped away at begins to fortify again. " —Gerald

CONTINUED >

Many of the students in that class were raised in homes with divorced parents, and they nodded their heads in knowing agreement, exchanging stories about how fast food became a regular part of their lives after the divorce. It appeared to be part of their collective memory of adolescence.

Their shared response isn't unusual, considering that almost one out of six adolescents today has experienced parental divorce. The impact of divorce can be devastating and long lasting. Research has shown that adolescents whose parents have divorced are more likely to have behavior problems, struggle with academics, and are more likely to use alcohol and drugs. They're more likely to become depressed and anxious, especially if they're caught between the battling parents.[15] It can be difficult for them to form close relationships with romantic partners. And when they do get married—even though they're committed to making the marriage work—they're more likely to get divorced.

Judith Wallerstein is probably the best-known authority on the impact of divorce on children. For over 25 years, she studied 131 people who, as children, experienced the divorce of their parents. In her landmark report of her findings, *The Unexpected Legacy of Divorce*, she says this, "Divorce is a life-transforming experience. After divorce, childhood is different. Adolescence is different. Adulthood—with the decision to marry or not and have children or not—is different. Whether the final outcome is good or bad, the whole trajectory of an individual's life is profoundly altered by the divorce experience."[16]

Relationships with Mom and Dad Change

When a divorce occurs, the mother usually retains custody. Studies have found that in that first year after the divorce, a mother tends to be more permissive in her parenting and is often less affectionate than she was before the divorce.[17] However, that evens out after a few years. It's also been found that if an adolescent has a good relationship with her mother, she'll do much better after the divorce than one who has a poor relationship.[18]

Most adolescents' relationships with their fathers decline after a divorce. One possible reason is that fathers often bear the brunt of the blame and anger from the adolescent, especially if they move out of the home. A girl will speculate, "If he'd just worked harder at the marriage…" or "If he'd stayed faithful…" then the marriage would have survived. They often don't understand all the nuances of marriage, and it may not be appropriate for them to know all the reasons that led to their parents' divorce.

Another reason a girl's relationship with her father declines after a divorce is because she's simply becoming more socially active outside the family unit. If her family were still intact, her path would have naturally crossed with her father's more often because they'd be living in the same house. Now, it's necessary for the father to make a deliberate effort to connect with his daughter on a regular basis. If the effort isn't made (on either side), it's less likely that she'll go out of her way to make plans that involve him.

Divorce can understandably bring about anger, with an adolescent sometimes taking sides and blaming one parent—or even both parents—for the divorce. Sometimes the anger comes from having to assume parental responsibility. In one case, a wife left her husband and three children. The middle child, a seventh-grader and the only girl in the family, was expected to cook the family meals. When an adolescent is forced into an adult role like this, anger and resentment toward the absent parent can build.

Anger can also result from the lack of security and structure due to a parent's physical or emotional absence. Says Wallerstein, "In many of the divorced families, girls did not receive the special protection we saw in intact families. Few had curfews or

CONTINUED >

- "Systematically organize your youth ministry around connecting adults and parents with teenagers. Adolescent girls need as many adult women in their lives as your church can connect them with. Adolescent girls need women who are available. You will be available, but it's more important for them to talk to an adult woman. A small group leader is a great start, but not nearly enough support for young women. When I say 'adult woman,' I am referring to a female over the age of 26. The problem is you won't understand adult women either. Take a posture of humility, for you are the learner here. Connect, encourage…listen, listen, listen." —Mark

special rules to report in. If they did, these were honored more in the breach than in the practice...The girls in intact families, in contrast, had a different kind of adolescence than their peers from divorced families. They had strictly enforced curfews that they mostly obeyed. Their weekends were carefully monitored. Right or wrong, parents were much more controlling."[19]

There also can be a sense of loss and grieving as familiar family traditions and structures no longer exist in their old form. Holidays and school vacations become a time of stress, with adolescents leaving their friends to go spend time with a noncustodial parent, or feeling the burden of not wanting to hurt one parent if they choose to spend a holiday with the other one. A divorce can also have a long-term destructive impact on sibling relationships. If the siblings are older, some may choose to live with the noncustodial parent. Thus, their lives begin to separate at that point.

Dating and Remarriage

When a parent begins to date again, it may create awkward feelings as the family structure changes once more in light of these new dynamics. If a girl is living with her mother, she can sometimes find that her mother begins to act more like a "friend" as she begins to date—seeking advice and insight from her daughter and trading dating stories. This role switching can be disconcerting to an adolescent. There can also be feelings of jealousy and resentment as the parent moves from focusing most of her time and energy on the children to splitting her attention between the children and the new boyfriend. This is especially true if the adolescent is forced to pick up more of the parental responsibilities around the home, such as babysitting her younger siblings.

When a parent remarries, other issues emerge. It takes about five years for a family to settle down after a remarriage (almost twice as long as it takes after a divorce).[20] Girls are less willing to accept a stepparent (mother or father) and have a hard time adjusting to the new family. They tend to withdraw and brood, shutting down all communication. Part of the reason could be that if a girl lived with her mother, then the close bond they had might now be threatened as her mother turns her attention and care toward her new husband. If the girl lived with her father, there's a threat of a new woman taking her place in her father's life and a concern that her father will no longer have time or attention for her.

As youth workers, we often can be the "safe adult" when a student is experiencing a divorce in her family. The parents are often so overwhelmed by the issues involved in separation and divorce that they, understandably, have very little leftover emotional energy to give to their children. We can provide a place where adolescents can be adolescents—where they can cry and vent and feel without worry. If a girl suddenly has to bear more of the parental responsibilities at home, there may be an opportunity for you to help her by delivering a meal for the family or baby-sitting her younger siblings so she can finish a homework project.

There may be other times where we have to step into a family situation and to challenge struggling parents not to rely on their adolescent children as confidants or "small adults," but rather encourage them to seek other sources of emotional support, such as a pastor or support group.

SIBLINGS

Kristi is the youngest of three daughters. She's pretty much on her own at home, now that both of her sisters are out of the house. Her oldest sister has been removed from her life for a while now; she just graduated from college and is living on her own. The middle sister, Kasey, just left for college. Kasey is the one Kristi struggled with. She was good at everything she tried. A strong student and aggressive athlete, she had a forceful personality that demanded her parents' attention. When Kristi's youth pastor asked her how she was doing—now that she was going to be the only child at home— Kristi's response was only mildly surprising. "I'm thrilled!" said Kristi. "Mom and Dad can finally spend time with me now!"

Siblings play an important role in an adolescent girl's life. Older brothers and sisters are role models for a young girl, showing her how to navigate the difficult terrain of adolescence. They can offer instruction on how to "manage" Mom and Dad when it comes to issues such as curfew and dating. They can provide a (somewhat) nonjudgmental listening ear as they listen to issues that might feel too overwhelming to share with the parents. If a girl feels as though she has a warm, supportive relationship with her siblings, this can assuage the negative effects of not having a relationship with her peers.

If siblings attend the same school, the older ones can provide their younger siblings with a certain amount of protection from bullies. They can also instruct a sibling on how to negotiate and navigate the school in a way that Mom and Dad can't (for example, what to wear, which history teacher to choose, and what bathrooms to never go into). In a conversation I had with a girl who was heading to an inner-city high school with close to 2,000 students, I asked if she was anxious. She shrugged her shoulders with indifference, "Amanda will be there." She had absolute certainty that her older sister would watch out for her and help her figure out the system.

Sometimes, however, older siblings are negative examples. For example, teenage girls with older sisters who became pregnant during their teen years are much more likely to be sexually active than other girls.[21] One study showed that an older brother's attitudes toward sexual activity had more influence on a younger sister than an older sister's attitudes. Having an older sibling who acts out in destructive ways seems to pave the way for younger siblings to follow suit. Sometimes they have more influence over an adolescent's choices than even the parents.

If there are younger siblings at home, they can offer adolescents an opportunity to try on adult roles and responsibilities. Girls in the United States and other cultures move into the caregiver role very easily, bearing the responsibility of watching out for their younger siblings. Having to baby-sit younger siblings, make meals, and care for them all help to give an adolescent a sense of responsibility and the chance to try on adult roles for a short period of time.

Conflict is also part of having brothers and sisters. In fact, it's the relationship that causes the most conflict for adolescents. It's with our brothers and sisters that we learn how to fight and how to resolve arguments. Siblings will yell and argue over name-calling, teasing, who owns what, chores, being perceived as the "favorite," invading one another's space. Brothers are more likely than sisters to threaten to use physical force in a sibling argument. But if you talk with any woman who grew up with sisters, she'll tell you stories about battles involving hair pulling and face slapping.

Stepsiblings

With the high rate of divorce and remarriage, it's likely that an adolescent from a divorced home will experience a blended family at some point. Usually, relationships between stepsiblings are fairly positive and without the extremes of full-sibling relationships. Stepsibling relationships tend not to be as deep or as intense as full- or even half-sibling relationships. Conflict can arise when the child who was the oldest sibling in the household becomes the second or even third oldest. The loss of perceived special status can be disheartening and cause conflict.

DID YOU KNOW...?

Research has shown that a girl with older brothers is stereotypically much more feminine and fits more traditional female gender roles than a girl with older sisters.[22]

SIBLING RELATIONSHIPS

There are five categories that describe adolescent sibling relationships:[23]

1. *The Caregiver* relationship typically involves an older sibling, usually a girl, who watches out for the younger ones and often takes on parental responsibilities.

2. *The Buddy* relationship is when siblings love to hang out with each other and have a strong friendship.

3. *The Critical* relationship is marked by teasing and conflict. Siblings know which buttons to push to get a rise out of their brother or sister and constantly do so.

4. *The Rival* relationship is competitive at its core. Siblings vie against each other for success, whether on the athletic field, in the classroom, or at home.

5. *The Casual* relationship is one where the siblings get along, but the relationship isn't that close. There isn't a strong connection between them and, for the most part, they operate in their own worlds.

The difficulty in youth ministry arises when two or more siblings are in the ministry together. Depending on the type of relationship they have (see sidebar), they can get along great and be role models for other students in the ministry. Sometimes the older one acts as a caregiver to the younger ones, even driving their little brothers and sisters to youth group.

However, it's just as likely that the siblings will compete for the attention of the leaders and the other students. Or one may adopt the role of the "good girl," while the other plays the "rebel," just to prove individuality. As siblings, they know what pushes each other's buttons, and they'll seek to irritate and embarrass each other in the midst of their peer group. When there's a high level of rivalry or judgmental attitudes, youth workers should separate the siblings, giving each teenager their own space and perhaps asking different adult volunteers to shepherd them so they have the freedom to develop outside the shadow of their older sister or brother.

IMMIGRANT FAMILY ISSUES

Have you ever heard the terms "one-point-five" (1.5) or "second-generation"? They're descriptors for families that recently immigrated to the United States. "One-point-five" refers to people who were born in another country but brought to the United States as children. They usually remember at least some of their homeland and customs. But, depending on their age, they may or may not speak English with an accent and may still be able to speak their home language.

"Second generation" refers to those born after their parents immigrated to the United States (the parents are called "first generation"). Depending on their family cultures, they may (or may not) know their home languages and embrace the customs of their home countries. Quite often, second-generation adolescents have a stronger affiliation with the United States than with their parents' country of origin. This can become a source of conflict as parents (and sometimes extended family) try to retain the culture of their homeland and try to protect their daughters from what they see as the negative influence of American culture.

They may also view a daughter's independence as possible abandonment—of both the family and of their culture. One study of 5,000-plus, second-generation adolescents found that conflict with parents is a strong predictor of low self-esteem and increased depression in adolescent girls. The amount of conflict increases when the family suffers economically because of the immigration.[24]

Daughters tend to struggle most in the adaptation process, perhaps because many cultures try to protect the innocence of their daughters and keep them safe and "pure," whereas their sons are encouraged to take risks. One second-generation girl, whose father is from Mexico, talked about her dad's authoritarian perspective: "I'm much closer to my mother. She understands me. My father talks about how certain things are 'inappropriate,' like staying out talking to boys in the park late at night. He says that's inappropriate for a young woman to do. I grew up with these boys. There was nothing bad that was going to happen. My mom understands that."

Some immigrant families have a fortress mentality when it comes to their children. They're adamant about trying to protect their kids from the influences of American culture. They form churches that are ethnically based, sometimes with services offered only in their home language. They have after-school programs that emphasize their homeland values. Any suggestions about bringing in other styles of worship are met with disdain or concerns that they'll lose the identity of their home culture.

DID YOU KNOW...?

Usually if a child immigrates before she's 11 years old, she should be able to pick up a new language and speak it without the accent of her native language. This is what's sometimes referred to as the "Kissinger Effect." Former U.S. secretary of state Henry Kissinger emigrated from Germany to the United States at age 12; he spoke with a heavy German accent his whole life. His brother was 10 years old when they moved, but he now speaks without any trace of an accent.

A GIRL'S VOICE

"Self-definition was an ambivalent process, and still is...I grew irritated when my parents' friends reminisced about the difficult days upon arriving in the U.S. (they were trained as nurses and accountants in Korea, but because of language barriers, they did janitorial work). With an internalized, self-denigrating attitude, I thought, 'This is America. Just get used to it.' Barbie dolls were scary-looking and ugly to me, but I still wanted creased eyelids and big, demure, Western-looking eyes." —Jenny Kim, "Kim Chee and Yellow Peril"[25]

Whether 1.5 or second generation, an adolescent will often adjust to Western culture much faster than her parents (most likely due to her immersion into the public school system). When a parent can't speak English well, the adolescent is relied upon to be the interpreter and the negotiator in the family. This role reversal can create insecure and tense family dynamics, since the adolescent is taking care of the parent in a variety of social settings. Because of her language skills, she now has more power in the new culture than her parents do.

In some cases, adolescents are the first generation to immigrate to the United States. Sometimes their family sends them to America for the educational opportunities; other times they come here to flee war and violence back home. The Lost Boys of Sudan are examples of this.[26] However, at a prayer vigil for Sudan, a young Sudanese woman stood up and challenged the audience, "Don't forget, there are the Lost *Girls* of Sudan as well." Adolescents who immigrate without the support of an extended family often have to deal with loneliness and loss.

In the words of Roselyn Domingo, who came to the United States by herself, "Staying here in America means that I will have to continue being separated from my family. Even if I have better opportunities here, how good can life be if I'm not with my family? I need a chance to grow up with my family—a family that was taken away from me during my childhood. At the same time, I want to provide a better future for my family, so that they do not have to suffer the bad conditions in the Philippines, such as flood and pollution. I know that taking care of them would mean, in some cases, sacrificing my own happiness."[27]

A person's ethnic heritage and background have a strong influence on her identity development, whether she wants it to or not. In cases of 1.5- and second-generation adolescents, their identity development can be especially difficult. It's not just that their values conflict with their parents', but they can also feel as though they're in conflict with the whole culture. For example, when they try to adopt the Western standards of dating, they aren't just arguing with their mothers and fathers, but with the generations that have come before them. In some cultures, such as the Chinese culture, devotion to family is emphasized as an individual's priority. That can come in direct conflict with the American culture that encourages an adolescent to be independent of her parents and family. This tension between the two cultures is evident in how girls identify themselves. Girls, more so than boys, will tend to hyphenate their identities (e.g., Korean-American, Mexican-American, and so on).

It's important to understand that when a family decides to immigrate, major changes take place in the family's system. There is a loss of the former culture and support systems. Depending on the number of family members who immigrate, there can also be a loss of the extended family that, in many cultures, helps raise the children in a family system. There can be a loss of everyday familiarity with foods and religious practices. There can also be a sense of loneliness, as an adolescent's peers may not understand the experiences she's encountered—either here or back "home."

There may be confusion when it comes to her roles as a young woman. In a home culture, an adolescent girl might be expected to stay at home, take care of her parents, and help with the family business until she marries. She might then move into her husband's family's home and live with them. So even though the family now lives in the United States, her parents might expect her to remain in that same role from their home country's culture. It can be difficult for her to navigate her family's expectations, while she may have her own dreams to go to an out-of-state college and focus on a career, rather than marriage and a family.

Immigrant families can also act as a safe place and a source of strength for adolescent girls, espe-

"For some reason, I equated 'American-ness' with 'whiteness' throughout my childhood. Calling myself 'Korean-American' instead of a categorical 'Korean' was seen as a treacherous sell out, as if I unconsciously wanted to be a white more than anything else. My parents' generation called me a 'banana': yellow on the outside, white on the inside. But I was insistent on this hyphenated identity, mainly because I felt that I was a *type* of American (i.e., Korean as adjective, American as noun)—a cultural hybrid. I knew African American and Latino children born in the U.S. like me were also 'American' in terms of citizenship. But collectively we would always be the Others. Why else would whites dominate the mainstream culture of the Gap, McDonald's, and TV sitcoms?"[28] —Jenny Kim, "Kim Chee and Yellow Peril"

cially if the family is a warm and supportive place with reasonable expectations and rules. One-point-five and second-generation adolescents can receive support not only from their immediate families, but also from extended family members and others in their ethnic community. A strong and healthy ethnic identity can provide a sense of identity and help girls as they struggle with their own personal identities.

THE YOUTH WORKER'S ROLE

Large, extended families are part of not just immigrant lives, but also the lives of many girls of color. A strong family orientation can be a source of strength for adolescent girls. It's a place where elders and customs are respected, and where a girl can realize that she's part of a legacy of strong women. For example, in African American families there is often a significant network of extended family members. This family can be a support to African American girls, providing them with role models, encouragement, and protection against the racism of American culture.

In the 1992 American Association of University Women (AAUW) study, African American girls reported the smallest drop in self-esteem from grade school to high school compared to other races.[29] Much of this strong sense of self-esteem can be related to the support of family.

Although youth ministry is never intended to replace the family system, sometimes it can be a support where the system is weak. Just as an extended family provides role models and encouragement—maybe even protection—so too can a youth ministry. In having leaders who come from a variety of generations and backgrounds, our adolescent girls can understand that they're a part of a long lineage of Christians.

CHAPTER TEN
FRIENDSHIP MATTERS

It was a Friday night and several of the local youth ministries had come together for a concert. Haley was there with her girlfriends from her church group. They'd spent the afternoon text messaging each other to figure out who was coming and what everyone was wearing. At age 12, Haley knew that wearing the wrong thing to a social gathering could turn a girl into a social exile. Once she learned what Brianne was wearing, she dug around her closet for something similar. It was unexpressed, yet acutely understood, that Brianne was the Alpha female in their group of friends. The rest of the girls were content to follow her confident lead.

Brianne had also been Haley's best friend for years. But this year, Brianne was spending more time with the friends she made while visiting other church groups. Haley was getting the message that she was no longer at the core of Brianne's circle of friends, but was quickly being pushed into the outer orbit.

The girls clustered in the corner of the gym, subtly eyeing the various youth groups as they arrived—critiquing the girls and checking out the guys. Haley struggled to adopt her confident and nonchalant persona. Suddenly, Brianne spied a group of guys she knew from another church sauntering in, and she waved them over. As the guys drifted across the gym floor, Brianne whirled around and pointedly stared Haley up and down. Then she hissed the words that would replay in Haley's mind for years afterward, "Haley, why don't you go stand somewhere else?" It clearly wasn't a question, but a command. The Queen Bee had spoken, and her message had stung Haley deeply: Haley was no longer acceptable to the group; rather she was an embarrassment and a liability to their likeability.

The rest of the girls turned away in discomfort and pity as they followed Brianne to go meet the guys. Haley spun away with a hair toss that was meant to communicate, "I hate you," but failed miserably in its transmission. She quickly made her way to the bathroom where she could be alone in her shame and confusion.

At one time or another, most females have experienced a variation of this "Haley" experience. Saying that adolescence is a time of turbulence for girls is an understatement, especially when it comes to friendships. Whereas in grade school, a girl could keep the same one or two best friends for years, once those girls reach middle school their friendship can dissipate in a day. Although this makes sense when girls' relationships are viewed through a developmental lens, it's important to keep in mind that the growth process can be confusing and sometimes agonizing to those girls in the midst of it.

HOW FRIENDSHIPS CHANGE FROM CHILD-HOOD TO ADOLESCENCE

We know that prior to early adolescence, children's friendships are predominantly based on shared activities, such as riding bikes, playing soccer, going to Scouts, or attending Sunday school.[1] In this pre-adolescent life, parents play a very influential role. Parents determine which activities a girl will be involved in, what neighborhood she lives in, where she goes to church, and, to a certain extent, who her playmates will be. At this stage of life, girls place a lot of significance on their parents' counsel.

Once a girl reaches early adolescence, the focus of her relational world begins to shift away from her parents and toward her peers. Her parents still maintain a strong presence in her life, but their influence diminishes. An adolescent girl will turn to her friends to keep her company before she'll go to her parents. In one study of over 1,000 adolescents from 12 to 19 years of age, more than 70 percent of them agreed to these statements:

- "My close friend understands me better than my parents do,"

- "I feel right now that in my life I learn more from my close friends than I do from my parents," and

- "I'm more myself with my close friends than with my parents."[2]

This same study found that adolescents will turn to their parents to talk about educational and vocational issues, but they'd rather talk to friends when it comes to discussing personal issues, such as their views on sex and their relationships with guys.

There's not only an increase in depth of sharing and interaction with peers, but also an increase in the amount of time spent with them. As a pre-adolescent, a girl may spend her school time with peers, but spends most of her leisure time with her family. Beginning in early adolescence, she spends her leisure time with her peers as well. In one study of 13-to-16-year-olds, the researchers found that the average length of time for an interaction with their parents was only 28 minutes a day, while the average interaction with friends was 103 minutes a day.[3] In other words, she'd rather hang out with her friends than with Mom or Dad.

For parents of adolescents experiencing this relational shift for the first time, the impact can leave them feeling shut out of their daughters' lives. Youth workers will often hear distraught parents say, "I can't get her to talk to me. She's always in her room, and then she's either on the phone or online with someone." Parents find themselves longing for the little girl who wanted to go everywhere and do everything with them. It may be hard for them to grasp that this emotional separation is a healthy indicator that their daughter is becoming more independent, a necessary move in the journey toward adulthood.

There is some good news for parents in the midst of this change. Studies have found that if adolescents have had a strong relationship with their parents, then they're more likely to have a strong relationship with their friends. If they've learned to trust in and confide in their parents, they'll take those same traits into their friendships.[4]

YOUTH WORKER TIP

In the early fall, schedule a parents' meeting for first-time parents of middle schoolers. Give them a heads-up about what changes they can expect to encounter with their child. Have some "veteran" parents and high schoolers available to answer their questions. Just as kids are trying to figure out whether or not they're normal, their parents are wondering the same thing!

Why the shift away from parents to friends? During adolescence, girls spend a lot of energy trying to figure out, "Am I normal?" In this quest, friends can be a safe haven, especially same-sex friends. Even if the other girls haven't had the same experiences, they do provide a listening ear and a reassuring sense of feeling understood by someone who's going through something similar. It's not unusual to hear comments like, "She gets me," or "She feels the same way I do." Girlfriends, especially during early adolescence, can provide a secure place to discuss the messiness of this new life, away from the perceived "prying questions" of anxious parents. With a good friend, there is a sense that a girl can share her deepest feelings and fears yet still be accepted.

A strong peer friendship can also provide an escape from a difficult home situation. Early adolescents are at a point where discussion about their emotions and the stressors in their lives comes more easily with their friends. As children, their conversations revolved around the activities they were involved in or the tangible realities of their lives (e.g., "My mom and dad are getting a divorce."). Now they're able to talk about how they feel about the situation with a greater intensity (e.g., "I'm relieved that my dad is moving out. My stomach felt like I'd swallowed some acid whenever I heard them fighting").

Not only are early adolescent girls turning to their friends before they'll turn to their parents, but the number of their friendships is also increasing. While as a child a girl may have several "good" friends, it's likely that she had only one or two "best" friends (or, in girl-speak, "BFF"—"Best Friends Forever"). But by the time she hits middle school, her capacity to have several deep friendships increases. ("Deep" as in a certain level of intimacy where girls mutu-

CONTINUED >

ally share their personal thoughts, feelings, and experiences.) Conflict arises when her best friend from grade school isn't ready to accept this expanding circle of friends.

Similar to our opening story in this chapter, a girl like Brianne may hit middle school ready to make new friends as a symbol of her developing social identity. In typical early adolescent fashion, the Briannes of the world can easily leave a slower developing or more introverted Haley in the dust. Brianne may or may not be intentionally cruel, but the effects on the friend left behind can be devastating. Brianne would probably describe the process as just a part of growing up and perhaps judge Haley for being immature (a harsh condemnation for any young adolescent). Haley, on the other hand, may be fighting against the changes that come with growing up. She may want to stay in her safe grade school world, where friendships revolve around playing soccer, not around flirting with the guys. Consequently, she may judge Brianne for being a shallow snob.

As youth workers, we must understand that both girls have valid perspectives based on where they are developmentally. It's also valuable to realize that Brianne and Haley's friendship may go back to being exclusive for a while, then another break will occur, then exclusivity, then… Youth workers need to realize that this conflict is a normal rite of passage and that by breaking up and reconnecting, the girls are learning valuable conflict resolution skills. Youth workers can assist girls by helping them reflect on the process and on their behavior—especially if either one of them, or both, starts behaving viciously. If one becomes a target, it might be helpful to give her confrontation skills to boost her self-confidence.

Boys Allowed

As girls progress into middle adolescence, they move from having predominantly same-gender friendships to mixed-gender friendships. It's not unusual for a girl to include a guy among her list of close friends—and without any romantic aspirations. Whereas before she felt comfortable sharing her intimate thoughts only with girlfriends, she now feels the freedom to expand her circle of deeper friendships to include guys. These cross-gender friendships serve a purpose beyond just getting a guy's perspective on life. They're also preparing her for a long-term romantic partnership, which may extend into marriage.

However, girl-guy friendships are not without their downside. These friendships may result in less intimacy and more conflict with their female friends. Research also shows that there's some misperception as to the level of intimacy in a girl-guy friendship. Girls say their friendships with guys have a higher level of intimacy than what the guys report.[11]

HOW GIRLS' FRIENDSHIPS DIFFER FROM BOYS' FRIENDSHIPS

Adolescent guys and girls are similar in that they both value close friendships with people with whom they can be open about their lives. Both genders look for friends to talk to about what they're really feeling. However, there are some particulars that differ when it comes to girls' friendships. Girls usually have more friendships than guys do, and those friendships have more depth and inter-reliance than what's typically found in boys' friendships.[12] Consequently, along with that deeper level of sharing comes an emphasis on trust. Thus, when trust is broken in a girl-girl friendship, it's tantamount to a break-up.

Girls, more so than guys, prefer smaller, more intimate groups and activities that provide opportunities for deeper conversations. This is why there's a preponderance of sleepovers for girls, especially among early adolescents. It's during occasions such as these that girls learn from each other how to navigate the turbulence of adolescence. Often seen as a rite of passage into the adolescent world, sleepovers pro-

CONTINUED >

for socialization rather than entertainment. Girls are online, but they're also on their pagers. They're watching TV, but they're also on the Internet."[8]

In one study, two 13-year-old girls, "Sam" and "Karrie" were interviewed. The authors' findings give us some insight into the role of IMing in an adolescent girl's world. "In general, Sam and Karrie believe that their IM relationships enhance their social status, establishing a kind of social currency that keeps them in the know. Karrie thinks that being online makes her more popular in some peers' minds. 'It depends on how you use it,' Karrie says. 'Like sometimes things happen on there, like funny things, and then you get better friends because of things you can talk about.' Sam, who plans to switch schools in the fall from the local parochial middle school to the public high school, says she's been using IM in order to get to know some kids from the new school, and learn about 'their inside jokes and stuff' and other pertinent social gossip. Knowing who is popular and who is going out with whom will allow her a smoother transition and will in turn guarantee a more solid social network when she starts school."[9]

vide opportunities for deeper communication away from authority figures. For younger girls, sleepovers also provide a chance to discuss with others both the facts and the myths of adolescence, frequently deliberating on topics they deem as too sensitive (and embarrassing) for parental ears.

At a sleepover girls can easily spend the entire night talking, supported by bouts of ingesting mounds of junk food and braiding each other's hair. On the other hand, boys' sleepovers focus more on activities—playing video games or basketball, watching movies, and so on.

Another difference between girls' and guys' friendships is that girls' friendships tend to be more empathetic. If one girl in the friendship cluster is struggling with a crisis, it has an impact on her friends' moods. This might explain why when one girl runs out of the room crying, several others follow in her wake; and soon you have an entire group of weeping seventh-graders out in the hallway. Should one of the friends appear to be unaffected by the girl's crisis, then that can be reason enough to ostracize her, at least temporarily, from the cluster. (The exception to this rule, of course, is if the unaffected friend is also the Alpha female of the group and the one causing the crisis). There's a definite sense of provisional solidarity: "When one feels pain, we all feel pain...and woe to the one who doesn't feel the pain with us."

Dangerous Attachments

Girls, more so than guys, tend to require a higher degree of nurturing in their friendships. Without trying to be stereotypical, this translates into a girl's need to sense that someone cares about them and will invest emotionally in the relationship. In a healthy friendship, this nurturing involves both giving and receiving, depending on the circumstances. However, this appropriate need can be distorted if she's had an unhealthy or nonexistent parental relationship. For example, if she has a father who was absent, either emotionally or physically, it's possible that she may seek out pseudo-nurturing from high-risk friendships (i.e., friendships where the nurturing comes with strings attached, such as sexual favors in exchange for perceived intimacy).

Youth workers especially need to be aware of this need for nurturing. If a girl is coming from a wounded background, she can easily misinterpret any pastoral attentions from a male (or female) youth worker as being more along the lines of an intimate friendship or even a romantic relationship. Youth workers need to be alert to the signs of a girl who overly attaches herself to adult leaders and regularly crosses appropriate boundaries:

- Repetitive phone calls with no clear purpose

- A desire for one-on-one time in a private setting

- Wheedling her way into a youth worker's family life

- Sharing inappropriate personal information with a male youth leader

When this violation of boundaries occurs, it's important to clarify the limits while still emphasizing care and concern for her: "You cannot call me more than once a day" or "You need to call and ask for permission before you stop by the house." The desire for nurturing is healthy; she's just trying to get the need met in an unhealthy manner, whether deliberately or unintentionally.

GIRLS AND RELATIONAL AGGRESSION

Melissa cautiously raised her hand—the only one out of the group of eight students who were crammed into the pastor's study for confirmation class. The pastor had asked some question about church history, and Melissa knew the answer. As the pastor looked

GUYS ASK—

"Why do girls always travel in herds to the bathroom?"

It gives girls a chance to step away from the big group and check in with each other. Plus, it can give them a sense of security ("I'm not alone") and a chance to bond. They're checking their hair, getting another opinion that they look okay, discussing whether or not the night is going okay, asking if the other girls think that "x boy" likes them, and so on. Are they talking about the guys? Yeah, probably. Sorry. But nobody's stopping the guys from doing the same thing.

FRONTLINE STORY

A junior high small group leader hosted a sleepover for her girls during one of the weeks leading up to her wedding. She was talking with another adult leader when she noticed the girls were all huddled in the corner and whispering. When they realized she was watching them, they broke from their hushed confab and the spokesperson stated, "Cathy, we have a question for you. Since you're getting married, we want to ask you a personal question—what is oral sex?"

Cathy took a deep breath. She'd known these girls for three years, and she knew their parents well. She also knew that if she didn't answer their question, they'd ask it at school instead, and she didn't want them hearing any myths. So, feeling the weight of the parents on her shoulders, she gave a brief, technical description. There were grimaces and squeals. "Ohmigosh!" screamed the girls. "We thought it was talking dirty on the phone!"

By the way, Cathy told the girls' parents about the conversation the next day. Better to hear it from her than to have one of the girls say, "Cathy told us about oral sex last night!"

down to check her response, Melissa caught Tiffany rolling her eyes at Michelle. Michelle kicked her to let her know she'd been seen. Tiffany turned to see Melissa glaring at her and responded with a shrug as if to say, "Whatever." The pastor looked up to continue the lecture, clueless that her office had just been the site of relational aggression.

Relational aggression among girls is nothing new. Any woman can tell you at least one vivid story of cruel behavior among girls at her junior or senior high school. In her book, *Queen Bees and Wannabes*, Rosalind Wiseman exposes the aggression that occurs in the hidden culture of an adolescent girl's social system. And she labels roles that are familiar to just about every female who's come through the American school system. For example, the "Queen Bee" (QB) operates "through a combination of charisma, force, money, looks, will, and manipulation."[14] She's the ruler of the social group (clique) and those around her do what she commands—sometimes out of fear and sometimes because they want to be associated with her reputation of popularity. She's never intimidated and can persuade the other girls in her group to do whatever she wants them to, even to turn on another member of the group.

Wiseman profiles several other roles that girls can play in their cliques. There is the "Sidekick" who is second in command to the QB. She dresses like her, talks like her, and carries out her commands when the QB isn't around. She does everything the QB tells her to do, and the two of them frequently gang up on other girls. However, Wiseman notes this crucial difference: When a "Sidekick" separates from a QB, she can change for the better.

The "Banker" gathers information about the other girls and uses it to advance her own agenda. If she hears gossip about someone, she'll "save it" to pass on during another conversation that could raise her social status. For example, she may reveal information like this in a group of girls after church: "Taesha,

I don't want to hurt your feelings, but I really think you should know that your boyfriend was making out in the parking lot with Christina after church last night. I'm just telling you for your own good." The "Banker" has just embarrassed Taesha in front of her friends, created a conflict with Christina, and upped her social status by looking as if she has insider information. She gains information by coming across as trustworthy and friendly, which is why adults often don't realize the damage she's doing.

The "Torn Bystander" at least has a conscience. She knows what's right and what's wrong, but she's still torn by her devotion to the group. Even though she knows that what the QB is doing is wrong, she feels powerless to stop it. However, the "Pleaser/ Wannabe/Messenger" will do anything to break into the group and gain the favor of the QB. She analyzes what the QB does and wears, mimicking her in an effort to gain the QB's approval and acceptance. What she doesn't realize is that while the QB may use the PWM to do her dirty work, she's also mocking her.

The unusual role in the group is the "Floater." She moves freely from one clique to another and is confident about who she is. She's nice to other girls and is genuinely likeable. She doesn't need the QB's approval; hence, the power issue is a moot point.

And then on the opposite end of the power spectrum from the QB is the "Target." Whether inside or outside the clique, she's often the victim of the clique's humiliating cruelty. Wiseman maintains that her role is necessary for maintaining the social structure of the group. She may be the Target because of what she wears, how she looks (including her ethnicity), or because she challenged the power structure of the group. It's important to note that a girl who's the Target will rarely tell her parents (or youth pastor) that there's abuse going on. She'll often just withdraw—if not physically, then emotionally.

PROGRAMMING ALERT

Examine your programming. Do you have activities that reach both genders or is there a bias toward the testosterone-based activities in the group? Do you have coffeehouse concerts as well as 3-on-3 basketball tournaments? What about a book discussion besides the dodge ball competition? You don't have to schedule a spa night to balance out the Play Station party, but you do need to be aware of the different needs of the kids in your ministry.

GIRLS AND TECHNOLOGY

The same traits that girls value in friendships also show up in how they view technology. In a report called *Tech-Savvy: Educating Girls in the New Computer Age*, published by the American Association of University Women Educational Foundation (AAUW), the researchers reported that when it comes to electronic games, "Girls have clear and strong ideas about what kinds of games they would design: games that feature simulation, strategy, and interaction." The report goes on to say, "These games, in fact, would appeal to a broad range of learners—boys and girls alike."[13]

"I left school on a Friday and came back on Monday, and I had no friends at all. I found out that we were not friends anymore when a girl had a sleepover for her birthday party and purposely handed out invitations in front of me. She said she didn't have one for me because she didn't like me…She was my best friend."[16] —Kari, on *The Oprah Winfrey Show*

"We fall into clans: Jocks, Country Clubbers, Idiot Savants, Cheerleaders, Human Waste, Eurotrash, Future Fascists of America, Big Hair Chix, the Marthas, Suffering Artists, Thespians, Goths, Shredders. I am clanless. I wasted the last weeks of August watching bad cartoons. I didn't go to the mall, the lake, or the pool, or answer the phone. I have entered high school with the wrong hair, the wrong clothes, the wrong attitude. And I don't have anyone to sit with. I am Outcast."[17] —Melinda Sordino, the high school female narrator in *Speak*

In naming these different roles, Wiseman gives youth workers a paradigm for beginning to understand some of the aggressive behaviors of the girls in their group. Whereas boys are more physically aggressive, girls are subtler in their aggression, and thus their behavior can go unnoticed.

Girls show aggression by deliberately "icing" a girl—ignoring her existence even if she's standing right there. They might give an evil glare or make threatening gestures once an authority figure's back is turned. They pass on gossip and start rumors that can devastate a girl's reputation. They hiss an insult such as, "Slut," as a girl walks by. And they do it so deftly that only the Target can hear it.

In her book *Fast Girls: Teenage Tribes and the Myth of the Slut*, Emily White explores how unfounded rumors about a girl's sexual behavior affect her life long past graduation.[15] Some of the interviewees, now women, talked about how they're still haunted by depression and thoughts of suicide after being labeled the "Target" or "Slut" during high school.

Youth workers need to be aware of who's the QB and who's the Target in their groups, as well as which students are playing the other roles. They need to understand that even though a girl may have all the right Bible answers and may play the role of a good Christian, she can still perpetuate relational aggression. Observe which girl the other girls model their dress and behavior after. Notice who holds the informal power (i.e., who calls the shots) with the girls in the ministry. Also, look around to see who's suddenly sitting alone after having been part of a group for months. Are there girls who disappear from the group after a conflict with the QB? Is there a girl who's being deliberately left out of any of the informal social events of the group? By observing subtle behaviors and listening to the quiet, catty remarks, a youth worker can learn who's playing which role.

GIRLS AND VIOLENCE

It was the first week of May 2003 when the media picked up the story. A high school touch football game in a wealthy northern Chicago suburb had turned into a brawl. High school seniors had pelted juniors with garbage, dead fish, and human waste. And one student caught it all on home video. The horrors of the day were replayed on the five and 10 o'clock evening news broadcasts across the country.

This annual football game had been a rite of passage at the high school since 1977, where seniors initiated the juniors into their last year of high school. Based on the video footage, it did seem to be an awful event, but frankly, adolescents typically do their fair share of awful things. Why did this grab so much media time? Simple. Both the perpetrators and the victims were girls.[19]

It used to be that girls displayed aggression through teasing, gossiping, and ostracizing each other. This hazing in northern Illinois revealed to the nation what girls all over have already known: Adolescent females have become more violent in the last few years. Sometimes the violent part of a hazing or initiation ritual is over a boy, but sometimes it's a fight for the fun of it—just like the guys.[20]

Angel

There are times when girls fight to protect themselves, to gain status, or to earn a certain reputation. Angel exemplified the kind of girl who fought to protect herself through her bad-girl reputation. She had punkish brown hair and deep brown eyes, but her Mickey Mouse T-shirt and quick smile softened her tough demeanor somewhat. One day Angel and I sat in a local diner eating hot fudge sundaes topped with blue-tinted whipped cream, and she told me her story.

A MALE YOUTH WORKER'S PERSPECTIVE...

Q: "What do you wish you had known about teenage girls before you started in ministry?"

A: "The complexity of their social structure. I knew that girls get in fights and tend to hold grudges more than guys, but I didn't realize how a fight between girls can affect every girl in your ministry. When I arrived at this church, I found that only about half of the girls who were in junior high came to youth functions. There was a fight between some girls, and they all took sides, and now half of them didn't come to youth group because of this.

"Another aspect of teenage girls I somewhat realized, but didn't understand the power it held, was the hierarchy of the social structure. Last year we had a group of seventh-grade girls that ran in a pack together. There was one girl that all the girls followed, and if she wasn't into whatever we were doing, then the rest weren't, either. So I learned to get this 'head girl' on board with our events or activities and the rest would follow." —Jon, a first-year youth pastor

GIRL BULLIES VERSUS BOY BULLIES

In his book, *Why Gender Matters*, Dr. Leonard Sax compares girl and boy bullies:[18]

GIRLS who bully typically—
- Have many friends
- Are socially skilled
- Act in groups to isolate a single girl
- Are doing well in school
- Know the girls they are bullying

BOYS who bully typically—
- Have few friends
- Are socially inept
- Act alone
- Are doing poorly in school
- Don't know the boys (or girls) they bully

"Sometimes I think that high school is one long hazing activity: if you are tough enough to survive, they'll let you become an adult. I hope it's worth it."[21] —Melinda Sordino, the high school female narrator in *Speak*

GIRLS IN GANGS[22]

- It's estimated that four percent of gang members are girls. That figure rises to nine percent if the girl is First Nation (Native American).

CONTINUED >

Her siblings had been part of a gang, but she'd managed to stay out. When I asked her how, she said bluntly, "Fighting." She learned quickly that if she could start the fight, the rest of the girls at school left her alone. She'd proven she was tough and not to be messed with.

Then she asked me how many fights I'd been in, but the only ones I could recall involved a couple of hair-pulling escapades during grade school. She looked at me skeptically, "You've never been in a fight? Ever? You've never started a fight? You've never been beat up?" For her, fighting had been a preemptive, protective measure to keep herself out of the local gang. She couldn't fathom a world without girl aggression.

THE YOUTH WORKER'S ROLE

As we witness increases in the level of both relational and physical violence among girls, it's vital that youth workers intervene. In Matthew 5:9, Jesus says, "Blessed are the peace*makers*." I take this statement to mean that we need to proactively deal with the rise in violence. Besides setting positive examples of constructive conflict resolution, rather than destructive, we need to establish zero-tolerance policies within our ministries—for both physical and relational aggression.

We must also understand that it's likely that, at some point in her life, a physically aggressive girl may have been the victim of some type of abuse—physical, sexual, or emotional. We need to talk about practical ways to fend off aggression and teach girls how to develop an exit plan from a situation that's escalating. We must approach the issue of relational aggression just as seriously as we do physical aggression, understanding that emotional bruises hurt just as physical ones do, although they often take much longer to heal.

It's vital that a youth ministry be a safe place for girls—both the Briannes and the Haleys of our communities—and to see healthy friendships modeled. Adolescent girls already have enough relational chaos to deal with at school and at home. May our ministries serve as havens where students can at least experience God's love and acceptance from their youth leaders, if not from the other students.

CONTINUED >

- Roughly one-third of all early adolescent gang members are female.
- Girls leave gangs at an earlier age than guys do.
- Only 72 percent of girls in gangs expect to graduate from high school (compared to 93 percent of girls who aren't in gangs).
- Twenty-five percent of girls not involved with gangs say they've hit or threatened to hit another student within the past year. Eighty percent of girls in gangs reported the same.

THE LOWDOWN ON GIRL VIOLENCE

- In 2003, eight percent of girls said they'd been in a physical fight in the last year.[23]
- Twenty-five percent of all teenagers (13 to 15 years old) who are arrested for aggravated assault are girls.[24]
- In 1900 one out of every 50 juveniles arrested for a crime was a girl. In 2003, it was one out of three.[25]
- Girls usually fight other females they know: friends, family members, or peers at school.
- Girls usually don't use weapons when they fight.[26]

CHAPTER ELEVEN
FAITH MATTERS

One late autumn afternoon I found myself sitting on the cold, tile floor of a bathroom, deep in conversation about faith and life. One thing I've learned in youth ministry is that God shows up in mysterious places. Sometimes it's a burning bush in a desert, other times it's an ancient bathroom at camp. But when he shows up, you pay attention.

We were in the girls' cabin on our youth ministry's fall retreat; I was leaning against the outside of the shower wall, and Angela was sitting a few feet away, lodged somewhat comfortably between the toilet and the sink. I'd found her crying in the bathroom when I was doing a last check on the cabin, making sure everyone had gone down to the lodge for the worship session.

Angela was a visitor to our youth group. She'd come on the retreat with one of our regular students— a friend of hers from school. Pretty and outgoing, she quickly found her place with the other students. I'd written her off as a shallow socialite, figuring she was only there for the boys, her friends, and just to have a good time. But I was wrong. She'd been to the main sessions of the retreat and watched from the back row as we prayed and worshiped together. Something that weekend had stirred her deeply.

When I found her huddled in the bathroom, she was in the midst of a faith crisis. Her belief system, which so far had successfully gotten her to this point in her life, was falling apart. We talked deeply about God, his love for us, and his desire to be close to us. The tears flowed as she prayed on that grungy tile floor and sensed on a soul level, perhaps for the first time, that the God of the universe wanted to be in a relationship with her. It was one of those holy moments that answers a youth worker's nagging question of why we put up with the crazy hours, low pay, and bad food. That day God was moving in a life, and I was privileged to be part of the process.

As I reflected on my conversation with Angela, I realized that on one level what happened was very personal and specific to her at that moment in time. But on another level, she was clearly fitting a larger pattern of how adolescent girls deal with issues of faith and spirituality. Her questioning and her faith crisis are very typical of what an adolescent experiences, albeit not always on a bathroom floor.

As we've seen in every section of this book, nothing about an adolescent girl is certain—except change. Her body is changing, her relationships are changing, and her emotions are changing. And at the same time, all of those changes impact her teenage faith as well. Maybe she learned to toddle in the church nursery, skinned her knees at Vacation Bible School, earned a Bible for memorizing verses and even a few gold foil stars for perfect Sunday school attendance. But once she hits adolescence, she'll still question what she believes. It's a very normal part of moving from childhood to adulthood.

PRE-ADOLESCENT FAITH

As a child, a girl's belief system is grounded in her family system. She's part of the same faith community (or communities) as her parents, and most likely she identifies with the same religious tradition as her extended family. If her parents are religious, she's probably religious. And vice versa: if her parents aren't religious or if they're divided about their beliefs, then she's not as likely to embrace religion on her own.[2] If she's raised in a trusting and loving family, she can grasp that God is trustworthy and loving. If she feels safe from outside dangers, she senses that God is the protector of the powerless. If she knows there will be food at the table when she sits down to dinner, she can understand that God provides.

Surrounded by family and by her faith community, she absorbs the stories of God, as well as the legacy and practices of her faith tradition. During

---

SPIRITUAL STRUGGLES OF ADOLESCENT GIRLS

Author and professor Patricia Davis has identified several areas in which an adolescent girl will typically struggle:[1]

- God's will

- Career choices

- Maintaining relationships in the midst of conflict

- Expressing her own faith in the face of a restrictive church

- Moral and ethical choices about sexuality and reproduction

"Girls whose families do not instill in them a sense that they are cherished, girls who are abused, and girls who are not taken seriously often revealed troubled relationships to God. Girls whose family religion is judgmental, harsh, and punitive often incorporated these feelings into their own relationships with God."[3]
—Patricia H. Davis, *Beyond Nice*

THE IMPACT OF RELIGION ON CHILDREN

A panel of researchers analyzed years of research done on children, including medical reports, and came to the following conclusions:

- "Young people who are religious are better off in significant ways than their secular peers. They are less likely than nonbelievers to smoke and drink and more likely to eat well; less likely to commit crimes and more likely to wear seat belts; less likely to be depressed and more likely to be satisfied with their families and school."

- "Religion has a unique net effect on adolescents above and beyond factors like race, parental education, and family income," says Brad Wilcox, a University of Virginia sociologist and panel member. "Poor children who are religious will do better than poor children who are not religious," he adds, "and in some cases better than nonreligious middle-class children…Too often, youth organizations try to foster virtue by appealing to self-interest," he says. "These programs don't seem to realize that adolescents are also looking for something bigger than themselves."[4]

the worship service, she learns when to sit, when to stand, when to sing, when to respond, when to be silent, when to give, and when to take—even if she doesn't fully grasp the underlying meanings behind those behaviors. Sitting in a pew or around the dining room table, she comes to understand that certain days hold special meanings, whether they're days of remembrance or of celebration. (Although if she's very young, she may only grasp that this was a special holiday because she got to choose a new dress and new shoes that pinch just a little.)

Not only does a young girl understand that there are rhythms and patterns to her family's religious tradition, but she also comes to understand that there are certain rules that govern her behavior—both inside and outside of church: "You put money *into* the basket, not take it *out*," "Bow your head and close your eyes when you pray," "Don't wade in the baptismal tank," "Don't eat meat on Fridays," or "Don't eat pork *ever*." Sometimes these rules are grounded in Scripture, other times they're from the particular faith traditions, and still others are ones that adults seem to create for their own purposes and then sprinkle them with "Jesus dust."

For example, when it comes to obeying authority, a girl might hear "God tells little girls to obey their parents. You don't want to make God angry do you?" or "The reason we dress up when we go to church is because it makes God happy." Or when it comes to monitoring her behavior, she might hear something like, "God loves little girls who sit quietly," or "When you put your sister's doll in the toilet, that makes Jesus sad."

EARLY ADOLESCENT FAITH

As a girl enters early adolescence, she begins to question both the religious and nonreligious rules. She'll push at them if they seem illogical or contradictory to her. For example, she may ask, "Why do we have to go to church every Sunday? Rachel's family goes on Saturday, and Diana's family doesn't go at all, and both of those families are fine." Or, "Why does my science teacher teach about evolution but my Sunday school teacher teaches about creationism?" This kind of questioning can be irritating, especially to a parent, but it's a sign that she's moving into more abstract thinking. It means she's no longer simply acquiescing to religious expectations, but she's struggling to understand the significance of the behaviors and rules.

This is what religious scholar James Fowler calls a *Synthetic-Conventional faith*; a stage or phase where religious symbols and liturgy begin to take on deeper meaning.[5] At this stage, a young adolescent girl begins to comprehend that kneeling is a sign of worship; that giving and serving are both part of the responsibility of being a member of a congregation; and that the cross around her neck isn't just a pretty decoration, but it's a sign of remembrance and identification.

When a girl questions her traditions, it's an indication that she's beginning to test what she believes and to investigate other possibilities. Up until early adolescence, imagination and truth run together for her, which is why she can just as easily believe in a man in a red suit who brings her toys once a year as she believes in a sinless man who hung on the cross to pay for her sins. It's not until she reaches early to mid-adolescence that she begins to emerge from the concrete, literal thinking that accepted exactly what trusted adults told her. Perhaps that's why Jesus is recorded, in three of the Gospels, issuing a dire warning to anyone who causes a child to stumble (Matthew 18:6; Mark 9:42; and Luke 17:1-2).

In Judy Blume's novel about a teenage girl, *Are You There God? It's Me, Margaret* (1972), the narrator is an 11-going-on-12 girl who's searching for God. Part of her search includes checking out her friends' religious traditions. This inquisitive behav-

WHAT COLOR IS GOD?

Patricia Davis has spent years studying the spirituality of adolescent girls. Here's what she found when it came to girls' perceptions of God:

"The color of God's skin was especially important to the African American and Hispanic girls who participated [in a study]. For these girls God (sometimes identified as Jesus) was either no color, all colors, or dark-skinned...Although these girls did not seem to resist the cultural message that God is male, they were indeed in touch with the fact that the traditional image of a white God was not true. They knew that *if* God had a skin color, somehow their own skin color was represented in God."[6]

ior is normal for an early adolescent girl. She may visit a mass or celebrate a friend's bat mitzvah or confirmation. She starts asking more probing questions about why her family worships one way and her friend's family worships another (if at all). She may question her parents about how they *know* their way is the right way, but will usually default to assuming they're correct in their beliefs. This questioning and searching means she's in the beginning stages of forming her own theology.

As a middle schooler, she's very concerned about issues of fairness and justice. Because she's learning to view situations from another person's perspective, she's troubled when someone is treated unfairly or unjustly, whether it's a close friend or someone living on the other side of the world. She's drawn to causes, such as animal rights, childhood poverty, or protecting the environment—desiring to speak up for those whom she feels have no voice, perhaps because she empathizes with that feeling.

This sensitivity to justice and fairness means she has a very clear idea of what's right and what's wrong, and she constantly examines the lives of those around her and judges them accordingly. Try to justify telling a social lie (e.g., telling someone her new haircut looks good when it doesn't) or breaking a law (e.g., going five miles per hour over the speed limit) to an early adolescent—it's a losing battle. In her eyes, you've broken a rule, but God says to obey the rules of the church and the government.

That same passion for right and wrong means that at this age she can easily make strong commitments, such as how she'll *never* have sex before marriage, she'll *never* cheat on a test, or she'll *never* smoke or drink. In her mind at that moment, she knows these behaviors to be wrong and she believes that when faced with these decisions, she has the capacity to simply choose to do what is right. However, because she also values her relationships, a crisis will arise when her strong commitments put her in conflict with persuasive friends. Often she'll resolve the crisis by choosing to stay in relationship with her friends (who are tangible), rather than standing behind her convictions (which are intangible).

On the positive side, that commitment to relationships is what often draws her to a youth group. There is something very appealing about hanging around with peers who reaffirm her faith beliefs and who provide her with positive social relationships. This emphasis on relationships becomes obvious when she's asked whether or not she's coming to a youth group event and her response isn't "What are we going to do?" but "Who's going to be there?"

During early and middle adolescence, she's searching for like-minded peers or peers who will increase her social capital (although she'll be hesitant to admit the latter). If she doesn't find those at her home church, then she may choose to link up with another ministry or organization where there are peers with whom she feels she has more in common, or ones that will increase her social attractiveness. Joining Christian clubs or groups apart from the church, such as Young Life or the Fellowship of Christian Athletes, becomes more appealing to her because, in her eyes, they might fulfill both her social *and* her spiritual needs

MIDDLE ADOLESCENT FAITH

By the time a girl reaches middle adolescence (15 to 17 years of age), it's evident that she's functioning as an abstract thinker. She's digging deeply into why she believes what she does, and why her family believes the way it does. She's searching for meaning, for belonging, for a deeper purpose, and for a community. If she doesn't find these in her home faith community, she'll look elsewhere. She might join another church, another denomination, or even another religion. Or, she may merge several belief systems together, creating her own theology.

WHAT ATTRACTS ADOLESCENTS TO CHURCH?

"I concluded from my year of research that when teens are attracted to churches, they are attracted because the churches engage them in intense states of self-transcendence, uniting emotional and cognitive processes. Churches 'catch' them on three hooks: a sense of belonging, a sense of meaning, and opportunities to develop competence. When churches' ministries with youth include these components, teens will restructure their time and attention to participate in them...I discovered that teens stayed engaged in their congregations if they perceived that they offered, at a minimum, either a sense of belonging or a coherence of meaning."[7]
—Carol Lytch, *Choosing Church*

As a high school student, issues of justice and mercy become even more important to her. She's idealistic, believing she can help change the world. So when an unjust or cruel act occurs, she finds it hard to reconcile that fact with her belief in an all-powerful God. If God does have unlimited power, then why did her friend die in a car accident? Why didn't God prevent it? Or, if God controls the weather, then why do so many die people in hurricanes and floods?

When confronted by these seeming contradictions, God or the church bear the brunt of her skepticism and doubt. We do her a disservice if we don't allow her to search out the reasons leading to her skepticism, or we don't dialogue with her about her doubt. Sometimes a person (or a church) may feel threatened by her questions and will respond by telling her that doubting is a sin. Others don't take her questions seriously. Instead they admonish her to just "trust God more" and have a stronger faith. But simplistic answers might result in her withdrawal from God and her exit from the church, either physically or emotionally (whereby she chooses to participate in the rituals of the church only as a means of pleasing her parents and reducing the amount of conflict at home).

ALTERNATIVE SPIRITUALITY

In an article for *The Washington Post*, Laura Sessions Stepp (a frequent writer on adolescent issues) reported on the role of religion among adolescents. One of the people she spoke with was 12-year-old Kathleen, whose mother used doughnut holes to bribe her to go to Sunday school:

> "My brother is like one of the sheep," Kathleen says one Sunday morning with all the disdain someone her age can muster. "He'll go along and do as he's told, pretty much. I'm one of the little lambs

that keeps wandering off and my mom is the shepherd pulling me back into the fold." She has considered becoming a Catholic or a Jew. "And I was an atheist for about a day." Becoming an atheist "felt weird," she says. "I had this empty space that I didn't know how to fill. What should I do? Meditate? Sing or dance?" She decided that she did need God, whom she defines as "a bigger power you can confide in, find comfort in, someone who makes you feel more safe and secure." Wicca, a form of pagan nature worship, could be the answer, she says. Because "in Wicca, you have a goddess and a god. God will still be there for me."[9]

Kathleen, like many adolescent girls these days, is spiritually inclined and searching. In a recent survey of more than 3,200 adolescents (13 to 17 years of age), 54 percent of the girls who responded said that religion was important to them (another 30 percent said it was at least somewhat important).[10] In their searching, girls are turning to alternative forms of religion that celebrate feminine power and have a strong element of romantic mystery to them, such as neo-paganism, witchcraft, and Wicca (all of which are derivatives of paganism).

Wicca is perhaps the most well-known form of paganism among adolescent girls in the United States. Although it's not a major force among U.S. adolescents (only .3 percent versus 52 percent of teens who affiliate with Protestantism and 23 percent who affiliate with Catholicism[11]), it's growing relatively quickly. In 1990 there were 8,000 Wiccans in the United States, but by 2001 there were 134,000. It's estimated that there are anywhere from 500,000 to 13 million Wiccans globally.[12]

Although there is some debate about whether or not Wicca and witchcraft are the same thing, Wicca does have its roots in witchcraft. One of its key

ADVICE FROM A YOUTH PASTOR

"I'm still learning here, but thankfully what I have learned is that (more than the male-dominated institutional church knows, and I am a male in the institutional church) the spiritual formation for young gals is much different than it is for males. What they *need* are mature female leaders who have power, space, and resources equal to the male leaders to create space for these young women. And if you want equality in the ministry, then they need—temporarily—more power, space, and resources to create space for this development to occur.

"On a biblical level—please, 'Newbie Fellas'—read some of the feminine voices that speak to the troublesome passages surrounding women having 'authority' over men, or speaking out in church, or being submissive. Much of our current hierarchies have been built on prooftexting without reading the next few sentences. And when they do that, most don't talk about, or know of, the cultural context of the certain community, culture, and time of history.

CONTINUED >

founders is Gerald Gardiner, a British civil servant who merged witchcraft, the occult, and ancient folklore with Masonic rites in the 1940s and '50s.[13]

Because both Wicca and witchcraft are pagan religions, they're earth-based. The implication is that there's a strong emphasis on living in harmony with nature and guarding the environment, which has long been an area of concern for many adolescent girls. Wiccans believe that people are here to serve the earth, not vice versa. This focus on valuing nature and the environment directly taps into adolescent girls' interest in justice issues.

Wicca also embraces the strength of the feminine. They believe that the divine is both feminine and masculine and that the divine exists in everyone. This is appealing for some girls who have grown up in churches where God has strictly been defined in only masculine terms and using only masculine analogies. Wiccans are very clear that there is a power beyond them, and that this power should only be used for good. Their basic creed of "Do what you want, as long as you don't harm anyone" brings a sense of empowerment and freedom to many of the girls who embrace it.

For girls who feel as though they don't have any power and that no one listens to their voices because they're girls, Wicca can appear as an interesting alternative. It seemingly celebrates who she is as a young female when so many other voices are demeaning her. If a girl is struggling in school or at home, she's looking for a magical solution or an outside source to help her cope. A belief that advocates poetic rituals, "magick" power ("personal power and responsibility for one's actions and environment"[14]), sexual freedom, *plus* claims that she is a goddess can feel like a viable option to her as she tries to survive adolescence.

THE YOUTH WORKER'S ROLE

We need to realize that this alternative form of spirituality is the adolescent girls' pop-culture religion. It may well be that she's attracted to the "trappings" of Wicca. The ritual and romanticism found in neo-paganism taps into something that was missing from the local church for many years. Youth group meetings that focus on athletic competitions, rote memorization, three-point sermons, and gross-out games may have reached a certain group of students, but there was another group that was alienated by those things.

There are students who long for a certain sense of mystery and for sacred rituals, who desire communities where beauty is valued more than entertainment and where faith is holistic.

As Christians we need to remember that our faith isn't just a series of theological premises that we agree to, but that there's also relationship and divine mystery and deep community. These are all elements that draw adolescent girls. The recent emphasis on worship in the Christian community is a healthy start toward pursuing the part of God that cannot be described but only experienced.

We need to be challenged by the Wiccans' value of nature and admit where we have abused the earth for our own purposes. However, we also need to have a proper view of stewardship and understand that we don't have to worship nature, but we do need to respect it as a part of God's creation.

We also need to observe whether we're empowering the girls in our ministries or discouraging them. Do we send either blatant or subtle messages to teenage girls that say we believe they are, in God's eyes, less important than the guys? How about in our own eyes? Are there certain roles that are off-limits to girls, such as preaching or leading worship? Is that

CONTINUED >

"I could go off here—because this is one of the main reasons my wife is now going to seminary. She was basically the second full-time pastor at our last ministry, but was treated like a 'complementary partner' and expected to help the young girls learn to do crafts, have nail parties, and be a good spouse. These things aren't bad at all, but when they become the focus, then we are on another great adventure of missing the point." —Mike, a youth pastor for several years

because of the church's theology or the personal preference of the youth pastor?

A dear mentor of mine, Dave Busby, had a favorite expression he used in talking about youth ministry. He would say that as youth workers, we are "Jesus with skin on."

An adolescent girl may not understand who God is yet, or she may feel distant, or she may just need to know that God hasn't forgotten about her during this stage of her life when everything else seems up for grabs.

In this season, we can be tangible reminders that there is a God who loves her on nasty hair days and when she feels like she doesn't have a friend in the world.

We can be tangible reminders that there is a God who will forgive her as she makes bad decisions and challenge her as she dreams about her future.

We can be tangible reminders that there is a God who will walk with her on this incredible journey of adolescence.

May we all be "Jesus with skin on" to a generation of adolescent girls.

NOTES

INTRODUCTION—NO TOURISTS NEED APPLY

1. "Adolescent," *The American Heritage® Dictionary of the English Language*, 4th ed. (Boston: Houghton Mifflin, 2000), http://www.bartleby.com/61/54/A0095400.html (accessed December 22, 2005).

2. Aristotle, *Rhetoric: Book* 2, chapter 12, as cited in G. Stanley Hall, *Adolescence: Its Psychology and Its Relations to Physiology, Anthropology, Sociology, Sex, Crime, Religion, and Education*, volume 1 (New York: D. Appleton & Co., 1904), 522-523.

3. G. Stanley Hall, *Adolescence: Its Psychology and Its Relations to Physiology, Anthropology, Sociology, Sex, Crime, Religion, and Education* 2 vols. (New York: D. Appleton & Co., 1904).

4. F. Philip Rice and Kim Gale Dolgin, *The Adolescent: Development, Relationships, and Culture*, 11th ed. (Boston: Allyn & Bacon, 2004), 24.

5. Jean Kilbourne, *Can't Buy My Love: How Advertising Changes the Way We Think and Feel* (New York: Touchstone, 1999), 130.

6. Rolf E. Muss, *Theories of Adolescence*, 5th ed. (New York: McGraw-Hill, 1988), 224.

7. Mary Pipher, *Reviving Ophelia* (New York: Ballantine Books, 1995), 21.

8. Figures based on the 2000 U.S. Census Bureau.

9. U.S. Census Bureau, *International Population Reports WP/02*, "Global Population Profile: 2002" (Washington, D.C.: U.S. Government Printing Office, 2004).

10. World Vision, *Girl Child Report*, "Every Girl Counts: Development, Justice and Gender," Loretta Rose (principal writer), (Ontario, Canada: World Vision, 2001), 6, http://www.wvi.org/imagine/pdf/GirlChild.pdf

11. Ibid.

12. Ibid.

13. Ibid., 12.

14. Ibid.

15. Anita L. Botti, "The Trade in Human Beings Is a Worldwide Scourge," *International Herald Tribune*, June 1, 2000, http://www.iht.com/articles/2000/06/01/edbotti.2.t.php (accessed December 23, 2005).

16. Sharon LaFraniere, "AIDS Threatens African Girls' Gains: Orphaned, Poor and Struggling to Survive," *International Herald Tribune*, June 4, 2005, http://www.iht.com/articles/2005/06/03/news/mozam.php (accessed December 23, 2005).

CHAPTER 1

1. Erik H. Erikson, *Childhood and Society* (New York: W.W. Norton & Co., 1950).

2. A.C. Lacombe and J. Gay, "The Role of Gender in Adolescent Identity and Intimacy Decisions," *Journal of Youth & Adolescence* 27 (1998): 795-802.

3. Erik H. Erikson, *Identity and the Life Cycle* (New York: W.W. Norton & Co., 1980), 127.

4. Jean Phinney and Mona Devich-Navarro, "Variation in Bicultural Identification Among African American and Mexican American Adolescents," *Journal of Research on Adolescence* 7, no. 1 (1997): 3-32.

5. *Children Now—Prime Time Diversity* Report, 2001-02. Cited in Motivational Educational Entertainment (MEE) and The National Campaign to Prevent Teen Pregnancy, *This Is My Reality: The Price of Sex—An Inside Look at Black Urban Youth Sexuality and the Role of the Media* (Philadelphia: MEE, January 2004): 44.

6. B. Doll, "Children without Friends: Implications for Practice and Policy," *School Psychology Review* 25 (1996): 165-183.

7. Robert S. Weiss, *Loneliness: The Experience of Emotional and Social Isolation* (Cambridge, MA: MIT Press, 1973). Cited in Jeffrey Jensen Arnett, *Adolescence and Emerging Adulthood: A Cultural Approach* (Upper Saddle River, NJ: Prentice Hall, 2001).

8. Christian Smith and Melinda Lundquist Denton, *Soul Searching: The Religious and Spiritual Lives of American Teenagers* (New York: Oxford University Press USA, 2005), 116.

CHAPTER 2

1. The American Academy of Pediatrics and Philip Bashe, *Caring for Your Teenager: The Complete and Authoritative Guide*, ed. Donald E. Greydanus (New York: Bantam Dell, 2003), 562.

2. U.S. Department of Health and Human Services, "Fast Facts: What is Acne?" (Bethesda, MD: National Institute of Arthritis and Musculoskeletal and Skin Diseases, March 2005), http://www.niams.nih.gov/hi/topics/acne/ffacne.pdf

3. Jeffrey Jensen Arnett, *Adolescence and Emerging Adulthood: A Cultural Approach* (Upper Saddle River, NJ: Prentice Hall, 2001), 34.

4. M.E. Herman-Giddens et al., "Secondary Sexual Characteristics and Menses in Young Girls Seen in Office Practice: A Study from the Pediatric Research in Office Settings Network," *Pediatrics* 88 (1997): 505-512.

5. C.M. Worthman, "Interactions of Physical Maturation and Cultural Practice in Ontogeny: Kikuyu Adolescents," *Cultural Anthropology* 2 (1987): 29-38.

6. E.B. Robertson et al., "The Pubertal Development Scale: A Rural and Suburban Comparison," *Journal of Early Adolescence* 12 (1992): 174-186.

7. Bruce J. Ellis and Judy Garber, "Psychosocial Antecedents of Variation in Girls' Pubertal Timing: Maternal Depression, Stepfather Presence, and Marital and Family Stress," *Child Development* 71, no. 2 (March/April 2000): 485-501.

8. Anne Frank, *The Diary of a Young Girl* (New York: Pocket Books, 1972), 117.

9. Jeanne Brooks-Gunn and Edward O. Reiter, "The Role of Pubertal Processes," in S. Shirley Feldman and Glen R. Elliott, eds., *At the Threshold: The Developing Adolescent*, 16-53 (Cambridge, MA: Harvard University Press, 1990).

10. Adapted from Ginny Olson, "Fish Guts and Pig Intestines: Rites of Passage for Adolescent Girls," *Youthworker Journal*, September/October 2005, 46, http://www.youthspecialties.com/articles/topics/adolescent_development/fish_guts.php

11. J.A. O'Dea and S. Abraham, "Association Between Self-Concept and Body Weight, Gender, and Pubertal Development Among Male and Female Adolescents," *Adolescence* 34 (Spring 1999): 69-79.

12. X. Ge, G.H. Elder, M. Regnerus, and C. Cox, "Pubertal Transitions, Perceptions of Being Overweight, and Adolescents' Psychological Maladjustment: Gender and Ethnic Differences," *Social Psychology Quarterly* 64 (2001): 363-375.

CHAPTER 3

1. Susan Bordo, *Unbearable Weight: Feminism, Western Culture, and the Body* (Berkeley: University of California Press, 1993), 26, quoted in Marie L. Hoskins, "Girls' Identity Dilemmas: Spaces Defined by Definitions of Worth," Health Care for Women International 23, no. 3 (April-May 2002): 234.

2. The National Center on Addiction and Substance Abuse (CASA) at Columbia University, *Food for Thought: Substance Abuse and Eating Disorders* (New York: CASA, December 2003), ii, http://www.casacolumbia.org/pdshopprov/files/food_for_thought_12_03.pdf

3. Ibid.

4. Jean Kilbourne, *Can't Buy My Love: How Advertising Changes the Way We Think and Feel* (New York: Touchstone, 1999), 129.

5. A.E. Field et al., "Exposure to the Mass Media and Weight Concerns Among Girls," *Pediatrics* 103 (March 1999). Cited in Marjorie Hogan, "Media Education Offers Help on Children's Body Image Problems," *AAP News*, May 1999, http://www.aap.org/advocacy/hogan599.htm (accessed December 29, 2005).

6. "When Perception is Reality," press release (based on an editorial by Dr. Alain Joffe at Johns Hopkins University), *Archives of Pediatrics and Adolescent Medicine* 159 (June 2005): 592-593.

7. Kilbourne, *Can't Buy My Love*, 132.

8. Harvard Medical School, "Sharp Rise in Eating Disorders in Fiji Follows Arrival of TV," news release, May 17, 1999, http://www.hms.harvard.edu/news/releases/599bodyimage.html (accessed December 29, 2005).

9. "Getting the Skinny on TV," *Discover* 20, no. 12, December 1999: 34-35.

10. Motivational Educational Entertainment (MEE) and The National Campaign to Prevent Teen Pregnancy, *This Is My Reality: The Price of Sex—An Inside Look at Black Urban Youth Sexuality and the Role of the Media* (Philadelphia: MEE, January 2004): 43.

11. Mary Pipher, *Reviving Ophelia* (New York: Ballantine Books, 1995), 56.

12. Lori Brand and Luoluo Hong, "Dieting, Dating and Denial: Whose Body Is It?" (Presented at the 75th Annual Meeting of the American College Health Association, New Orleans, LA, on May 28-31, 1997). And Debra K. Katzman and Leora Pinhas, *Help for Eating Disorders: A Parent's Guide to Symptoms, Causes and Treatments* (Toronto: Robert Rose, 2005), 42. And "Ken and Barbie at Life Size," *Sex Roles* 34 (3-4), (February 1996): 287-294.

13. A. Mazur, "U.S. Trends in Feminine Beauty and Overadaptation," *Journal of Sex Research* 22 (1986): 281-303. Cited in Norine G. Johnson, Michael C. Roberts, Judith P. Worell, eds., *Beyond Appearance: A New Look at Adolescent Girls* (Washington, D.C.: American Psychological Association, 1999), 86.

14. H.R.M. Lerner et al., "Early Adolescent Physical Attractiveness and Academic Competence," *Journal of Early Adolescence* 10 (1990): 4-20. Cited in F. Philip Rice and Kim Gale Dolgin, *The Adolescent: Development, Relationships, and Culture,* 11th ed. (Boston: Allyn & Bacon, 2004).

15. H.R.M. Lerner et al., "Physical Attractiveness and Psychosocial Functioning Among Early Adolescence," *Journal of Early Adolescence* 11 (1991): 300-320. Cited in F. Philip Rice and Kim Gale Dolgin, *The Adolescent: Development, Relationships, and Culture*, 11th ed. (Boston: Allyn & Bacon, 2004).

16. Sascha de Gersdorff, "Fresh Faces," *Boston Magazine*, May 2005.

17. The American Society for Aesthetic Plastic Surgery, "Cosmetic Surgery Quick Facts—2004 ASAPS Statistics: Highlights of the ASAPS 2004 Statistics on Cosmetic Surgery," http://www.surgery.org/press/procedurefacts-asqf.php (accessed January 1, 2006).

18. Gersdorff, "Fresh Faces."

19. Anne M. Hahn-Smith and Jane E. Smith, "The Positive Influence of Maternal Identification on Body Image, Eating Attitudes, and Self-Esteem of Hispanic and Anglo Girls," *International Journal of Eating Disorders* 29 (2001): 429-440.

20. G.B. Schreiber et al., "Weight Modification Efforts Reported by Black and White Preadolescent Girls: National Heart, Lung, and Blood Institute Growth and Health Study," *Pediatrics* 98 (1996): 63-70.

21. "How Do You Feel About Your Body?" *Teen People*, August 2005, 186.

22. Ruth H. Striegel-Moore et al., "Recurrent Binge Eating in Black American Women," *Archives of Family Medicine* 9, no. 1 (January 2000): 83-87.

23. Ruth H. Striegel-Moore et al., "Recurrent Binge Eating in Black American Women," author's comment, *Archives of Family Medicine* 9, no. 1 (January 2000): 83-87.

24. Schreiber et al., "Weight Modification Efforts," 63-70.

25. Alice Chung, "Anorexic" in *Yell-Oh Girls! Emerging Voices Explore Culture, Identity, and Growing Up Asian American*, ed. Vicki Nam (New York: HarperCollins, 2001), 147.

26. Danice K. Eaton et al., "Association of Body Mass Index and Perceived Weight with Suicide Ideation and Suicide Attempts Among US High School Students," *Archives of Pediatrics and Adolescent Medicine* 159 (June 2005): 513-519.

27. Selena Bond and Thomas F. Cash, "Black Beauty: Skin Color and Body Images Among African-American College Women," *Journal of Applied Social Psychology* 22 (1992): 874-888. And Sarita Sahay and Niva Piran, "Skin-color Preferences and Body Satisfaction Among South Asian-Canadian and Europe-

an-Canadian Female University Students," *Journal of Social Psychology* 137 (1997): 161-172.

28. Mikiko Ashikari, "Cultivating Japanese Whiteness," *Journal of Material Culture* 10, no. 1 (March 2005), 73-91.

29. Lindsey Tanner, AP Medical Writer, "For Toned Look, Some Teens Use Supplements," August 1, 2005, http://www.boston.com/yourlife/health/diseases/articles/2005/08/01/for_toned_look_some_teens_use_supplements/ (accessed December 29, 2005).

30. Mark Sappenfield and Adam Karlin, "Steroids Now Often Used for Slimming, Not Just Sports," *Christian Science Monitor*, June 16, 2005.

31. Nanci Hellmich, "Girls Do Better in Gym Class without Boys," *USA Today*, August 23, 2005.

32. U. S. Department for Health and Human Services, "Children and Teens Told by Doctors that They Were Overweight—United States, 1999-2002," *Morbidity & Mortality Weekly Report* 54, no. 34 (Sept. 2, 2005): 848-849.

33. Ibid.

34. Center for Disease Control and Prevention, as quoted in the *Kaiser Family Foundation Report*, www.kff.org/entmedia/entmedia022404pkg.cfm

35. Cited in *Teen People*, August 2005, 26.

36. Eric Stice, Katherine Presnell, and Heather Shaw, "Psychological and Behavioral Risk Factors for Obesity Onset in Adolescent Girls: A Prospective Study," *Journal of Consulting and Clinical Psychology* 73, no. 2 (April 2005): 195-202. Cited in Katrina Woznicki, "Why Adolescent Girls Become Obese," http://www.medpagetoday.com/tbprint.cfm?tbid=860 (accessed December 30, 2005).

37. J.J. Brumberg, *Fasting Girls* (Cambridge, MA: Harvard University Press, 1988). Cited in Norine G. Johnson, Michael C. Roberts, Judith P. Worell, eds., *Beyond Appearance: A New Look at Adolescent Girls* (Washington, D.C.: American Psychological Association, 1999).

38. Debra K. Katzman and Leora Pinhas, *Help for Eating Disorders: A Parent's Guide to Symptoms, Causes and Treatments* (Toronto: Robert Rose, 2005).

39. P.M. Lewinsohn et al., "Adolescent Psychopathy: I. Prevalence and Incidence of Depression and Other DSM-III-R Disorders in High School Students," *Journal of Abnormal Psychology* 102 (1993): 133-144. And The McKnight Investigators, "Risk Factors for the Onset of Eating Disorders in Adolescent

Girls: Results of the McKnight Longitudinal Risk Factor Study," *American Journal of Psychiatry* 160 (Feb. 2003): 248-254.

40. Norine G. Johnson, Michael C. Roberts, Judith P. Worell, eds., *Beyond Appearance: A New Look at Adolescent Girls* (Washington, D.C.: American Psychological Association, 1999), 97.

41. Pipher, *Reviving Ophelia*, 174.

42. Katzman and Pinhas, *Help for Eating Disorders*, 10.

43. Pediatric Academic Societies, "Pro-Eating Disorder Website Usage, Health Outcomes in an Eating Disorder Population," *Newswise*, May 6, 2005, http://www.newswise.com/articles/view/511368/ (accessed December 30, 2005).

44. "Falling from My Pedestal," a case study in Andrew C. Garrod et al., *Adolescent Portraits: Identity, Relationships, and Challenges*, 5th ed. (Boston, MA: Allyn & Bacon, 2004), 150.

45. Marie L. Hoskins, "Girls' Identity Dilemmas: Spaces Defined by Definitions of Worth," *Health Care for Women International* 23, no. 3 (April-May 2002): 231-247.

46. Katzman and Pinhas, *Help for Eating Disorders*.

47. C.G. Fairburn and Paul J. Harrison, "Eating Disorders," *The Lancet* 361 (Feb. 1, 2003): 407-416.

48. A.E. Becker et al., "Binge Eating and Binge Eating Disorder in a Small-Scale, Indigenous Society: The View from Fiji," *International Journal of Eating Disorders* 34 (December 2003): 423-431.

CHAPTER 4

1. Karen Conterio, Wendy Lader, and Jennifer Kingson Bloom, *Bodily Harm: The Breakthrough Healing Program for Self-Injurers* (New York: Hyperion Books, 1998), 16.

2. Steven Levenkron, *Cutting: Understanding and Overcoming Self-Mutilation* (New York: W.W. Norton & Co., 1998), 25.

3. Ibid., 23.

4. Focus Adolescent Services, "Self-Injury" page on the Web site: http://www.focusas.com/SelfInjury.html (accessed December 30, 2005).

5. Conterio, Lader, and Bloom, *Bodily Harm*, 138-140.

6. Dr. Lisa Machoian, *The Disappearing Girl* (New York: Penguin Group, 2005), xxii.

CHAPTER 5

1. J.J. Padgham and D.A. Blyth, "Dating During Adolescence." Cited in Richard M. Lerner, Anne C. Peterson, and Jeanne Brooks-Gunn, eds. *Encyclopedia of Adolescence* vol. 1 (Garland Reference Library of Social Science) (New York: Taylor & Francis, 1991), 196-198.

2. Taylor, interview with the author, August 2005.

3. Bonnie Macmillan, *Why Boys Are Different and How to Bring out the Best in Them* (Hauppauge, NY: Barron's Educational Series, 2004), 150.

4. J. Neeman, B. Kojetin, and J. Hubbard, "Looking for Love in All the Wrong Places: A Longitudinal Study of Adjustment and Adolescent Romantic Relationship," in W. Furman (chair), *Adolescent Romantic Relationships: Conceptualizations, Characterizations, and Functions*, symposium conducted at the meeting of the Society for Research on Adolescence, Washington, D.C., March 1992. Cited in Jeffery Jensen Arnett ed., *Readings on Adolescence and Emerging Adulthood* (Upper Saddle River, NJ: Pearson Education, 2002).

5. Laura Sessions Stepp, "Risk-Taking Friends May Be Hazardous to Teens," *The Washington Post*, August 20, 2004.

6. Laura Sessions Stepp, "Guys Can Never be Sure What Turns a Young Woman Off: Deal-Breakers Include Really Dumb Remarks, Too Little Hair and, of Course, Too Much Hair," *The Gazette* (Montreal, Quebec), April 18, 2004.

7. Teri Quatman, Kindra Sampson, Cindi Robinson, and Cary M. Watson, "Academic, Motivational, and Emotional Correlates of Adolescent Dating," *Genetic, Social, and General Psychological Monographs* 127, no. 2 (2001): 211-234.

8. Motivational Educational Entertainment (MEE) and The National Campaign to Prevent Teen Pregnancy, *This Is My Reality: The Price of Sex—An Inside Look at Black Urban Youth Sexuality and the Role of the Media* (Philadelphia: MEE, January 2004): 31.

9. Alex Kuczynski, "She's Got to be a Macho Girl," *The New York Times*, November 3, 2002.

10. Laura Sessions Stepp, "Modern Flirting," *The Washington Post*, October 16, 2003.

11. Rachel Kramer Bussel, "Casual-Sex Myths," Lusty Lady column, *The Village Voice*, March 11, 2005.

12. Anne Jarrell, "The Face of Teenage Sex Grows Younger," *New York Times*, April 2, 2000, section 9, page 1.

13. Leonard Sax, *Why Gender Matters: What Parents and Teachers Need to Know about the Emerging Science of Sex Differences* (New York: Doubleday, 2005), 119.

14. Benoit Denizet-Lewis, interview by Neal Conan, *Talk of the Nation*, NPR, June 10, 2004, http://www.npr.org/templates/story/story.php?storyId=1952884

15. Benoit Denizet-Lewis, "Friends, Friends with Benefits and the Benefits of the Local Mall," *The New York Times Magazine*, May 30, 2004, http://209.157.64.200/focus/f-news/1144851/posts

16. Jeffrey Jensen Arnett, *Adolescence and Emerging Adulthood: A Cultural Approach, 2nd ed.* (Upper Saddle River, NJ: Prentice Hall, 2004).

17. Judith R. Vicary, Linda R. Klingaman, and William L. Harkness, "Risk Factors Associated with Date Rape and Sexual Assault of Adolescent Girls," *Journal of Adolescence* 18, no. 3 (June 1995): 289-306. And "Staying Connected: A Guide for Parents Raising an Adolescent Daughter," from APA Online: http://www.apa.org/pubinfo/girls/girls_violence.html (Copyright American Psychological Association, 2004.)

18. Jay G. Silverman, Anita Raj, and Karen Clements, "Dating Violence and Associated Sexual Risk and Pregnancy Among Adolescent Girls in the United States," *Pediatrics* 114, no. 2 (August 2004): 220-225.

19. Erica Goode, "Study Says 20% of Girls Reported Abuse by a Date," *New York Times*, August 1, 2001; and Michael Lasalandra and Susan O'Neill, "Study: 1 in 5 Teen Girls Assaulted by Date," *Boston Herald*, August 1, 2001.

20. Maura O'Keefe, "Predictors of Dating Violence Among High School Students," *Journal of Interpersonal Violence* 12, no. 4 (August 1997): 546-68.

21. Alan Guttmacher Institute, "Facts in Brief: Teen Sex and Pregnancy" (Revised September 1999), *Sex and America's Teenagers* (New York: Alan Guttmacher Institute, 1994), http://www.agi-usa.org/pubs/fb_teen_sex.html

22. B.V. Marin, K.K. Coyle, C.A. Gomez, S.C. Carvajal, and D.B. Kirby, "Older Boyfriends and Girlfriends Increase Risk of Sexual Initiation in Young Adolescents," *Journal of Adolescent Health* 27, no. 6 (Dec. 2000): 409-418.

23. Donell Marie Kerns, "Adolescent Male Sexual Aggression: Incidents and Correlates," (thesis, UW-Madison, 1994).

24. Erica Goode, "Study Says 20% of Girls Reported Abuse by a Date," *New York Times*, August 1, 2001.

25. Jay G. Silverman, Anita Raj, Lorelei Mucci, and Jeanne E. Hathaway, "Dating Violence Against Adolescent Girls and Associated Substance Use, Unhealthy Weight Control, Sexual Risk Behavior, Pregnancy, and Suicidality," *JAMA: Journal of the American Medical Association* 286, no. 5, (August 1, 2001): 572-579.

26. Ibid.

27. B. Albert, S. Brown, and C. Flanigan, eds., *14 and Younger: The Sexual Behavior of Young Adolescents (Summary)* (Washington, D.C.: National Campaign to Prevent Teen Pregnancy, 2003), 12, http://www.teenpregnancy.org

28. J. Rosenberg, "One-third of Teenagers Experience Abuse Within Heterosexual Relationships," *Perspectives on Sexual and Reproductive Health* Vol. 34, no. 2 (March/April 2002), http://www.guttmacher.org/pubs/journals/3410802.html

29. Mary Pipher, *Reviving Ophelia* (New York: Ballantine Books, 1995), 230.

30. Ibid.

CHAPTER 6

1. Matt Apuzzo (Associated Press Writer), "Study: Many Who Pledge Abstinence Substitute Risky Behavior," *Newsday*, March 21, 2005.

2. Advocates for Youth, *How Can I Talk About...?* "Virginity Pledges," A review of the research by Drs. Brückner and Bearman published in the *Journal of Adolescent Health* (2005) and *American Journal of Sociology* (2001), http://www.advocatesforyouth.org/news/talkingpoints/virginitypledges.htm (Last updated: June 16, 2005).

3. Ibid.

4. Ceci Connolly, "More U.S. Teens Delay Having Sex, Study Finds," *The Washington Post*, December 11, 2004, http://www.washingtonpost.com/wp-dyn/articles/A55856-2004Dec10.html

   Citing results from U.S. Department of Health and Human Services and Joyce C. Abma et al, *Teenagers in the United States: Sexual Activity, Contraceptive Use, and Childbearing,* 2002 (using data from the National Survey of Family Growth), December 2004, http://www.cdc.gov/nchs/data/series/sr_23/sr23_024.pdf

5. Alan Guttmacher Institute, "Facts in Brief: Teen Sex and Pregnancy" (Revised September 1999), *Sex and America's Teenagers* (New York: Alan Guttmacher Institute, 1994), http://www.agi-usa.org/pubs/fb_teen_sex.html

6. Ibid.

7. F. Philip Rice and Kim Gale Dolgin, *The Adolescent: Development, Relationships, and Culture*, 11th ed. (Boston: Allyn & Bacon, 2004), 194.

8. Emily White, *Fast Girls: Teenage Tribes and the Myth of the Slut* (New York: Berkley Books, 2002), 50-51.

9. B.V. Marin et al., "Older Boyfriends and Girlfriends Increase Risk of Sexual Initiation in Young Adolescents," *Journal of Adolescent Health* 27 (2000): 409-418.

10. K.A. Moore, A.K. Driscoll, and L.D. Lindberg, "A Statistical Portrait of Adolescent Sex, Contraception, and Childbearing," (Washington, D.C.: National Campaign to Prevent Teen Pregnancy, 1998). Cited in Deborah L. Tolman, *Dilemmas of Desire: Teenage Girls Talk about Sexuality* (Harvard University Press, October 31, 2005), 11.

11. G. Wade Rowatt, Jr., *Adolescents in Crisis: A Guidebook for Parents, Teachers, Ministers, and Counselors* (Louisville, KY: Westminster John Knox Press, 2001), 100.

12. W.D. Mosher, A. Chandra, J. Jones, "Sexual Behavior and Selected Health Measures: Men and Women 15-44 Years of Age, United States; 2002," *Advance Data from Vital and Health Statistics*, a publication of the Centers for Disease Control, no. 362, Table 6 (September 15, 2005).

13. W.D. Mosher, A. Chandra, J. Jones, "Sexual Behavior and Selected Health Measures: Men and Women 15-44 Years of Age, United States; 2002," *Advance Data from Vital and Health Statistics*, a publication of the Centers for Disease Control, no. 362 (September 15, 2005).

14. Centers for Disease Control and Prevention, "Surveillance Summaries," *Morbidity & Mortality Weekly Report* 53, no. SS-2 (May 21, 2004): 18, http://www.cdc.gov/mmwr/PDF/SS/SS5302.pdf

15. National Center for Health Statistics, *Sexual Behavior and Selected Health Measures: Men and Women 15-44 Years of Age, United States,* 2002 (Washington, D.C.: U.S. Department of Health and Human Services, 2005).

16. Alexandra Hall, "The Mating Habits of the Suburban High School Teenager," *Boston Magazine*, May 2003.

17. L. Remez, "Oral Sex Among Adolescents: Is It Sex or Is It Abstinence?" *Family Planning Perspective* 32 (2000): 298-304.

18. *Middle School Confessions*, Directed by Ellen Goosenberg Kent (HBO Family documentary, 2002).

19. Ibid.

20. Leonard Sax, *Why Gender Matters: What Parents and Teachers Need to Know about the Emerging Science of Sex Differences* (New York: Doubleday, 2005), 120.

21. The National Campaign to Prevent Teen Pregnancy, "Survey: Teens Say Parents Most Influence Their Decisions About Sex," news release by U.S. Newswire, December 16, 2004.

22. Jennifer Korneich et al., "Sibling Influence, Gender Roles, and the Sexual Socialization of Urban Early Adolescent Girls," *Journal of Sex Research* 40 (Feb. 2003): 101-110.

23. Diana E.H. Russell, *Sexual Exploitation: Rape, Child Sexual Abuse, and Workplace Harassment* (Beverly Hills, CA: SAGE Publications, 1984). Cited in Norine G. Johnson, Michael C. Roberts, Judith P. Worell, eds., *Beyond Appearance: A New Look at Adolescent Girls* (Washington, D.C.: American Psychological Association, 1999).

24. M.J. Seng, "Child Sexual Abuse and Adolescent Prostitution: A Comparative Analysis," *Adolescence* 24 (1989): 665-675.

25. Henry J. Kaiser Family Foundation, "Pregnancy & Childbirth: Teen Pregnancy Rate Dropped 30% in 1990s, Likely Continued Dropping in 2003, 2005, NCPTP Predicts," *Daily Women's Health Policy Report*, May 26, 2005, www.kaisernetwork.org/daily_reports/rep_index.cfm?hint=2&DR_ID=30336

26. "Teenagers Need Contraceptive Advice, Not Just Abstinence Counseling," *British Medical Journal*, http://bmj.bmjjournals.com/cgi/content/full/331/7509/129-c/DC1 (accessed July 20, 2005).

27. Alan Guttmacher Institute, and J.D. Klein and the Committee on Adolescence, "Adolescent Pregnancy: Current Trends and Issues," *American Academy of Pediatrics* 116, no. 1 (July 2005): 281-286.

28. Marlena Studer and Arland Thornton, "Adolescent Religiosity and Contraceptive Usage," *Journal of Marriage and Family* 49, no. 1 (Feb. 1987): 117-128.

29. Jeffrey Jensen Arnett, *Adolescence and Emerging Adulthood: A Cultural Approach*, 2nd ed. (Upper Saddle River, NJ: Prentice Hall, 2004), 301.

30. C.A. Bacharach, C.C. Clogg, and K. Carver, "Outcomes of Early Childbearing: Summary of a Conference," *Journal of Research on Adolescence* 3 (1993): 337-348.

31. Deborah Roempke Graefe and Daniel T. Lichter, "Marriage Among Unwed Mothers: Whites, Blacks and Hispanics Compared," *Perspectives on Sexual and Reproductive Health* 34, no. 6 (Nov/Dec 2002), http://www.guttmacher. org/pubs/journals/3428602.html

32. S.K. Henshaw and K. Kost, "Parental Involvement in Minors' Abortion Decisions," *Family Planning Perspectives* 24 (1992): 196-207.

33. Meg Meeker, *Epidemic: How Teen Sex Is Killing Our Kids* (Washington, D.C.: Regnery Publishing, 2002), 3.

34. Stuart Collins, et al., "High Incidence of Cervical Human Papillomavirus Infection in Women During Their First Sexual Relationship," *British Journal of Obstetrics and Gynecology* 109 (2002): 96-98.Cited in Meg Meeker, *Epidemic: How Teen Sex Is Killing Our Kids* (Washington, D.C.: Regnery Publishing, 2002), 37.

35. Centers for Disease Control and Prevention, *Tracking the Hidden Epidemics 2000: Trends in STDs in the United States* (Washington D.C.: U.S. Department of Health and Human Services, 2000). And H. Weinstock, S. Bermann, and W. Cates, Jr., "Sexually Transmitted Diseases Among American Youth: Incidence and Prevalence Estimates, 2000," *Perspectives on Sexual and Reproductive Health* 36, no. 1 (Jan/Feb 2004).

36. Alan Guttmacher Institute, "Facts in Brief."

37. National Center for HIV, STD, and TB Prevention, "STD Prevention for Adolescents," NCHSTP Program Briefing, 2001.

38. Meeker, *Epidemic*, 36-7.

39. U.S. Department of Health and Human Services, "Women's Health in the U.S.: Research on Health Issues Affecting Women," National Institute of Allergy and Infections Diseases, National Institutes of Health, NIH Publication No. 04-4697, 2003.

40. D.T. Fleming et al., "Herpes Simplex Virus Type 2 in the United States, 1976-1994," *New England Journal of Medicine* 337 (1997): 1105-1106.

41. Lawrence Corey and H. Hunter Handsfield, "Genital Herpes and Public Health," *Journal of American Medical Association* 283 (2000): 791-94. Cited in Meg Meeker, *Epidemic: How Teen Sex Is Killing Our Kids* (Washington, D.C.: Regnery Publishing, 2002), 73.

42. National Center for HIV, STD and TB Prevention: Divisions of HIV/AIDS Prevention, "HIV/AIDS Among Youth," http://www.cdc.gov/hiv/pubs/facts/youth.htm#1

43. Centers for Disease Control and Prevention, *HIV/AIDS Surveillance Report* 2003 15 (Atlanta: U.S. Department of Health and Human Services, 2004): 1-40. Also at http://www.cdc.gov/hiv/stats/2003surveillancereport.pdf

44. L.A. Valleroy, D.A. MacKellar, J.M. Karon, R.S. Janssen, and D.R. Hayman, "HIV Infection in Disadvantaged Out-of-School Youth: Prevalence for U.S. Job Corps Entrants, 1990 through 1996," *Journal of Acquired Immune Deficiency Syndromes* 19 (1998): 67-73. Cited in *National Center for HIV, STD and TB Prevention: Divisions of HIV/AIDS Prevention*, "HIV/AIDS Among Youth," http://www.cdc.gov/hiv/pubs/facts/youth.htm#1

45. Alan Guttmacher Institute, "Facts in Brief."

46. Centers for Disease Control and Prevention, *Tracking the Hidden Epidemics 2000: Trends in STDs in the United States* (Washington D.C.: U.S. Department of Health and Human Services, 2000).

47. Ibid.

48. Meeker, *Epidemic*, 176.

49. Motivational Educational Entertainment (MEE) and The National Campaign to Prevent Teen Pregnancy, *This Is My Reality: The Price of Sex—An Inside Look at Black Urban Youth Sexuality and the Role of the Media* (Philadelphia: MEE, January 2004): 56.

50. Author interview.

51. W.D. Mosher, A. Chandra, J. Jones, "Sexual Behavior and Selected Health Measures: Men and Women 15-44 Years of Age, United States; 2002," *Advance Data from Vital and Health Statistics*, a publication of the Centers for Disease Control, no. 362, Table A (September 15, 2005).

52. Amanda Gardner, "CDC Survey: Oral Sex Substitutes for Intercourse with Many Teenagers," (September 15, 2005), http://www.Forbes.com

53. Motivational Educational Entertainment, *This Is My Reality*, 26.

54. Ritch C. Savin-Williams, *The New Gay Teenager* (Cambridge, MA: Harvard University Press, 2005), 2.

55. Norine G. Johnson, Michael C. Roberts, Judith P. Worell, eds., *Beyond Appearance: A New Look at Adolescent Girls* (Washington, D.C.: American Psychological Association, 1999).

56. Ritch C. Savin-Williams, *The New Gay Teenager* (Cambridge, MA: Harvard University Press, 2005), 72-74. He cites: J.H. McConnell, "Lesbian and Gay Male Identities as Paradigms," in S.L. Archer ed., *Interventions for Adolescent Identity Development* (Thousand Oaks, CA: Sage, 1994), 103-118.

57. Savin-Williams, *The New Gay Teenager*, 41.

CHAPTER 7

1. Mary Pipher, *Reviving Ophelia* (New York: Ballantine Books, 1995), 57.

2. Betty Allgood-Merten, Peter M. Lewinson, and Hyman Hops, "Sex Differences and Adolescent Depression," *Journal of Abnormal Psychology* 99 (1990): 55-63.

3. Kara Gavin, "Is Your Child Overscheduled and Overstressed?" press release, University of Michigan Health System, July 25, 2005, http://www.med.umich.edu/opm/newspage/2005/hmchildstress.htm

4. Personal interview, author.

5. Michelle Chang, "Identity Crisis," in *Yell-Oh Girls! Emerging Voices Explore Culture, Identity, and Growing Up Asian American*, ed. Vicki Nam (New York: HarperCollins, 2001), 229.

6. The American Academy of Child & Adolescent Psychiatry and David Pruitt, *Your Adolescent: Emotional, Behavioral, and Cognitive Development from Early Adolescence Through the Teen Years* (New York: HarperCollins, 2000), 197.

7. Suniya S. Luthar and Bronwyn E. Becker, "Privileged but Pressured: A Study of Affluent Youth," *Child Development* 73 (2002): 1593-1610.

8. "Teenage Depression Can Be Enduring, but Is More Often Short-Lived," *UCLA News*, news release, May 27, 2005. Report given by Professor Constance Hammen at the American Psychological Society's 17th annual convention in Los Angeles, California, May 26-29, 2005, http://newsroom.ucla.edu/page.asp?RelNum=6188&menu=fullsearchresults

9. Dr. Lisa Machoian, *The Disappearing Girl* (New York: Penguin Group, 2005).

10. Cathy Schoen, Karen Davis, Karen Scott Collins et al., *The Commonwealth Fund Survey of the Health of Adolescent Girls* (New York: The Commonwealth Fund, 1997), http://www.cmwf.org/publications/publications_show.htm?doc_id=221230 Cited in Norine G. Johnson, Michael C. Roberts, Judith

P. Worell, eds., *Beyond Appearance: A New Look at Adolescent Girls* (Washington, D.C.: American Psychological Association, 1999), 9.

11. Luthar and Becker, "Privileged but Pressured," 1595.

12. "Teen Sex, Drug Use May be Cause of Depression, Not the Effect," Health Behavior News Service news release, Sept. 16, 2005. Based on D.D. Hallfors et al., "Which Comes First in Adolescence—Sex and Drugs or Depression?" *American Journal of Preventative Medicine* 29, no. 3 (2005): 163-170.

13. K.R. Nilzon and K. Palmérus, "The Influence of Familial Factors on Anxiety and Depression in Childhood and Early Adolescence," *Adolescence* 32 (1997): 935-943. Cited in F. Philip Rice and Kim Gale Dolgin, *The Adolescent: Development, Relationships, and Culture,* 11th ed. (Boston: Allyn & Bacon, 2004).

14. C.M. Oldenburg and K.A. Kerns, "Associations between Peer Relationships and Depressive Symptoms: Testing Moderator Effects on Gender and Age," *Journal of Early Adolescence* 17 (1997): 319-337. Cited in F. Philip Rice and Kim Gale Dolgin, *The Adolescent: Development, Relationships, and Culture*, 11th ed. (Boston: Allyn & Bacon, 2004).

15. P.F. Gjerde and P.M. Westenberg, "Dysphoric Adolescents as Young Adults: A Prospective Study of the Psychological Sequelae of Depressed Mood in Adolescence," *Journal of Research on Adolescence* 8 (1998): 377-402. And P.F. Gjerde, J. Block, and J.H. Block, "Depressive Symptoms and Personality During Late Adolescence: Gender Differences in the Externalization-Internationalization of Symptom Depression," *Journal of Abnormal Psychology* 97 (1988): 475-486.

16. Charlene Laino, "Internet Addiction May Mask Teen Depression," WebMD online article reporting on the research presented at the American Psychiatric Association's 2005 Annual Meeting, May 25, 2005, http://www.webmd.com/content/Article/106/108167.htm

17. Machoian, *The Disappearing Girl,* xviii.

18. Erica Goode, "Study Links Prescriptions to Decrease in Suicides," *The New York Times*, October 14, 2003.

19. Machoian, *The Disappearing Girl*, 176.

20. The Substance Abuse and Mental Health Services Administration, "900,000 U.S. Teens Planned Suicides During Major Depression," a news release about the federal National Survey on Drug Use and Health Report *Suicidal Thoughts Among Youths Aged 12-17 with Major Depressive Episode* (September 9, 2005). The report is available online at http://www.oas.samhsa.gov

21. U.S. Bureau of the Census, *Statistical Abstract of the United States*, 2003 (Washington, D.C.: Government Printing Office, 2003). Cited in F. Philip Rice and Kim Gale Dolgin, *The Adolescent: Development, Relationships, and Culture,* 11th ed. (Boston: Allyn & Bacon, 2004), 410.

22. P.S. Bearman and J. Moody, "Suicide and Friendships Among American Adolescents," *American Journal of Public Health* 94, no. 1 (January 2004): 89-95.

23. Goode, "Study Links Prescriptions."

24. D. Stein et al., "The Association Between Adolescents' Attitudes Towards Suicide and Their Psychosocial Background and Suicidal Tendencies," *Adolescence* 27, no. 108 (Winter 1992): 949-959.

25. United States Health and Human Services, "The Surgeon General's Call to Action to Promote Sexual Health and Responsible Behavior: A Letter from the Surgeon General, U.S. Department of Health and Human Services," July 9, 2001, 9, http://www.surgeongeneral.gov/library/sexualhealth/default.htm (Select "Text of the Call to Action" link.)

26. National Center for Health Statistics (NCHS) and the Centers for Disease Control and Prevention, Worktable GM291 (1999), http://www.cdc.gov/nchswww/datawh/staab/unpubd/mortabs/gmwk291.htm, cited in Erica Goode, "Study Links Prescriptions to Decrease in Suicides," *The New York Times*, October 14, 2003. And http://www.cdc.gov/ncipc/factsheets/suifacts.htm

27. Bearman and Moody, "Suicide and Friendships," 89-95.

28. Ibid.

29. D.L. Peck and K. Warner, "Accident or Suicide? Single-Vehicle Car Accidents and the Intent Hypothesis," *Adolescence* 30 (1995): 463-472.

30. M.J. Rotheram-Borus and P.D. Trautman, "Hopelessness, Depression and Suicidal Intent Among Adolescent Suicide Attempters," *Journal of the American Academy of Child and Adolescent Psychiatry* 27, no. 6 (1988): 700-704. And P.D. Trautman, M.J. Rotheram-Borus, S. Dopkins, and N. Lewin, "Psychiatric Diagnoses in Minority Female Adolescent Suicide Attempters," *Journal of the American Academy of Child and Adolescent Psychiatry* 30, no. 4 (July 1991): 617-622, as cited in Dr. Lisa Machoian, *The Disappearing Girl* (New York: Penguin Group, 2005).

31. Machoian, *The Disappearing Girl,* 173-174.

CHAPTER 8

1. Barbara Strauch, *The Primal Teen: What the New Discoveries About the Teenage Brain Tell Us About Our Kids* (New York: Doubleday, 2003).

2. Ibid.

3. David Walsh, *Why Do They Act That Way? A Survival Guide to the Adolescent Brain for You and Your Teen* (New York: Free Press, 2004).

4. Strauch, *The Primal Teen*, 33.

5. Allie Shah, "Why Some Teens Lash Out," *Star Tribune*, March 24, 2005.

6. Strauch, *The Primal Teen*, 111.

7. Leonard Sax, *Why Gender Matters: What Parents and Teachers Need to Know about the Emerging Science of Sex Differences* (New York: Doubleday, 2005), 113. He cites: "See, for example, Carol Dwyer and Linda Johnson, 'Grades, Accomplishments, and Correlates,' in *Gender and Fair Assessment*, ed. Warren Willingham and Nancy Cole (Mahwah, NJ: Erlbaum, 1997), 125-56."

8. Eva M. Pomerantz, Ellen R. Altermatt, and Jill L. Saxon, "Making the Grade but Feeling Distressed: Gender Differences in Academic Performance and Internal Distress," *Journal of Educational Psychology* 94, no. 2 (2002): 396-404.

9. David Sadker and Karen Zittleman, "Gender Bias Lives, for Both Sexes," *Education Digest* 70, no. 8 (April 2005): 27-31.

10. Douglas B. Downey and Anastasia S. Vogt Yuan, "Sex Differences in School Performance During High School: Puzzling Patterns and Possible Explanations," *The Sociology Quarterly* 46 (2005): 310.

11. Diane F. Halpern, "A Cognitive-Process Taxonomy for Sex Differences in Cognitive Abilities," *Current Directions in Psychological Science* 13, no. 4 (2004): 136.

12. Catherine E. Freeman and the National Center for Education Statistics, *Trends in Educational Equity of Girls and Women: 2004* (NCES 2005-016) (Washington, D.C.: U.S. Department of Education and the Government Printing Office, 2004).

13. Downey and Yuan, "Sex Differences in School Performance," 310.

14. Ibid.

15. Leonard Sax, *Why Gender Matters: What Parents and Teachers Need to Know about the Emerging Science of Sex Differences* (New York: Doubleday, 2005).

16. C. Freeman, *Trends in Educational Equity.*

17. Joan Freeman, "Cultural Influences on Gifted Gender Achievement," *High Ability Studies* 15, no. 1 (June 2004): 13.

18. Sadker and Zittleman, "Gender Bias Lives," 27-31.

19. C. Freeman, *Trends in Educational Equity.*

20. Ibid.

21. Halpern, "A Cognitive-Process Taxonomy," 138.

22. Ibid., 135.

23. C.H. Sommers, "The War Against Boys," *Atlantic Monthly*, May 2000, 59-74.

24. Peter D. Hart Research Associates and the Horatio Alger Association, *The State of Our Nation's Youth*, 2005-2006 (Alexandria, VA: Horatio Alger Association, 2005), 18, http://www.horatioalger.org/pdfs/state05.pdf

25. John G. Wirt et al. and the National Center for Education Statistics, *The Condition of Education*, 2004 (NCES 2004-077) (Washington, D.C.: U.S. Department of Education, 2004). Cited in Douglas B. Downey and Anastasia S. Vogt Yuan, "Sex Differences in School Performance During High School: Puzzling Patterns and Possible Explanations," The Sociology Quarterly 46 (2005): 318.

26. C. Freeman, *Trends in Educational Equity.*

27. National Center for Education Statistics, "Earned Degrees Conferred," Projection of Education Statistics to 2011 (Washington, D.C.: U.S. Department of Education, 2003), section 4, http://nces.ed.gov/programs/projections/ch_4.asp Cited in Leonard Sax, *Why Gender Matters: What Parents and Teachers Need to Know about the Emerging Science of Sex Differences* (New York: Doubleday, 2005), 8.

28. Halpern, "A Cognitive-Process Taxonomy," 135.

29. American Association of University Women, *Shortchanging Girls, Shortchanging America: Executive Summary* (Washington, D.C.: American Association of University Women, 1991). Cited in Barbara Kerr, *Smart Girls: A New Psychology of Girls, Women and Giftedness* (Scottsdale, AZ: Great Potential Press, 1994).

30. Sadker and Zittleman, "Gender Bias Lives," 27-31.

31. Mary Pipher, *Reviving Ophelia* (New York: Ballantine Books, 1995), 64.

32. J. Freeman, "Cultural Influences," 12.

33. Ibid., 13.

34. Sadker and Zittleman, "Gender Bias Lives," 27-31.

35. Margrét Pála Ólafsdóttir, "Kids Are Both Girls and Boys in Iceland," *Women's Studies International Forum* 19, no. 4 (1996): 357-69. Cited in Leonard Sax, *Why Gender Matters: What Parents and Teachers Need to Know about the Emerging Science of Sex Differences* (New York: Doubleday, 2005), 49-51.

36. Sax, *Why Gender Matters.*

37. Halpern, "A Cognitive-Process Taxonomy," 138.

38. Downey and Yuan, "Sex Differences in School Performance," 310.

39. Ibid.

40. Sax, *Why Gender Matters.*

41. J. Freeman, "Cultural Influences," 16.

42. E. Pomerantz, E. Altermatt, and J. Saxon, "Making the Grade but Feeling Distressed: Gender Differences in Academic Performance and Internal Distress," *Journal of Educational Psychology* 94, no. 2 (2002): 402. Cited in Leonard Sax, *Why Gender Matters: What Parents and Teachers Need to Know about the Emerging Science of Sex Differences* (New York: Doubleday, 2005), 81.

43. Sari Solden, *Women with Attention Deficit Disorder: Embracing Disorganization at Home and in the Workplace* (Grass Valley, CA: Underwood Books, 1995).

44. Ronald Kotulak and Jon Van, "Girls Are Quieter About ADD," *Chicago Tribune*, May 17, 1999.

45. Jerome Kagan and Susan B. Gall, eds., *The Gale Encyclopedia of Childhood & Adolescence* (Farmington Hills, MI: Thomson Gale, 1997).

46. Jeffrey Jensen Arnett, *Adolescence and Emerging Adulthood: A Cultural Approach* (Upper Saddle River, NJ: Prentice Hall, 2001), 336.

47. S.S. Luthar, E. Zigler, and D. Goldstein, "Psychosocial Adjustment Among Intellectually Gifted Adolescents: The Role of Cognitive-Developmental and Experiential Factors," *Journal of Child Psychology and Pyschiatry* 33 (1992):

361-373. Cited in Joan Freeman, "Cultural Influences on Gifted Gender Achievement," *High Ability Studies* 15, no. 1 (June 2004): 16-17.

48. Barbara Kerr, *Smart Girls: A New Psychology of Girls, Women and Giftedness* (Scottsdale, AZ: Great Potential Press, 1994).

49. J. Freeman, "Cultural Influences," 7.

50. Shanti Zaid and the Colorado Historical Society, "'Aunt' Clara Brown,'" http://www.coloradohistory.org/kids/brown.pdf

CHAPTER 9

1. Patricia Hersch, *A Tribe Apart: A Journey into the Heart of American Adolescence* (New York: Ballantine Books, 1999), 18.

2. Center on Addiction and Substance Abuse, *The Formative Years: Pathways to Substance Abuse among Girls and Young Women Ages 8-22*, (New York: CASA, 2003), 59, http://www.casacolumbia.org (They document five studies that talk about the benefits of teens having dinner with their parents.) Cited in Leonard Sax, *Why Gender Matters: What Parents and Teachers Need to Know about the Emerging Science of Sex Differences* (New York: Doubleday, 2005), 161.

3. Kenneth W. Griffin et al., "Parenting Practices as Predictors of Substance Use, Delinquency and Aggression Among Urban Minority Youth: Monitoring Effects of Family Structure and Gender," *Psychology of Addictive Behaviors* 14, no. 2 (2000): 174-84. Cited in Leonard Sax, *Why Gender Matters: What Parents and Teachers Need to Know about the Emerging Science of Sex Differences* (New York: Doubleday, 2005).

4. Terri Apter, *You Don't Really Know Me: Why Mothers and Daughters Fight and How Both Can Win* (Boston, MA: W.W. Norton & Co., 2004), 33.

5. Grace K. Baruch and Rosaline C. Barnett, "Adult Daughters' Relationships with Their Mothers: The Era of Good Feelings," *Journal of Marriage and Family* 45 (1983): 601-606.

6. Carol Gilligan, *The Birth of Pleasure: A New Map of Love* (New York: Knopf, 2002), 108.

7. Ann C. Crouter et al., "How Do Parents Learn about Adolescents' Experiences? Implications for Parental Knowledge and Adolescent Risky Behavior," *Child Development* 76, no. 4 (July-August 2005): 869-882.

8. Eirini Flouir and Ann Buchanan, "Father Involvement and Outcomes in Adolescence and Adulthood," *End of Award Report* (Oxford: Economic and Social Research Council, Oct. 24, 2001). As cited in Terri Apter, *You Don't Really Know Me: Why Mothers and Daughters Fight and How Both Can Win* (Boston, MA: W.W. Norton & Co., 2004).

9. Leonard Sax, *Why Gender Matters: What Parents and Teachers Need to Know about the Emerging Science of Sex Differences* (New York: Doubleday, 2005).

10. J. Snarley, *How Fathers Care for the Next Generation* (Cambridge, MA: Harvard University Press, 1993). Cited in Norine G. Johnson, Michael C. Roberts, Judith P. Worell, eds., *Beyond Appearance: A New Look at Adolescent Girls* (Washington, D.C.: American Psychological Association, 1999).

11. Suniya S. Luthar and Bronwyn E. Becker, "Privileged but Pressured: A Study of Affluent Youth," *Child Development* 73 (2002): 1593-1610.

12. Apter, *You Don't Really Know Me.*

13. F. Philip Rice and Kim Gale Dolgin, *The Adolescent: Development, Relationships, and Culture*, 11th ed. (Boston: Allyn & Bacon, 2004).

14. Ibid., 267.

15. Christy M. Buchanan, "The Impact of Divorce on Adjustment During Adolescence," in Ronald D. Taylor and Margaret C. Wang, eds., *Resilience Across Contexts: Family, Work, Culture, and Community* (Mahwah, NJ: Lawrence Erlbaum Associates, 2000). As cited in Jeffrey Jensen Arnett, *Adolescence and Emerging Adulthood*, 2nd ed. (Upper Saddle River, NJ: Prentice Hall, 2004), 222. And R. Needle, S. Su, and W. Doherty, "Divorce, Remarriage, and Substance Use: A Prospective Longitudinal Study," *Journal of Marriage and the Family* 52 (1990): 157-169.

16. J. Wallerstein, J. Lewis, and S. Blakeslee, *The Unexpected Legacy of Divorce: A 25-Year Landmark Study* (New York: Hyperion, 2000), xxvii.

17. Christy M. Buchanan, "The Impact of Divorce on Adjustment During Adolescence," in Ronald D. Taylor and Margaret C. Wang, eds., Resilience Across Contexts: Family, Work, Culture, and Community (Mahwah, NJ: Lawrence Erlbaum Associates, 2000), 179. As cited in Jeffrey Jensen Arnett, *Adolescence and Emerging Adulthood*, 2nd ed. (Upper Saddle River, NJ: Prentice Hall, 2004), 224.

18. Christy M. Buchanan, "The Impact of Divorce on Adjustment During Adolescence," in Ronald D. Taylor and Margaret C. Wang, eds., *Resilience Across Contexts: Family, Work, Culture, and Community* (Mahwah, NJ: Lawrence

Erlbaum Associates, 2000). As cited in Jeffrey Jensen Arnett, *Adolescence and Emerging Adulthood*, 2nd ed. (Upper Saddle River, NJ: Prentice Hall, 2004).

19. Wallerstein, Lewis, and Blakeslee, *The Unexpected Legacy of Divorce*, 108.

20. E. Mavis Hetherington, "Family Functioning and the Adjustment of Adolescent Siblings in Diverse Types of Families," *Monographs of the Society for Research in Child Development* 64, no. 4 (1999): 2.

21. P.L. East, "Do Adolescent Pregnancy and Childbearing Affect Younger Siblings?" *Family Planning Perspectives* 28 (1996): 148-153; or P.L. East, "The Younger Sisters of Childbearing Adolescents: Their Attitudes, Expectations, and Behaviors." *Child Development* 67 (1996): 267-282. Cited in F. Philip Rice and Kim Gale Dolgin, *The Adolescent: Development, Relationships, and Culture*, 11th ed. (Boston: Allyn & Bacon, 2004).

22. J.L. Kornreich et al., "Sibling Influence, Gender Roles, and the Sexual Socialization of Urban Early Adolescent Girls," *Journal of Sex Research* 40, no. 1 (Feb. 2003): 101-110.

23. R.B. Stewart et al., "That Was Then, This Is Now: An Empirical Typology of Adult Sibling Relationships," paper presented at the biennial meeting of the Society for Research on Child Development in Indianapolis, Indiana, March 1995. Cited in Jeffrey Jensen Arnett, *Adolescence and Emerging Adulthood: A Cultural Approach* (Upper Saddle River, NJ: Prentice Hall, 2001), 190-191.

24. R.G. Rumbaut, "The Crucible Within: Ethnic Identity, Self-Esteem, and Segmented Assimilation Among Children of Immigrants," *International Migration Review* 28 (1994): 748-794. Cited in Norine G. Johnson, Michael C. Roberts, Judith P. Worell, eds., *Beyond Appearance: A New Look at Adolescent Girls* (Washington, D.C.: American Psychological Association, 1999).

25. Jenny Kim, "Kim Chee and Yellow Peril," essay in Vicki Nam ed., *Yell-Oh Girls! Emerging Voices Explore Culture, Identity, and Growing Up Asian American* (New York: HarperCollins, 2001), 186-187.

26. For more information about the Lost Boys of Sudan, check out these Web pages http://www.unicef.org/sowc96/closboys.htm http://www.redcross.org/news/in/africa/0108lostboyspage.html

27. Roselyn Domingo, "Separation Anxiety," in *Yell-Oh Girls! Emerging Voices Explore Culture, Identity, and Growing Up Asian American*, ed. Vicki Nam (New York: HarperCollins, 2001), 62.

28. Kim, "Kim Chee and Yellow Peril," 186.

29. American Association of University Women, *Shortchanging Girls, Shortchanging America: Executive Summary* (Washington, D.C.: American Association of University Women, 1991), http://www.aauw.org/research/SGSA.pdf

CHAPTER 10

1. Jeffrey Jensen Arnett, *Adolescence and Emerging Adulthood: A Cultural Approach* (Upper Saddle River, NJ: Prentice Hall, 2001).

2. James Youniss and Jacqueline Smoller, *Adolescent Relations with Mothers, Fathers, and Friends* (Chicago: University of Chicago Press, 1985). As cited in Jeffrey Jensen Arnett, *Adolescence and Emerging Adulthood: A Cultural Approach* (Upper Saddle River, NJ: Prentice Hall, 2001), 225-226.

3. D. Burhmester and J. Carbery, *Daily Patterns of Self-Disclosure and Adolescent Adjustment* (Paper presented at the biennial meeting of the Society for Research in Child Development, Washington, D.C., in March 1992).

4. Arnett, *Adolescence and Emerging Adulthood.*

5. David M. Considine, *Media Literacy and Adolescents: Teenagers & Screenagers,* http://www.ci.appstate.edu/programs/edmedia/medialit/ml_adolescents. html

6. Peter D. Hart Research Associates and the Horatio Alger Association, *The State of Our Nation's Youth,* 2005-2006 (Alexandria, VA: Horatio Alger Association, 2005), 37, http://www.horatioalger.org/pdfs/state05.pdf

7. Pamela Paul, "Nouveau Niche," *American Demographics* (July 1, 2003), 6.

8. Ibid.

9. Cynthia Lewis and Bettina Fabos, "But Will It Work in the Heartland? A Response and Illustration," *Journal of Adolescent & Adult Literacy* 43, no. 5 (February 1, 2000): 462-469.

10. Motivational Educational Entertainment (MEE) and The National Campaign to Prevent Teen Pregnancy, *This Is My Reality: The Price of Sex—An Inside Look at Black Urban Youth Sexuality and the Role of the Media* (Philadelphia: MEE, January 2004): 34-35.

11. Jennifer J. Thomas and Kimberly A. Daubman, "The Relationship Between Friendship Quality and Self-Esteem in Adolescent Girls and Boys," *Sex Roles: A Journal of Research* 45 (July 2001): 53-66.

12. John Janeway Conger and Nancy L. Galambos, *Adolescence and Youth: Psychological Development in a Changing World,* 5th ed. (New York: Longman Publishing Group, 1996).

13. American Association of University Women Educational Foundation, *Tech-Savvy: Educating Girls in the New Computer Age* (Washington, D.C.: American Association of University Women, 2000), http://www.aauw.org/research/girls_education/techsavvy.cfm

14. Rosalind Wiseman, *Queen Bees and Wannabes: Helping Your Daughter Survive Cliques, Gossip, Boyfriends, and Other Realities of Adolescence* (New York: Three Rivers Press, 2002), 25.

15. Emily White, *Fast Girls: Teenage Tribes and the Myth of the Slut* (New York: Berkley Books, 2002).

16. "The Hidden Culture of Aggression in Girls," *The Oprah Winfrey Show*, April 24, 2002, "Why It's Hard to Be a Girl" photo gallery, slide 1, http://www.oprah.com/tows/pastshows/tows_2002/tows_past_20020424.jhtml

17. Laurie Halse Anderson, *Speak* (New York: Penguin Group, 1999), 4.

18. Leonard Sax, *Why Gender Matters: What Parents and Teachers Need to Know about the Emerging Science of Sex Differences* (New York: Doubleday, 2005), 75.

19. For more information, go to http://en.wikipedia.org/wiki/Glenbrook_North_High_School or http://www.oprah.com/tows/pastshows/200305/tows_past_20030527_b.jhtml

20. Deborah Prothrow-Stith and Howard R. Spivak, *Sugar & Spice and No Longer Nice: How We Can Stop Girls' Violence* (San Francisco: Jossey-Bass, 2005).

21. Anderson, *Speak,* 191.

22. Gary D. Gottfredson and Denise C. Gottfredson, *Gang Problems and Gang Programs in a National Sample of Schools* (Ellicott City, MD: Gottfredson Associates, 2001), http://www.gottfredson.com/gang.htm And Christian E. Molidor, "Female Gang Members: A Profile of Aggression and Victimization," *Social Work* 41, no. 3 (May 1, 1996): 251-258.

23. Centers for Disease Control and Prevention, "Surveillance Summaries," *Morbidity & Mortality Weekly Report* 53, no. SS-2 (May 21, 2004). Cited in http://www.girlsinc.com/ic/content/GirlsandViolence.pdf

24. Girls Incorporated, "Girls and Violence," fact sheet, May 2001, http://www.girlsinc.com/ic/content/GirlsandViolence.pdf

25. Prothrow-Stith and Spivak, *Sugar & Spice*, 46.

26. Gary D. Gottfredson and Denise C. Gottfredson, *Gang Problems and Gang Programs in a National Sample of Schools* (Ellicott City, MD: Gottfredson Associates, 2001).

CHAPTER 11

1. Patricia H. Davis, *Counseling Adolescent Girls* (Minneapolis: Augsburg Fortress Press, 1996), 40.

2. P.E. King, J.L. Furrow, and N. Roth, "The Influence of Families and Peers on Adolescent Religiousness," *Journal of Psychology & Christianity* 21 (2002): 109-120; C.A. Clark and E.V. Worthington, Jr., "Family Variables Affecting the Transition of Religious Values from Parents to Adolescents: A Review," *Family Perspectives* 21 (1987): 1-21. Cited in Adolescence and Emerging Adulthood, 2nd ed. (Upper Saddle River, NJ: Prentice Hall, 2004).

3. Patricia H. Davis, Beyond Nice: *The Spiritual Wisdom of Adolescent Girls* (Minneapolis: Augsburg Fortress Press, 2001), 5.

4. Laura Sessions Stepp, "An Inspired Strategy; Is Religion a Tonic for Kids? You Better Believe It, Say Teens and Scholars," *The Washington Post,* March 21, 2004.

5. James Fowler, *Stages of Faith: The Psychology of Human Development and the Quest for Meaning* (San Francisco: Harper & Row, 1981).

6. Davis, *Counseling Adolescent Girls*, 42.

7. Carol E. Lytch, *Choosing Church: What Makes a Difference for Teens* (Louisville, KY: Westminster John Knox Press, 2004), 25.

8. Mary Pipher, *Reviving Ophelia* (New York: Ballantine Books, 1995), 71.

9. Stepp, "An Inspired Strategy," 2004.

10. "National Survey of Youth and Religion, 2002-2003," as cited in Christian Smith and Melinda Lundquist Denton, *Soul Searching: The Religious and Spiritual Lives of American Teenagers* (New York: Oxford University Press USA, 2005).

11. Ibid.

12. Ikechukwu Enenmoh, "A Wiccan Life: ISU Wiccan Is Part of the Fastest-Growing Religion in the United States," *Iowa State Daily*, October 17, 2005.

13. Barbara Taormina, "From Cradle to Coven," North Shore Sunday on TownOnline.com, October 28, 2005; Lucas, "Principles of Wiccan Belief: A Fresh Perspective for a New Generation," part of the "Adult Pagan Essay Series," October 23, 2005, http://www.witchvox.com

14. Lucas, "Principles of Wiccan Belief: A Fresh Perspective for a New Generation," part of the "Adult Pagan Essay Series," October 23, 2005, http://www.witchvox.com

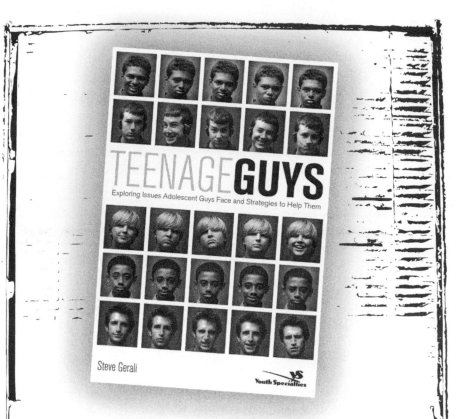

When was the last time you saw your desk? How much will that next retreat cost? When was your next review supposed to be? Discover how to manage your ministry with comprehensive directions and worksheets for budgeting, scheduling, organizing, managing, and more. Includes *The Youth Assistant Special Edition CD-ROM*, with mroe than 80 forms, checklists, and samples featured in the book.

Youth Ministry Management Tools
Everything You Need to Successfully Manage and Administrate Your Youth Ministry
Ginny Olson, Diane Elliot, Mike Work

RETAIL $39.99
ISBN 0-310-23596-0

visit www.youthspecialties.com/store
or your local Christian bookstore

Youth Specialties